Dig for Pirate Treasure

By ROBERT I. NESMITH

BONANZA BOOKS · NEW YORK

To DOROTHY, CORINNA, PEGGY, CYNTHIA,
MELISANDE, DENISE, CHERYL, PENNY,
LYN, JESSICA, LUCINDA, STEPHANIE,
ROBERT AND HARVEY. A happy crew
who think the author is really an old pyrate.

To The Reader

THE author would be happy to hear from any finders of actual treasure who have interesting stories of their discoveries, ashore or at sea.

Please *do not* ask for identification of old coins unless they are from Spanish colonial mints before 1824. And please *do not* mail coins without writing first. The author is not an expert on lost mines or treasure other than pirate loot and sunken cargoes.

Additional information on treasures referred to in this book *cannot* be given, as any information known to the author appears in the text.

Preface

IT is the romance of adventure that leads small boys, young men, middle-aged men, and retired old men to search for treasure. Robert Louis Stevenson once remarked that a man who had not hunted treasure as a boy was never a child.

Treasure can be sought alone in the woods by the light of the moon, or in the burning sun of a tropical beach with an exploration syndicate. It can be dug up with a spade, a plow, or a twelve-ton steam shovel. It may be found behind the henhouse in your own back yard or stumbled over on the distant shores of some palm-fringed isle. It can be located in the clear green water with a glass-bottomed bucket from a skiff, or under the sea with goggles and swim fins. It can be dredged from the ocean depths with the latest in modern salvage equipment.

With maps or without; with carefully planned expeditions or strolling the beach; with willow wands or a metal detector, an abundance of treasure trove is found annually.

Some of the costliest professional expeditions in history have turned up nothing—and amateurs digging with their fingers have uncovered thousands in cash. The odds against finding a single doubloon may be a thousand to one against you, but the thrill of adventure is yours, come success or failure.

Mention treasure, and visions appear of pirates' loot and sunken galleons loaded with gold. But modern-day treasure hunting is not imaginary. It is active and alive. As this is written many expeditions are working all over the globe and thousands of individuals are tramping the shores or gliding under the sea.

This book does not attempt to cover such treasures as King Tut's Tomb, the Dead Sea Scrolls, or the Kohinoor Diamond. Neither are the valuable and priceless Roman finds of the British Isles included, nor lost mines and hidden caches of the old West.

These tales are about the pirates and the Spanish galleons and their treasures, how they were lost or hidden and of the modern searches to recover them.

It was Captain J. E. Austin of the submarine *S-48* and Simon Lake of Bridgeport who first introduced me in 1922 to the pirates, their cutthroat crews and sunken treasure ships. While I was filming the *S-48* trials for Fox Newsreel, Captain Austin practically accepted me as an unofficial member of his trial crew and we became good friends. It was Austin who gave me a copy of *Black Bartlemy's Treasure* by Jeffrey Farnol. The first line, "The Frenchman beside me had been dead since dawn," started me on the trail of piracy, buccaneering, and treasure.

Once on this downward path, I never have been able to stop. For some thirty-odd years my days have been spent making industrial photographs in swamps, in mountains or underground, on land, at sea or in the air; but my nights have been devoted to the lives and exploits of the greatest adventurers and villains in history.

Piratical books, drawings, manuscripts, pamphlets, charts, reports of trials, and clippings overflowed my library. Then came treasure chests, flint-lock pistols, cutlasses, and snickersnees. Then I found a piece-of-eight and the buried-treasure department was formed. It was only natural that along the way I met many kindred spirits like Dwight Franklin, Charles B. Driscoll, Montfort Amory, Edward A. Wilson, Raymond Dow, Bradford Babbitt, A. J. S. McNickle, H. J. Altgelt, Mr. and Mrs. W. Alexander, Jr., C. M. Brookfield, F. C. C. Boyd. W. C. Blaisdell, A. H. Blackington, Tom Beaton, Dorothy Borsodi, J. F. Clow, Tram Combs, Norman A. Dodge, Sir R. H. Davis, Emily Driscoll, Roy Daniels, William Kelleher, Edwin A. Link, Stuart Mosher, Dr. A. F. Pradeau, O. K. Rumbel, Wayte Raymond, David Stick, and W. H. Vernor. Their help with material and their enthusiasm have been greatly appreciated and I am proud to have had their friendship.

Special thanks go to John S. Potter, Jr., of the Atlantic Salvage Company, Ltd., for his permission to use information from *The Treasure of the Rande;* to Waldo Logan for his tale of Silver Shoals; to Mendel L. Peterson for information in "History Under the Sea"; to Gay Crampton and J. L. Highsaw for their experiences; to Edward Rowe Snow for the history of Blackbeard's skull; to Mrs. Charles B. Driscoll and Bernard Blood for contributions to the Foul Anchor Archives; to Elton Manuel for his Newport pirate records; to F. L. Coffman, of Quest Associates, for expedition reports; to Pablo de Jesus of Manila for his Philippine research; to Arthur McKee, Jr., for many happy hours at Plantation Key; to N. S. Binnendijk (Lloyd's Agency, Amsterdam) for material on H.M.S. *Lutine;* and to the many treasure hunters who have written and sent reports.

The assistance of the following institutions and organizations is gratefully acknowledged: The American Numismatic Society; Archives of the Indies at Seville; Royal Academy of History, Madrid; British Museum Manuscript Department; Henry E. Huntington Library; New York

Public Library Reserve Room; Pierpont Morgan Library; Provincial Library of British Columbia; Vancouver Public Library; U.S. National Museum, the Smithsonian Institution; Wichita City Library; Atlantic Salvage Company, Ltd.; Algomah Instrument Co.; Bludworth Marine; Fisher Research Laboratory; Lloyd's of London; Siebe, Gorman & Co., Ltd.; Lucius Pitkin, Inc.; Sam Tour & Co.; S. K. Trohn Refining Co.; and the Treasure Trove Club.

For reading and editing the manuscript, my sincere thanks go to my friends Beth Foster and Edwin Carpenter, Jr.

Robert I. Nesmith

Foul Anchor Archives.
Rye, New York

Contents

Illustrations

CHAPTER 1

Dig for Pirate Treasure

Digging for pirate loot has been a popular pastime for many years. Even if you don't hit a water-soaked iron chest full of gold on your hunt, there may be treasure right in your own backyard. The odds may be long but somebody will find a bonanza this year —or next. Millions in hidden riches is waiting to see daylight—so why not join the hunt?

IN A DIM garret on the waterfront of Panama the old mate of the brig *Morning Star* is dying. His skinny hand points limply to the battered sea-chest in the corner and with his last gasp he croaks, "Treasure—jewels —the chart—" and sets sail on his last voyage beyond the seas.

The ancient mariner may die in Halifax or Havana or Vancouver. He may have sailed on the *Mary Dier* or the *Revenge* or the *Bachelor's Delight*. Perhaps cook, cabin boy, seaman, or second mate, he is always the sole survivor of some piratical crew. The story is the same. Always there is a crudely drawn map of an island, outlined in faded ink on old vellum, or maybe in blood on porpoise hide.

Where is the island? The map does not show. No latitude. No longitude. Only a few cryptic signs and numerals in almost illegible script. But there, at the spot marked X,

30 paces N.N.E. in line with the tree and the rock, must lie the wealth of Panama, Long John Avery's jewels, or the solid gold Virgin of Lima.

And another pirate treasure excursion is born. Out with the picks, shovels, and bulldozers. Make the dirt fly. As long as the party has the chart of some defunct buccaneer or dead pirate's mate, investors will back the hunt and middle-aged, respectable citizens will take off for some God-forsaken island on high adventure.

The romance of pirate treasure is strong. But the fact is clear. Lost treasures are seldom found with faded charts. *If the map showed where treasure was buried, the treasure would not be lost.*

Don't get me wrong. Pirate treasure, hoarded treasure, war treasure, sunken treasure, is found regularly in coins, bars, paper money, jewels, and ancient relics, and more worth billions is still undiscovered.

If piracy is the world's second oldest profession, treasure hunting must be the third. It is an ancient and established avocation. It runs in cycles. A news feature or magazine article about Lafitte or Blackbeard or Billy Bowlegs will arouse interest enough to start adventurous folks off on digging parties. A deluge of treasure discoveries reported in 1885 led one skeptical news editor to comment: "A handbag marked C. Columbus will turn up next."

The popular idea of a pirate is more picturesque than accurate. They were only the roughest and toughest seamen of their times. But because of the daring deeds and the Robin Hood characteristics attributed to them in the minds of the populace, they received more publicity than was sometimes warranted. Ask the average person today to name a pirate and nine out of ten will reply, "Captain Kidd." Blackbeard might be a close second, and in Tampa if you failed to name Gasparilla, you could be ostracized by the Chamber of Commerce. Of the fifteen hundred common pirates reported in 1717 as actively preying on Atlantic coastal shipping, but a handful are remembered today.

It is the common belief that pirates cached their ill-gotten wealth on lonely beaches and distant islands and in haunted caves. Some *did* bury it. It was heavy to tote around. For every fact in pirate history, there are hundreds of old wives' tales of hairy-eared seamen roaming around in the dark of night, planting bags of gold by moonlight and tossing outlandish coins across the tavern bars for rum.

The buccaneers and pirates spent most of their wealth when they returned to port. Lolonais, a very bloody buccaneer, divided 260,000 pieces-of-eight among his crew at the end of a successful voyage, and an eyewitness wrote:

The whole dividend being finished they arrived at Tortuga one month later to the great joy of most of the island. As to the common pirats, in three weeks they had scarce any money left, having spent all in things of little value or at play. [The governor bought their cargo for a twentieth of its worth, the innkeepers trebled the price of brandy, and] they lost and spent the riches they had got in much less time than they were taken by robbing. The taverns and stews, according to the custom of pirats, got the greatest part. . . .

It was easy come, easy go, and another expedition against the Spaniards was recruiting. "Come one, come all! A golden chain or a wooden leg!" And under the pirate disability plan, the loss of a leg paid $800.

In a division of spoils, jewels and gold were favored. Silver was the least desirable, it was too heavy and too bulky. Sir Francis Drake on his expedition into the South Sea stopped at an island near Panama, and Basil Ringrose, a buccaneer author, reported "that he here made the dividend of that vast quantity of plate [silver], which he took in the Armada of this sea, distributing it to each man of his Company by whole Bowls full. The Spaniards affirm to this day [1680], that he took at that time 12 score tons of plate and 16 bowls of coined money a man; his number being then forty-five men in all . . . they were forced to heave much of it overboard, because his ship would not carry it all. Hence this island was called by the Spaniards Isle of Plate from this dividend, and by us, Drake's Isle."

An unconfirmed report circulated in 1930 that the crew of an old and battered tug quietly anchored off Drake's Island and in a few days by stealthy dredging, unknown to the authorities, lifted 18 tons of silver and gold from the site. The bullion value was reported as over a quarter of a million dollars. If this report was true, there must still be tons of silver waiting in the mud for some lucky skin diver to gather.

Drake's men knew the value of the silver which they tossed over the side but the buccaneers in the *Bachelor's Delight* under the famous Captain Bartholomew Sharp threw away a fortune unwittingly. In July 1681, Sharp was cruising against the Spaniards in the South Sea and captured the ship *Santo Rosario*. She was loaded with brandy, oil, wine, fruit, and other commodities including 700 heavy pigs or bars of metal. The buccaneers, thinking this was a load of tin or lead, threw it aside, keeping only one bar to mold into bullets. To their dismay it was then discovered that the metal was unrefined silver when part of the bar sold in London for 75 pounds sterling. When they parted with the *Santo Rosario* they left behind a million dollars in treasure and a Spanish crew snickering in their sleeves.

A good lead for a treasure hunt was written in 1737 by an author who was active in the days when the demons of the sea were still alive. Clement Downing, a midshipman aboard H.M.S. *Salisbury*, sent to Madagascar to suppress piracy, left this tip for diggers:

At Guzarat I met with a Portuguese named Anthony de Sylvestre; he came with two other Portuguese and two Dutchmen to take on in the Moor's service, as many Europeans do. This Anthony told me he had been amongst the pirates, and that he belonged to one of the sloops in Virginia when Blackbeard was taken. He informed me that if it should be my lot ever to go to York River or Maryland, near an island called Mulberry Island, provided we went on shore at the watering place, where the shipping used most commonly to ride, that there the pirates had buried considerable sums of money in great chests well clamped with iron plates. As to my part, I never went that way, nor much acquainted with any that ever used those parts; but I have made inquiry, and am informed that there is such a place as Mulberry Island. If any person who uses those parts should think it worth while to dig a little way at the upper end of a small grove, where it is convenient to land, he should soon find whether the information I had was well grounded. Fronting the landing place are five trees, amongst which, he said, the money was hid. I cannot warrant the truth of this account; but if I was ever to go there, I should find some means or other to satisfy myself, as it could not be a great deal out of my way. If anybody should obtain the benefit of this account, if it please God that they ever come to England, 'tis hoped they will remember whence they had this information.

This clue to Blackbeard's lost loot may be a cold trail 220 years later. Mulberry Island and the five trees may be washed away but many expeditions have dug on lesser evidence.

The real pirates of history seldom survived long enough to recover their buried plunder and enjoy their old age in comfort.

Captain Avery, the "Arch Pyrat," was swindled out of his jewels when he retired and died a pauper.

Blackbearded Edward Teach was killed on the deck of his ship.

Dapper Bartholomew Roberts, who had three ships and the largest gang in history, died in battle and his body was tossed overboard.

Thomas Tew was shot in two by a cannon ball in a Red Sea fight.

Captain Halsey died with fever.

Captain Fly was hanged at Boston from the yard-arm and his pupil, Captain Bannister, was hanged. Captain Lewis was murdered by his crew.

Fenn was hanged at Antigua and his predecessor, Captain Anstis, was shot by his men while taking a siesta.

Ned Low's crew of twenty-five were executed at Newport, and Low, marooned by his men, was later picked up and hanged by a French man-of-war.

Of Lowther's crew, eleven were hanged at St. Kitts and four were condemned to the galleys for life. Lowther committed suicide.

Alexander Rob, an unimportant pirate who was gibbeted with the Scotchman John Gow, left good advice in his last dying words: "Brother Sailors, if ever it should be your hard fortune to be taken by pirates, suffer yourselves to be shot to death, rather than join them in their villainy, which has been the cause of my ruin; for God knows, the life of a pirate is a short, very sad, and miserable life."

James D. Jeffers, alias Charles Gibbs, and Thomas Wansley, a pair of not-too-bright pirates, murdered the captain and mate of the brig *Vineland* and stole 54,000 Mexican dollars. Off Long Island, they fired and scuttled the brig and came ashore near Barron Island in 1831. They talked too loud in a tavern, were arrested by the sheriff and brought to jail in New York City. It was testified at their trial that five thousand dollars in bags had been tossed overboard to lighten their boat when she hit a bar. The balance, in canvas bags, was buried hurriedly on the beach, with some old clothes to mark the spot. A Mr. Johnson, who lodged the pirates overnight, testified that the next morning he went with Wansley to get the clothes but "does not believe they took away the money." Did Johnson get it later? Did some of the gang dig it up? Or is it still there?

Gibbs was one of the biggest liars in all pirate history.

While in prison he confessed to over four hundred fictitious murders and claimed a heroic U.S. Naval enlistment. Actually he had kept a waterfront dive in Boston but failed in business before going to sea. When he and Wansley were hanged on Ellis Island, in New York harbor, half of the city turned out to witness the event. The bodies of the pirates were given to the Medical College and Brower, the sculptor, made a death mask of each pirate's face. The casts have been lost but a reporter for the *New Yorker* magazine recently turned up Gibbs's skull in the museum section of a New York Trade Society Library. Among a hodgepodge of relics presented to the Society over a period of many years, such as a lump of fused glass and teeth from the great fire in the Crystal Palace, a jackknife containing a pair of spectacles and two blades, and a revolver from the battle of Bull Run, was "the skull of James D. Jefferson [sic], known as Gibbs the Pirate."

"Its nothing much as a skull," said the librarian, ". . . but then Jefferson [sic] may have been nothing much as a pirate. Would you care to see a blue tile from the Temple of Heaven, in Peking . . . ?"

How fleeting is fame!

When Gibert, DeSoto, Ruiz, and their crew were tried in Boston for the piracy of the American brig *Mexican* of Salem, they were convicted of carrying away $10,000 in silver. Their trial before Judge Story took fourteen days and there was much testimony about dividing the treasure, with the mate receiving $3,000, the officers $1,000 each and the crew from $300 to $400 per man. This took place on the slave coast of Africa and the money in bags was buried in the woods behind Cape Lopez. Another $4,000 was hidden in the yard of a local Negro prince. Five of the gang later dug up the money and sailed for the island of Fernando Po with their loot as ballast. On the way the coin was tossed overboard to escape detection where it was soon recovered by divers. This pirate trial like many others furnished scant leads to searchers for digging parties.

Any pirate who returned laden with wealth could slip the swag to pals ashore just in case he was picked up by the sheriff as a sea rover. Colonial records mention members of piratical crews as landing and burying their money, but generally state that the owners returned to the spot when suspicion died down and recovered it.

Any seaman in colonial times who was apprehended by the King's men with bags of coin or bullion in his possession was immediately seized as a sea robber and his money taken from him. Once the money fell into the clutches of His Majesty's Naval Officers or the sheriff's men, it was gone for good.

Three well-heeled buccaneers who had suffered months of cruising in the South Sea, battling the Spaniards and crossing the Isthmus of Panama through jungles and swamps, found out that they should have buried their hard-earned gains before landing in Virginia.

When Captain Davis, of the *Bachelor's Delight*, with Lionel Wafer and John Hingson ended a two years' cruise, famous in buccaneer annals, they stopped at Philadelphia. Instead of staying there and enjoying life, they took their sea-chests and sailed for the James River in Virginia. Wafer, an author-surgeon, who wrote *A New Voyage and Description of the Isthmus of America* in 1699, ended his famous book with these words: "There I thought to settle [Virginia]: But meeting with some Troubles, after a three Years residence there, I came home for *England* in the Year, 1690."

The three years' residence was the jail at Jamestown. They were picked up on the river by Captain Simon Rowe commanding His Majesty's Ship *Dunbarton* and because of their money were immediately under suspicion. Wafer had one bag of silver plate, dishes, and lace weighing 74 pounds, and three bags of various valuables weighing 84 pounds; he said that he owned about 160 pounds of silver plate and 1,100 pieces-of-eight. Captain Davis had three bags of Spanish money and a parcel of silver in a chest weighing 142 pounds, and Hingson owned 800 pieces-of-eight and plate weighing 106 pounds. That was all the evidence the law needed.

They were not brought to trial but were thrown into jail and it was not until 1689 that they were freed and returned to England. After another year or two in Newgate Prison, the King, in March, 1692, finally ordered their release and the restoration of their money *with the exception of 300 pounds* and *a fourth part of the amount still held by Captain Rowe.* This sum was ordered "to be devoted to the building of a college in Virginia, or such other charitable objects as the King shall direct." The records of the College of William and Mary show that the amount of 300 pounds was received from the buccaneers, "Davis, de la Wafer and Hinson."

Virginia's hospitality to Captain Davis and his pals, if noised about in buccaneer circles, should have warned future visitors loaded with Spanish silver to sneak ashore in the dark of the moon and plant their money above high-water mark, rather than to devote their profits to "charitable objects as the king shall direct."

Treasure hunters will please note that this is the same Captain Davis reported to have buried his silver on Cocos Island in the Pacific. The huge sum of 300,000 pounds' weight in silver dollars, 733 bars of gold, and 7 kegs of gold coin is mentioned in one treasure-hunting prospectus. If this is true, Davis was only carrying small change when he visited Virginia.

Iron treasure chests with complicated hand-wrought lock mechanism still exist. They were fairly common before banks came into use and were utilized by well-to-do families to safeguard their valuables. Such chests were also in use, sometimes bolted to the deck in the captain's cabin on ships, to carry money on voyages.

I hunted for years for such a treasure chest and finally bought one in New Orleans. I like to think that it once belonged to the Lafitte brothers, but when I bought it, it was empty. I used it to store rare editions of my pirate library. Until I attempted to move it, I did not realize its weight. Then I began to wonder how the pirates in picture and story could lift a chest of gold.

Two cubic feet of gold doubloons would easily fit in my chest and allow space for the coins to clink merrily together. In treasure tales, the chest is tossed into the captain's gig, rowed ashore, carried up the beach by two pirates to be buried in a deep hole above high-water mark. There is something fishy about this!

The U.S. Assay Office informed me that two cubic feet of gold weighs 2,408 pounds. Added to the weight of the iron chest, it would make a ton and a quarter of dead weight. Granted that the hairy-chested pirates were husky —two pirates, four pirates, or even the entire port watch could not lift such a chest an inch off the deck. This proves nothing except that artists, even great ones like Howard Pyle, can be as fanciful as authors. If you are lucky enough to dig up a chest of gold, round up your friends to help haul it away.

The three treasure chests of varied sizes that I dug up (in antique shops) now rest with others in the pirate collection of my author friend, the treasure-hunting Flying Santa Claus, Edward Rowe Snow of Marshfield, Massachusetts. Snow is one of the few men who have actually dug up treasure on a beach, not once but twice.

He has hunted treasure along the Atlantic coast for twenty years and in 1940 picked up a clue from a charac-

ter called "Peg-leg John" Nuskey about a treasure hidden
by Captain James Turner, otherwise known as the "King
of Calf Island." Turner appeared in Boston in 1846 and
took a job as keeper of Bug Light. He later died in soli-
tude in 1882 leaving a legend that he had buried money
nearby. Snow followed clues for years and searched until,
one day, in the cellar of a deserted house on Middle
Brewster, he found a vellum bound seventeenth-century
book in Italian. Bookworms and rats had eaten many of
the pages but Snow took it to the Boston Public Library
for appraisal and identification. There, Miss Harriet Swift
noticed pin holes through certain letters on page 101. The
holes pricked out certain letters which made a message
which Snow deciphered (after many trials) to read "GOLD
IS DUE EAST TREES STRONG ISLAND CHATHAM OUTERBAR."
Snow and his brother went to work with an electronic
metal-detector. After six tries they dug up a small metal
chest full of old silver coins buried above high-water mark
near Chatham on Nauset Beach. Most of the coins were
early American silver pieces dated between 1799 and the
1820's with a few earlier pieces-of-eight. I spent an
exciting evening with Snow looking over the 316 rust-
covered coins while he told me of his search for the treasure of the "King of Calf Island," a legend that came true.

In thirty years' search, I have only met one other person
who saw and handled doubloons that were dug up in a
buried chest. Due to the natural secretiveness of the finders of valuable treasure, it is seldom that one can meet a
person who saw even a part of a true pirate hoard. So
when I listened to the tale of Mr. J. L. Highsaw of Mem-
phis, I felt like the man who shook the hand of the man
who shook the hand of John L. Sullivan.

In 1931 Mr. Highsaw was vacationing at a resort hotel
on the Gulf Coast. After supper he went out to walk on
the beach in the moonlight. To a silent man who paused

near him, he remarked, "I wonder if any of the old tales of pirate treasure buried along the coast could be true?"

The stranger introduced himself and led him to his son and wife a short distance away. "Here's the key," he said to his son; "go up to the hotel and bring back the bag."

In a few minutes the young man returned with a heavy pouch. The stranger opened the bag and said to Mr. Highsaw, who was wearing a stiff straw hat, "Take your hat off and let me fill it with pirate gold." Then into the hat he poured over a hundred Spanish gold doubloons, saying; "Feel these. Bury your hand in them. They are real pirate treasure!" And as Mr. Highsaw looked at the gold in the moonlight, the stranger explained.

A few years before, when his son married, the old folks gave the newlyweds a tract of land and built them a home near the edge of a river on the Florida coast. While the house was being finished, the father and some workmen were digging a well. About twenty feet down in the sandy soil they struck something hard. The obstruction, when uncovered, proved to be an iron chest. The rusty lid was chiseled off with difficulty, and there in the chest, cradled in the decayed satin lining, were 3,700 Spanish gold doubloons, dated in the 1740-1760's.

The finder stated that he took samples to the U.S. Mint in New Orleans (the mint closed in 1909), where he was told that they did not buy foreign coins. They informed him that they did purchase gold in bars. He then selected 144 of the coins for souvenirs and heirlooms, and melted the balance into ingots which he sold as bullion for $48,000.

Had he sold the doubloons slowly and in small lots to coin collectors or dealers, he should have realized at least $150,000 from his lucky strike. How I would have liked to examine that collection of pirate gold before it was melted!

The source of most of the pirate and galleon treasure was the gold and silver from Spanish America. When Spain held the West Indies, Mexico, and Central and South America, she owned the greatest storehouse of metallic wealth that the world had ever seen. With native slave labor she wrung from the soil tons by the thousands of the purest gold and silver. It flowed in a steady stream to Spain and all over the civilized world. Much of it was sidetracked by the English, Dutch and French privateers. The buccaneers and in later days the pirates stole their share. Much that was buried, secreted, and lost on land and at sea is continually being discovered.

Peruvian friends tell me that hardly a day passes but that gold and silver is brought into Lima by natives, who have found it in out-of-the-way places, and sold to the local silversmiths. The same is true in all the towns and cities in the old Spanish colonies.

Mexico, for example, is positively sitting on buried treasure. Rumors and tales of rich finds there are legion but it is always difficult to separate truth from fancy. The finders keep their mouths shut. Hoarding of hard money has been prevalent in Mexico since the first mint in America began coining there in 1536. The republican silver pesos of Mexico minted between 1823 and 1910 have been gradually withdrawn from circulation, until today *five hundred million dollars' worth* is hidden or buried. This is only natural. When the United States gold coinage was called in, and gold was officially rated at $35 an ounce, thousands of U.S. gold coins were missing. After the bank holiday of 1933, many citizens put away silver dollars in vaults and hidden nooks. Treasure in millions goes underground during wars, and Civil War treasures are still plowed up in the Southern states by farmers. This may not be as romantic as pirate treasure but gold is gold wherever it is found.

About 1950, while demolishing an old adobe house on church property in Mexico City, workmen discovered between the walls a few thousands of silver half-real and one-real coins. The earliest were minted about 1560 and the latest around 1600. From the condition of the thousand coins loaned to the writer for study, it could be seen that they had been deposited in the wall a few at a time over many years and that the hoard had rested in its final hiding place for over three hundred years.

Mexico City workmen, in excavating for the foundation of a new opera house, uncovered a few hundred silver coins. These were pieces-of-eight and smaller denominations of the coinage of Philip III of the years 1600 to 1611. Among the 107 pieces of various sizes obtained by the writer from this hoard were some of the earliest *dated* coins (1607-1611) of the Mexico City mint. Had they been found along the New England or Florida coasts, the finders would have surely declared them pirate profits. Such discoveries are not unusual in Mexico and my friend A. J. S. McNickle tells the tale of meeting in Mexico City an out-of-towner who was in search of a good lawyer. He had recently sold the old family ranch, and the new owner hired workmen to brace and repair a leaning wall. The wall suddenly collapsed and a keg of gold hidden in it fell on a workman and crushed him. The former owner was trying to prove that the barrel of gold belonged to himself and not to the new owner, but the lawyers he consulted offered him scant success as he had sold the property "lock, stock and *barrel.*"

The latest news of treasure received from Mexico reads:

Two as yet unidentified bricklayers have reportedly become millionaires overnight.

The two workers, who formed part of a demolition crew, were tearing down one of the old houses in the Lagunilla market area when they came upon two metal chests loaded with old gold coins, necklaces, earrings and other jewelry.

Witnesses say the workers called the foreman in charge and among the three they loaded the chests—reportedly weighing 50 or 60 kilos each—into a car and drove away.

In November 1936 at a bend known as El Mesuno, near Bartolomeo de Honda along the right bank of the Magdalena River in Colombia, an unusual treasure in gold coins was discovered by workmen in clearing or dredging along the river edge. The pieces consisted of *pistoles* or double *escudos* struck at the mint in 1635 at Santa Fé de Bogctá. The lot was estimated as worth $15,000. In Spanish colonial days, goods and treasure were sent by muleback from Bogotá to Honda, and then boated downstream to Cartagena for shipment to old Spain. This gold was no doubt lost in transit by the sinking of a small boat. Some forty specimens brought to the United States were examined by the writer and found to be in perfect mint condition as struck, and obviously uncirculated.

The news wires from Panama in 1937 carried an exciting story of a discovery made by three prospectors, an American, a Frenchman, and a German. The report stated that they had stumbled onto fabulous wealth hidden in the lost La Estrella mine near Piedra Candelas in Chiriquí Province. First announced as 35 bars of gold, the "find" grew to 80 bars and then to 120 bars weighing fifty pounds each and worth a total of $3,000,000. Soldiers were rushed to guard the treasure for the government and later reports stated that the finders had quarreled, one had been shot and another had disappeared. The third, found three days' journey from the mine, denied any knowledge of the gold. The mine was regarded by the natives as cursed. If the tale was true, the curse was working overtime.

A similar story of the discovery of a treasure chest full of Spanish coins made by William Sneed, a hotel man of Lakeland, Florida, flashed over the AP wires a few years ago. Snead had supposedly brought up the chest in the Suwanee River, the loot of Billy "Bowlegs" Rogers, or Gasparilla, and had a pocketful of coins to prove it. The next day, when reporters questioned Snead for more details, his only answer was, "It was all a mistake." At least, it was not as big a mistake as the three millions in gold from La Estrella.

One of the most famous hunts for treasure started in 1927 in Old Panama, when Lieutenant George Williams, Fred Kelly, and Wallace Bain began excavating, under the terms of a four-year concession from President Chiari of Panama. They dug in the ruins of the old city which had been captured, sacked, and burned by Sir Henry Morgan, the buccaneer. Williams and Kelly had originally left London in 1926 on a hunt for the Cocos Island treasures but never reached the island. Williams had a metal detector of his own invention and used it to good advantage in Panama.

In a 1928 report Williams wrote, "I have been very busy in Old Panama and have unearthed some wonderful stuff including gold pots, candlesticks, silver bells and many historical things." In digging under the old church, he also reported, "I have made some very good finds lately including a gold candlestick which contained a secret hiding place in which was an old parchment bound with gold wire. Also a solid gold ball seven inches in diameter with a cross on top and leaves of gold underneath. This represented the world. A complete skeleton was also unearthed in the tunnel 60 feet below the surface."

The year following, Williams was digging gold relics from Indian graves in Coclé, Panama, and was invited to search in old Guatemala City and in El Salvador with his "machine." He also planned to search the old Cruces gold trail that ran from Panama through the jungle to Nombre de Dios and Porto Bello.

In 1930 he wrote that for every dollar invested in treasure hunting he had been repaid in a four-figure sum but his stable of racing horses and sixteen greyhounds ate up his profit rapidly. When he discovered that his "machine" could locate treasure he stated, "I can now afford to bet $500 on a horse race where before I could only play $5." At the time, Williams was operating from Ancon and planning a U.S. syndicate to include several museums for a search of Indian burial mounds.

By 1935, Lieutenant Williams was selling his "treasure finders" to hunters in the United States. One buyer claimed the apparatus did not work and his inquiry to the U.S. Consul at Panama brought the reply that after Williams's explorations of Old Panama were made "he is said to have issued exaggerated reports concerning his findings there, but there is no record of any treasure being discovered." If Williams's reports were true he dug up enough gold to maintain his stables of horses and dogs— a new way of financing the sport of kings.

Beaches are likely spots for treasure gathering and many a doubloon or rusted piece-of-eight has been picked up with no more effort than reaching for it. Old-timers along the shores of New England and Cape Cod have frequently found coins and now and then summer visitors are lucky. Recently a honeymooning couple strolling along a beach were picking up flat stones and skipping them into the water. One piece was thrown by the young husband who told me: "I sensed at once it was not a stone and waded around until I recovered it. Can you tell me what it is?" It was a badly corroded and blackened silver piece-of-eight coined in Peru in the 1660's, an authentic pirate souvenir for the finder's children to admire when he tells them

of finding it on his honeymoon. I have no doubt that it
came from the wreck of the pirate ship *Whidah*.

When the ship *Whidah* had been captured in the Wind-
ward Passage by the pirate Captain Bellamy, she sailed for
New England with treasure aboard. The crew of 180 men
were called together, $100,000 was divided, and the
money was put into bags which were then stowed in
chests between decks. Bellamy then captured a small wine
ship, the *Mary Ann*, off Nantucket Island, and Paul
Williams, Bellamy's quartermaster, was put in command
of another captured sloop. On April 26, 1717, the pirates
were off Cape Cod when the weather turned foggy and
stormy and the ships became separated. The *Mary Ann*
ran ashore near Orleans and the men on board reached
shore and scattered. Seven of the pirates were captured
and jailed at Barnstable. The *Whidah* crashed on a bar
some ten miles to the north, about two and one-half miles
south of the present life-saving station at Wellfleet.

Of the 146 pirates aboard the *Whidah*, only two managed to reach shore alive. These were John Julian, an
Indian, born on Cape Cod, and Thomas Davis, a Welsh-
man who had been forced to join the pirates against his
will. Six of the captured pirates were tried and hanged in
Boston and 102 bodies that washed ashore were buried
on the Cape. For many years the wreck of the *Whidah*
was visible at low tide and surprisingly enough no large
amount of coins was found at the time. Gold and silver
pieces of early dates and from Spanish mints have been
washed ashore all along the ocean side of Cape Cod for
years since, and if you have sharp eyes and are along Cape
Cod after a storm maybe you will find a real pirate coin
in the sand, like the honeymooners.

The tide uncovered gold coins at Beachmont, Massachusetts, in 1884. They were scattered over an area about
seventy feet square and were of Spanish origin and dated

in the early 1700's. Whether they were from a miser's hoard, pirate loot, or a wrecked ship was not determined. But the beach swarmed with eager diggers for many days.

When William Cottrell, a lobsterman, found a Portuguese gold "half-Joe" on a private beach near Highlands, New Jersey, in 1948, he returned with his son, Lloyd, and found six more pieces. They were joined by four clam-diggers who each uncovered a coin. The news of the gold strike leaked out, and a crowd of hunters descended on the location armed with rakes, screens, shovels, clam-forks, and pails. Young men, old men, boys, and women worked feverishly in the mud and sand and in practically no time the beach was pockmarked with holes. The owner of the property arrived to find his beach a shambles and appealed to Police Chief Monahan. The chief ordered the diggers to desist, stop, and halt their efforts but his demands had as much effect as King Canute in commanding the tide to stay its rise. The New Jersey State Troopers were called. They advised the owner to post "No Trespassing" signs, and promised to issue summonses to persistent interlopers. In all, some twenty-six gold johannes of Portugal dated between 1730 and 1768 were found, each worth about $75. A magician's token was also uncovered which was featured by a Newark newspaper in a photograph as being the rarest and most valuable of the pieces recovered. As these tokens can be bought for about ten cents each, the paper was flooded with telephone calls from owners of similar pieces all willing to sell them for $75 each. The Portuguese "Joes" were apparently thrown up on shore by a dredge while clearing a channel in the Shrewsbury River. If the owner of the beach realizes that he has his own gold mine, he will carefully sift the beach every Spring before the tourist season begins.

The Crampton family were about to close their summer home on the beach at Mantoloking, New Jersey, in late

September, 1949. Nine-year-old Gay Crampton and her little friend, Judy Ross, decided to take their last swim of the season. It was late afternoon and the tide was low. As the little girls started down the beach, Mrs. Crampton, from a near-by dune, warned them to keep away from a "large black blob" in the shallow water. The children noticed some twisted metal objects which had washed ashore but decided they were nothing of value. When a boy and his father took an interest in the "blob," the little girls were too curious to stay away and went to investigate. As Gay told the story later:

It looked like a rock about three feet in diameter, composed of a hardened tar-like substance that had picked up small stones and sand. The boy ran for a crowbar to dislodge it from the sand and we all worked fast against the rising tide and the setting sun. Fortunately the lump was not as heavy as stone and we gradually heaved it closer to the beach, where it was possible to break off small pieces.

I ran to mother with a piece and small round objects fell from it into her lap. She rubbed one in the sand and a gold coin appeared with the words "Georgius III Dei Gratia" faintly visible. It was dated 1789.

In other chunks were different sizes of shoe, hat and belt buckles neatly packed together. Some dainty cuff links, gold rings—too small for any of our fingers—and tiny buttons came out of lump after lump. We also found some hairpins, so fragile that they broke when we touched them. By the time we had divided the treasure and trudged home, the tide was high and the sun had set.

If only I had had a camera to photograph Daddy's face when he saw our discoveries! After he stopped asking questions, he said this was the real stuff—as he could tell by the design of the buckles. We were ecstatic until he inspected them more closely and found the buckles were pewter and brass, the buttons glass and pewter, the cuff links brass and the coins—brass!

He imagined that we had found a bale of goods from a burned ship, and that the resin or packing had solidified and protected them from the salt water all these years.

"But secretly we felt that we had discovered gold," said Gay, who is now a young lady of eighteen.

The buckles, buttons, rings, and cuff links are all interesting relics of the American Colonial period. The counterfeit English sovereigns dated 1789 were probably concealed in the bale of trade goods to evade the customs examiners. They were well enough made to fool the unwary, but counterfeit coins during that period were very dangerous to fool with. The crime of counterfeiting English money in those days was deemed high treason and the sentence for the crime was death. "To counterfeit is Death" was a motto which had little effect on coiners, and old newspapers contain many items warning the public.

One of many items found in the *Massachusetts Sentinel* is dated July 30, 1785. "New-York, July 20. On Saturday last was executed, pursuant to his sentence, Benjamin Lewis, for counterfeiting money, a crime of such baleful tendency as seldom admits of a mitigation."

It is not surprising that treasure and marine relics are found along the New Jersey shores. The coast is littered with thousands of ancient and modern wrecks loaded with valuables. The mystery of where and how the Gay Crampton bale was lost may never be solved. Another and more grisly story appeared in the 1733 newspapers. From Cape May, New Jersey, the report came that the bodies of three men had washed ashore. One was well-dressed with gold buttons in his cuffs, two gold rings on his fingers, silver shoe buckles, and a watch and some gold coins in his pockets. He had been shot through the head and the other two bodies were decapitated. About the same time in July, a sloop drove ashore fifteen miles to the northward of the Cape. A brig was reported off Bombay Hook which tacked about and put to sea. A brigantine bound from Bristol with a number of convicts on board was in the vicinity.

It was suspected that the convicts had mutinied and murdered the master and men, or that an act of piracy had been committed by another crew. A later news item reported that nothing further could be learned. There were many missing men and missing ships in those days of piracy. How and where they met their ends, only Davy Jones knows.

Florida, the treasure hunter's Paradise, is well pockmarked by diggers searching for the hidden hoards of Billy "Bowlegs" Rogers, the Gasparilla treasure, "Calico" Jack Rackam's gold, and the booty of Black Caesar, the pirate of the Keys. Rumors of finds circulate now and then but it is hard to pin them down, and any real discoveries of value are kept dark by the discoverers.

Recently, half of the town of Green Cove Springs watched eagerly while a steam shovel probed Main Street for a pirate hoard estimated at $4,000,000. The idea originated with 80-year-old G. B. Mobley, who contended that pirates coming to the area for fresh water buried their swag there. Mobley located the spot with a divining rod and made an unsuccessful try for the treasure in 1945. The city granted Mobley permission to dig a second time in exchange for 10 per cent of any money recovered and a bond that the hole would be refilled. Nothing of value was uncovered.

Boys playing pirates and poking around in deserted houses, woods, and gardens or digging caves have a good percentage of success. In Monterey, California, in January 1948, a few hundred people dug and delved on the large estate of the late W. H. Martin, who had buried coins fifty years earlier. His heirs declared the property "open territory" and the big scramble was on. By the fourth day, it was estimated that $6,000 in U.S. gold pieces had been found by the diggers. The largest strike in this modern gold rush was made by twelve-year-old Mike Mairoana,

when he uncovered $740 in U.S. gold coins in a rusty tin
can.

Two cub scouts were reported to have found $11,200
in gold in a ruined French abbey during a hike in 1954.
Part of the money went to the Benedictine monks who
owned the abbey.

When Michael Barry of Victor, New York, was a small
boy he hid his valuable belongings in an old stove pipe
above the ceiling in a second-floor bedroom. When Michael reached the ripe age of twelve he went exploring
and brought forth a rusty wrench, a water pistol, and an
old comic book. Then he thrust his arm farther back in
the pipe and drew out a rusty can containing $700 in
U.S. gold coins. The family then remembered that Michael's great-grandmother, when in her eighties, would
rock in her chair and point to the ceiling and say, "There's
gold up there!" Sure enough, there was!

In March 1951, two small boys searching in an abandoned fourteen-room house of a deceased millionairess in
Yonkers, New York, discovered three tin cake boxes holding $33,841 in coins and paper money. The lads turned
the money over to their parents, who hastened to the
police with it. The Central National Bank, administrators
of the estate, promised that the boys would be well rewarded for their honesty. Prior to the boys' discovery,
$25,300 had been found under the floorboards of a bed-
room. Guards were placed at the house. When it was demolished and the guards withdrawn, a tragic accident
occurred. A group of teen-agers were digging in an em-
bankment on the property when a sudden cave-in buried
two of them—victims of their treasure-hunting zeal.

Lawsuits often result from treasure discoveries. In 1934,
a quantity of U.S. gold coins was found in the cellar of
an abandoned old Baltimore house. The finders were
Henry Grob, age 15, and Theodore Jones, 16. Altogether

3,558 coins with a face value of $11,425.50 were dug out of the cellar wall. Litigation over the title to the money followed. This hinged largely on whether the coins were buried before or after the ancestors of the owners of the house had received their title. A court order was issued forbidding any sale of the gold but the relatives of one boy privately sold $185 worth of it at face value. The two owners, Mrs. Elizabeth H. French and Miss Mary P. Findley, offered to reward the boys with 25 per cent of the find, but the Second Circuit Court of Baltimore, with Judge Eugene O'Dunne, settled the case by awarding the entire hoard to the finders.

Then, by court order, the coins were sold at public auction, realizing $19,558.75 for 438 lots. All the coins were dated before 1857. This should have been the end of a youthful success story in the Horatio Alger style—poverty to riches—but it does not end here.

In May, 1935, the month when the auction took place, the two boys met again and "felt lucky." They returned to the same cellar, which since their first visit had been well dug over by many unsuccessful hunters. Once again the boys came up with U.S. gold to the value of eight to ten thousand dollars. There was more litigation, and again the boys were awarded the full treasure on the assumption that it was part of the original hoard. The Court of Appeals upheld the lower court's decision in the boys' favor at the end of 1937. The second find was sold privately for an unnamed sum and the coins are now scattered among many happy coin collectors.

One of the most famous historic treasure discoveries was made on a Maine farm in November, 1840, and was named The Castine Hoard. Stephen Grindle and his son, Samuel, were hauling wood for the winter on their farm near the Second Narrows of the Bagaduce River. By an old trail across the rocky land Stephen picked up a silver

French crown. Digging around the spot uncovered twenty additional coins before dark. A severe snow storm occurred during the night which rendered further investigation impractical. Early in the spring of 1841, the search was resumed.

The money had been picked up near a large rock which was partially buried in the ground about twenty-five yards from the river. Now four or five hundred silver coins of France, Spain, Spanish America, Portugal, Holland, England, and Massachusetts were found. From the location of the coins, some of which had been washed a distance away in the ground, it appeared that the hoard was placed on or near the rock in a bag or container that had rotted. The coins are believed to have been left by someone fleeing from Fort Castine, after the year 1701. Grindle sold the coins for their silver value, and probably realized something over $500. In today's market they would bring at least ten times that amount. The location was well searched in following years but no more treasures were found. Dr. Joseph Stevens purchased at the time of discovery a specimen of each variety and eighteen of these are on exhibit at the Maine Historical Society in Portland.

A farmer's plow turned up some silver and gold coins on Richmond Island, in Casco Bay, Maine, in 1855. The latest date was 1642: in all there were 21 pieces of gold and 31 of silver. There was also a signet ring, with the inscription:

> United Hearts
> Death only Partes.

The island was first settled by Walter Bagnall, who founded a trading post in 1628. Bagnall made a practice of cheating the Indians and he was murdered by a party of Redskins in 1631. The following year, Dixie Bull, the pirate who captured the village of Pemaquid, was leading

the law a merry chase and an expedition on his trail
stopped at Richmond Island. They missed Dixie but they
did capture and hang "Black Will," an Indian, concerned
in the murder of Bagnall.

Coin collectors are always eager to acquire complete
hoards when possible, because of their historical value.
Dr. P. I. de Jesus, President of the Philippine Numismatic
and Antiquarian Society, has in the last few years been
successful in obtaining three lots of buried Spanish-Colo-
nial pieces-of-eight. The first lot of 2,590 coins was unearthed in 1952 in the oldest section of Manila. The
second lot of 93 pieces was dug up in Bataan Province
and the third of 48 coins was from an unknown location.
In 1887 and in 1920, conical gold nuggets, believed to
have been used in the Philippines before the arrival of
the Spanish conquerors, were found. It is this sort of treasure that is worth many times its bullion value to his-
torians.

Dungeon Rock in Lynn, Massachusetts, is a monument
to two determined treasure hunters, Hiram and Edwin
Marble. An obscure pirate named Thomas Veale returned
from the sea and took up his abode in a deep cave under
a rock ledge. He supposedly hid his treasure nearby. An
earthquake, unusual to New England, shook up the rocks
in 1658 and pirate Veale was entombed. This legendary
story brought the Marbles to Dungeon Rock. They obtained rights to the land and began digging in 1852.
With painstaking effort they chipped, hacked, and blasted
through solid rock until by 1863 they had tunneled to a
depth of 135 feet. After sixteen years Hiram died and his
son, Edwin, continued the work until the year 1880. The
twenty-eight years of willing and backbreaking slavery in
the dark, cold, and wet ledge of solid stone was wasted
effort, it seems now. But the Marbles were obsessed with
one idea—that the gold was there and that they would

eventually reach the treasure of pirate Veale. They never did.

News headlines such as these are not unusual:

FARMER PLOWS UP CIVIL WAR SILVER, or

GOLD CERTIFICATES FOUND IN OLD SOFA, or

NEW EXPEDITION OFF FOR KIDD'S LOOT, or

DOCUMENT SIGNED BY BUTTON GWINNETT FOUND IN BARN SELLS FOR $50,000, or

TREASURE ISLAND MAP BRINGS $3,200.

Modern electrical detectors of metal and underwater devices are putting treasure hunting up to date and thousands of seekers are joining the hunt for the billions that have never come to light. It's all treasure whether it comes from the garden, the attic, or from under the old henhouse. Even if your grandfather was not a pirate he may have hid his savings in the cellar so he could sleep soundly at night.

Only the more romantic treasure seekers who can hear Long John Silver's parrot, Captain Flint, screaming "Pieces-of-eight!" along the lonely beaches on windy nights and who have no fear of Blackbeard's ghost will go after the loot of the pirates.

CHAPTER 2

Spain's Golden Galleons

Along the route of the treasure galleons from Havana to Spain lie the rotted and coral-encrusted hulls of dozens of sunken ships. This true tale of one galleon and how it was lost was learned from one of Florida's best-known treasure divers, Art McKee, of Plantation Key.

ART McKEE anchored the *Treasure Princess* over the galleon wreck and as she swung in the tide I could look down through the glass bottom and see a pile of rocks and some cannon. We were three and a half miles offshore at Treasure Harbor, Plantation Key, Florida, and the wreck on the reef below us lay in about five fathoms of clear green water.

McKee had been working at the site for three years bringing up all kinds of relics, and I had been studying the pieces-of-eight in an effort to date and identify the wreck. The coins had proved that she was one of the Spanish plate fleet that sank in the hurricane of July 1733.

Wes Bradley, the mate, started up the two compressors, one for the water jet and the other to pump air for two Miller-Dunn diving hoods. We put on thick navy-blue sweaters (although the water was about 80°) and high tennis shoes. I asked Art if the dark sweaters were to

30

prevent sharks from taking us for white meat, and he laughed.

"Don't worry about sharks, they seldom show up in this neighborhood. You'll be glad to have the sweater because after a while on the bottom, you get really chilled. The greatest danger is from sea-urchins that have spines like needles, and from coral scratches and poisoning. If your air cuts off you have a couple of minutes to come up to the surface on the air in your helmet. If your ears hurt, push your nose against the face-glass and blow till they pop. Let's go!"

He stuck his head into the diving hood and jumped backward off the ladder. After a few years as a professional diver, Art does not waste any time. I had been dropped five thousand feet underground in a copper mine but this thirty feet of water seemed deep, so I slid down the weighted shot-line.

McKee was waiting for me on the bottom and I followed him across the ocean floor, trailing air hose. The light-green brightness and visibility surprised me. Thousands of small fish swam around us. My feet seemed lighter than my head, and I wondered if the water, which was up to my chin in the hood, would come up over my mouth. Then I realized that my head was in a miniature diving bell and remembered that early divers used buckets. By the time I became accustomed to the sensations, we reached the wreck.

Hollywood has done us wrong. Here was no towering, ornate, gilded stern; no hull, no masts or spars, and no skeleton dangling from a yard arm. In over two hundred years, the worms, waves, rust, and rot had ruined the picture. Only a pile of rounded rock ballast, surmounted by three big rusted cannon, with white coral crust over all, remained of the Spanish plate ship.

We climbed up on the ballast and Art gave me a

sign-language description of the sights. The hill of stones appeared to be about fifteen feet high, and, at a guess, covered an area one hundred feet long by forty feet wide. It was surely a large galleon which in its day could stow tons of cargo and carry over two hundred people. At one end, we climbed down into a cavelike hole previously dug out and McKee started his jet hose. As he carefully washed away the sand, queer-shaped lumps of coral-covered objects appeared. If a piece looked as though anything was enclosed he handed it to me to put in a bucket. I sat down beside Art and dug with my hands, but my location only produced a few lead bullets or grape-shot.

According to the treasure stories, a decayed chest should have dumped golden doubloons into our laps, but it was not our lucky day. Not even a giant octopus lived on the wreck, but four big mutton snappers did and one of them kept crowding us in an eager search for worms. He would eat from Art's hand, and was such a nuisance that he had to be practically pushed out of the way.

Below the level of the sand, the wood of the hull was still intact. The two-foot-square keel had been exposed with some of the planking that the worms had not completely eaten. I was not producing anything of value and began to feel a little watersoaked, so signaled to Art, climbed the line up to the *Treasure Princess*, and got aboard. I was surprised to find that I had been under for nearly two hours. Wes Bradley was anxious to go down and work with McKee.

I watched them through the glass bottom, and as twilight came, I could hardly distinguish the white helmets. When the moon came up they finally quit and we hauled up two last buckets of loot. It was late September, the hurricane season, and their final chance to work that year.

On the way back to Treasure Harbor we looked over the lumps of coral and found a flint-lock pistol, initialed

H.M. on the butt, some silver ornaments, and a few blackened pieces-of-eight. Not an impressive day's haul but sure proof that plenty of material is still buried in the sand. Until the coral was cracked open, the day's work could not be valued.

From this one wreck McKee has recovered over twenty cannon of various sizes; nearly a thousand silver coins (all struck before 1733); gold rings and medals; silver statues, ornaments, candlesticks, and jewelry; pewter plates, platters, mugs, belt and shoe buckles; buttons, bullets, barshot, and daggers, swords, pistols, and gun barrels; tons of cannon balls and grape shot; nautical instruments and ship's gear; a three-ton anchor—all sorts of relics of historical value.

When discovered, most of these items are cemented together in clumps of hard coral, with spikes, coins, cannon balls, and all sorts of items from silver knives and forks to pins and broken glass and crockery in one mass. The gold has not been affected by centuries under water. Lead, pewter, and copper objects may be coral-coated but come up in fairly good condition. Silver objects and coins when found attached to iron are hardly blackened but when found alone turn to a black silver sulphide. Many of the coins are only a compressed black dust enclosed in a coral shell. When melted in a crucible, these return to metallic silver with little loss in their original weight. When assayed, some of these coins show a content of 95 per cent silver and 2.56 per cent gold. Iron and steel objects, even when found in good condition, quickly rust when brought up into the air, and in a short time completely flake apart. Wood, except when covered by sand on the ocean bottom, has completely disintegrated.

In one small spot, by careful jetting, McKee salvaged a three-carat natural teardrop-shaped emerald mounted in a delicately carved gold earring; a heart-shaped silver per-

fume flask and chain; a gold ring originally set with nine
rubies, but with only three left in the setting; a quarter
doubloon or *pistole* of gold dated 1728 from the Lima
mint; a pewter thimble, and a small pair of rusted scissors.
I wondered if some fair *señorita* had left her jewel casket
behind when rescued or went to a watery grave in the
clear green gulf.

In the buccaneer days of the seventeenth century, the
galleons sailed from Spain in a fleet and ordinarily reached
Cartagena two months later. On their arrival, the general
in charge notified Porto Bello and sent messengers overland to Lima and other Spanish colonies. The towns along
the Pacific sent the South Seas Armada with gold, silver,
and precious stones, and native produce, to Panama. The
treasure was transferred by mule train across the Isthmus
to Porto Bello, and the galleons spent two weeks loading.
Merchants from various cities came at this time to trade
and as the galleons only sailed once a year, it was a big
event. An eyewitness, writing in 1655, counted two hundred mules in one day, laden with wedges of silver which
were unloaded in the market place and permitted to lie
about like heaps of stones in the streets. In 1700, the
volume of business transacted by merchants at the Porto
Bello fair was estimated to amount to over a hundred
million dollars.

If reports came that English, Dutch, or buccaneer ships
were in the Caribbean, the fleet did not sail for Spain.
When the galleons were loading, all ports were closed
for fear the whereabouts of the flota and the value of its
cargo might leak out to enemies. Goods from China via
Manila, which had been landed at Acapulco in the Pacific,
together with the bullion and coin of Mexico, were loaded
at Vera Cruz.

The Mexican flota and the Cartagena galleons met at

Havana and, protected by heavily armed warships, sailed in a convoy for Spain past Key West, through the Bahama channel along the Florida coast and out into the Atlantic.

It would be hard to exaggerate the millions in treasure that never reached Spain. Single ships known to have been lost held as much as $3,000,000 in gold and silver. It is not stretching the truth to state that gold and silver in doubloons, pieces-of-eight, ingots, and bars, valued today at more than $65,000,000, are awaiting some lucky finders, on the Florida coast. There is probably a like amount scattered along the shores of Padre Island, Texas, and the edges of the Bahamas and the Antilles.

It would take years of research in Spanish archives to find the facts of lost galleons and the treasure they carried to the bottom. One fabulous item alone would be well worth salvaging: the gold table of 3,310 pounds' weight that was lost at sea with Bobadilla. Although there was only one such table, there must have been tons in treasure lost in the following occurrences:

In 1592, the loss of some ships of the fleet of Santo Domingo and New Spain sent by General Juan de Urive.

In 1605, the unfortunate accident to the flagship of the Honduras ships in a thunderstorm when a bolt of lightning struck the mainmast and she sank, only saving 11 of the 101 people on board.

In 1622, shipwreck of the galleons of Spain.

In 1628, the misfortune that happened to the fleet of New Spain under General Don Juan de Benavides Bazan, which was lost in the harbor of Matanzas.

In 1640, when the *Viga* and the *Galgo* ran aground on the island of Bermuda.

In 1641, the *Almiranta* which was dismasted in a hurricane, after coming out of the Bahama Channel in latitude 30°, and lost on the Abrojos.

And there were many others.

Here is the story of McKee's galleon and how the coast of Florida became littered with treasure ships.

In July 1733, the annual galleon fleet under the command of Admiral Don Rodrigo de Torres had gathered in the harbor of Havana ready to sail for Old Spain. There were eighteen huge merchant ships and dispatch boats, protected against pirates by two sixty-gun warships. Their holds bulged with silver bars and coin; gold in ingots, nuggets, dust, and doubloons.

As the sunrise gun at Morro Castle echoed across the harbor on July 13, the last passengers and crew members hurried on board. With sounds of shouted orders, blocks creaking, gulls screaming, the anchors were weighed and the great white sails were raised. With a fanfare of trumpets and a signal gun, the fleet left port . . . their red-and-white ensigns proudly displayed against the blue Caribbean sky.

The fleet had sailed at this time of the year to avoid the hurricane season. But the general had been advised by old-timers who could smell a storm brewing to await the next quarter of the moon. The advice was ignored. That day they had favorable winds, and on the 14th the wind freshened. By the 15th, when the ships were well into the Bahama Channel, the hurricane struck.

All that night, the heavy-laden, round-bottomed galleons were smashed by gigantic waves. They became separated from each other in the darkness. The sailors battled the gale to save sails and rigging, the religious prayed, and the lookouts strained their eyes for the low-lying Florida coast. Some of the ships were unmasted, some capsized. Many were swamped, and at least seventeen were lost. When daylight came, the once proud fleet of Admiral de Torres lay scattered along the Florida keys, the hulls torn out on the sharp coral reefs. Of the twenty-ship flota only three were saved.

The Boston *Weekly News-Letter* of October 18, 1733, printed this news item:

> New York—Oct. 8, 1733. We have news from Carolina, via Philadelphia that lately the Spanish flota consisting of 21 sail of ships (4 whereof were men-of-war) were cast on shoar upon the coast of Florida, excepting 2 ships; that the Spaniards have saved 12 million pieces of eight and carried the same to the Havanna with other Merchandizes, Rigging, &c.; that one Ship, Men & Cargo all perished.

The official report from Havana to Cadiz lists twenty ships in the flota and records that they came off luckier than might have been expected. The ships that grounded on the reefs in twenty to thirty feet of water were reached by skin divers and salvage crews, who recovered much of the treasure and cargo when the weather cleared. However there should still be much gold and silver left in those sunken and rotted hulls.

List of the 1733 Spanish Galleon Wrecks

Capitana (d'Rui) Went ashore in 3½ fathoms of water and was leaking so badly that unless she had grounded, all would have drowned. No one was lost and the treasure was taken out.

El Duque Lost and only three seamen were saved.

El Infante Grounded in 3¼ fathoms of water and lost all her cargo and supplies. People and treasure were saved.

San Joseph y Las Animas alias *el Conde* Grounded in six fathoms and lost entire cargo and supplies. The supercargo and three seamen were drowned.

Chaves Ran aground on sand bar in six fathoms with decks awash, all hands saved in life boats. Part of cargo saved.

Tres Puentes   Grounded in three fathoms with decks awash and saved some of supplies and cargo. All hands saved.

Herrera   Grounded in three fathoms on Matacumbe. All hands, supplies, and part of cargo saved. To this key the people saved from the *Capitana, Infante* and *Duque* were brought as there was no fresh water on the island where they came ashore.

A sloop with cargo for Florida   Cut down her masts and was beached without injury to her hull and saved crew and cargo.

Murgia   Ran aground with no serious damage and was saved.

San Pedro   Went ashore and overflowed. Lost supplies and cargo, but saved people.

El Poder de Dios   Although it hit bottom at the entrance to Ariste (?), kept afloat. Only the mizzen mast came down. Ship was saved.

El Almirante (*Gallo*)   Ran aground and was swamped. Lost supplies but saved people.

El Lerri   Grounded and was partially swamped. Lost supplies and cargo but saved people.

San Francisco   Ran aground and partially flooded. People, supplies and some cargo saved.

Sanchez-Madrid   Ran aground without making water. Later she was swamped. People, cargo, and supplies were saved.

Sanchez   Wrecked and sunk on Key Vacas. Nothing saved but the people.

El Sueco de Arizon   Wrecked on Key Vacas, damaged and half sunk. Saved supplies, people, and part of cargo.

El Navio (*Floridana*)   Sailing for St. Augustine with cargo. One man reached shore at Key Vacas on a floating spar and from him it was learned that the ship went to the bottom and all on board drowned.

El Populo   A small ship about which nothing was heard.

El Aviso del Consulado   Dispatch boat. Lost but a lifeboat was found beached with supplies and equipment from which it was supposed that the crew escaped and went overland for St. Augustine.

The *San Francisco* and the *San Ignacio* named in another record are not mentioned in the official report. It is difficult to identify Spanish ships as they used an official name and a common or nickname which is sometimes confusing.

Another hurricane had played havoc with the fleet of eleven ships in a convoy in charge of General Don Juan Ubilla and Captain Don Manuel de Echevez, which left Havana on July 27, 1715. On July 30 when well into the Bahama Channel they met a hurricane similar to the one that was to wreck de Torres' ships.

Of the eleven ships, only one, the *Grifón,* escaped the storm when her captain skillfully kept her out of the hurricane center. Eight galleons were smashed to bits between Cape Canaveral and Palm Beach; two disappeared in the sea with no trace.

The Spanish report states that thus "great hopes and success ended in destruction and misery." General Ubilla perished with a thousand persons, and silver worth 14,000,000 pesos went down with the ships. As a result, there were many mercantile failures in Seville, Cadiz, Vera Cruz, and Cartagena.

Spanish salvage and rescue crews from Havana were sent to the scene. Skin divers recovered some four millions in treasure. While the salvage was going on, news of the wrecks reached the English at Jamaica and Governor

Spotswood at Williamsburg, Virginia. This brought Henry Jennings, Benjamin Hornigold, and most of the privateers, pirates, and seamen in the West Indies and Virginia like vultures to the Florida coast.

Reports were that Jennings with two ships and three sloops had located the Spanish camp on shore and had raided it, making off with $350,000 of the salvaged treasure. Meanwhile, various interlopers were fishing on the wrecks from small boats and a ship on the way to Havana was captured with 3,000 *onzas* in gold. Official reports flew thick and fast to the British Admiralty in London but the authorities in America seemed to think it was all legal loot and winked at the pirating.

Captain Belcher of H. M. S. *Diamond* reported in part:

> . . . there was two sloops fitted out of Jamaica, one belonging to Capt. Edward James, the other to Capt. Jennings, which had my Lord Hamilton's commission for suppressing of piracies . . . But their design, as they said themselves, was upon the wrecks. They went to sea and in a shorter time than could be expected, returned again with a considerable sum of money . . .
>
> But the common report . . . was that they had been in the Gulph, had landed their people upon the Key, on the Florida Shore, and forced from the Spaniards the money . . . which they had saved out of the wrecks, and amounted to about 100,000 Dollars which . . . I thought was the greatest Piracy . . . but by those that had their share of the money thought just. Since then there have been at least Twenty Sloops fitted for the Wrecks, and if I had stayed a week longer [at Jamaica] . . . I should not have had enough men to have brought me home. I lost ten in two days before I sailed . . . being all mad to go a-wrecking, as they term it. . . .

How much treasure is still on the 1715 wrecks in Florida cannot be computed. To this day there are reports of finding silver buried hurriedly on shore by the Spanish. Some of these 1715 wrecks might be worth locating, as it is doubtful that all the bullion could have been recovered with primitive methods. Somewhere, the following galleons lay along Florida shores:

The 1715 Spanish Galleon Wrecks

Capitana   Wrecked. Only a handful were saved and General Ubilla and 225 people were drowned.

Almiranta   Although wrecked near shore, she broke up and 123 men were lost.

Storeship *Lima*   Ran aground at the mouth of a river. The sea swept 60 men overboard and 35 drowned.

First tender   Wrecked. The 25 men saved floated ashore on part of the deck when she broke up.

Second tender   Wrecked and 12 men drowned.

Almiranta, de Echevez   Sank in deep water and 124 men lost.

Concepción, de Echevez   Sank and Capt. Manuel de Echevez and 135 men were lost.

La Holandesa, de Echevez   She rode out the hurricane under bare masts but was wrecked ashore with no loss of life.

La Francesca, de Echevez   Disappeared with all on board.

San Miguel, de Echevez   Disappeared with all on board.

Grifón   Rode out the storm and escaped.

Wrecks in shallow water are being located regularly in Florida waters largely because of the perfection of various types of skin-diving apparatus. Underwater photography, spear fishing, and exploration are becoming so popular that many men, women, and children are finding it fun to rival the fish in the sea and Florida has become a happy hunting ground.

The treasures found by Art McKee are not for sale. When he first began to find wrecks, he formed a corporation, McKee's Museum of Sunken Treasure, with a few far-sighted backers and many armchair treasure hunters. A Fortress of Sunken Treasure was built at Treasure Harbor, Plantation Key, where his discoveries are on exhibit. The State of Florida granted him a five-year ocean-bottom lease extending from Molasses Reef Light about twelve miles southwest along the edge of the Gulf Stream at the ten-fathom mark to Alligator Reef Light.

McKee got into the Florida waters professionally as a diver on the water pipe line to Key West. When the job was finished he took a position as Director of Recreation at Homestead, Florida. On his days off he took a diver's holiday exploring around the ocean bottom. This is his own story of how he got into treasure hunting, told to me while we sorted coral and examined relics in the museum.

"Well, being a professional diver," said Art, "I had all kinds of folks coming to me with plans to get treasure. Most of them said they knew right where it was and if I would go down and bring it up, they would give me half of the million dollars we would find. I was working and not too anxious to go off on any million-to-one shots.

"Finally I was approached by a man who really had a good lead from a chart (I am not at liberty to tell you his name or where the wreck lay). He offered me diver's wages for a ten-day job. That suited me and off we went. When we got to the site, I went down in shallow water and found a couple of cannon in the coral. They had been chipped by someone previously to see if they were bronze or brass as those are valuable. Never having seen a wreck on the ocean bottom before, I thought the cannon had been tossed off a galleon on the edge of this reef to lighten ship, but believe me, I was fooled. I worked around through the coral without finding anything and just when I was about to quit, I noticed down in deeper water off the reef's edge what looked like more cannon.

"The next morning I dropped over the edge of the reef into eighty feet of water, wearing deep-sea diving gear. Nobody had been there before as the coral was not broken down and there were a lot more cannon lying around. On the second day, I noticed a big rounded coral growth and as I walked past, hit it with my pick. The pick punctured the coral and broke out a piece and I could see underneath a hollow place where there had been barrel staves which had rotted. I hit the coral a couple more whacks and broke off more and inside was hard black pitch or tar, with gold coins sticking out of it. I broke off a hunk of the pitch and sent it topside and they got eighteen gold doubloons out of it. I was sure excited. I had never seen gold on the ocean bottom before and this glistened like new. I broke up the mass and we found over sixteen hundred gold doubloons altogether. I took a few, which you saw in the museum, as part payment. The owner kidded me about not going fifty-fifty with him on the deal. The coins were hidden in that barrel of pitch and stored in the hold with the cargo, maybe to keep them from being stolen if the ship was boarded by pirates or by the crew of a ship of an enemy nation. Maybe they were being smuggled into some country past the tax collectors.

"One night I was talking to the Miami Stamp and Coin Club and when they saw my doubloons and heard the story, some of them said, 'How about it, can't you get the owner to sell us a couple?' When I told them he had sold the coins to melt up or use for gold-plating, you should have heard them groan."

"No wonder," I said. "Although those early Spanish Colonial doubloons from Mexico, or Granada, or Chile contain about an ounce of gold and are worth at most thirty-five dollars for the metal, they are in very fine condition, they are from rare mints, and with scarce dates they sell to collectors for all the way from sixty to five hundred dollars each. Tell me, Art, where did you get those large silver bars? You showed me two and said that you sold one to the Smithsonian Institution in Washington."

His answer told me all I could have wished:

"Those silver bars came from a different place, and it was really Charlie Brookfield who found them. I was just the guy who went down and picked them up. We were looking for cannon and I was walking around on the bottom in shallow-water gear when Charlie spotted the first bar through a glass-bottomed bucket. He noticed it because of its shape, like a loaf of sandwich bread, as it lay in a lot of rounded rock ballast. He pointed it out and I picked it up and sent it up to the fellows on deck. I could hear them banging and clanking on it as they knocked the coral off to see what it was. It was heavy and I thought it was a bar of lead. Nobody said a word and I finally climbed up and went over the rail gear and all, I was so excited. When we saw it was silver, we clapped each other on the back all around, and shook hands about a dozen times. Finally one of the fellows said, 'Did you see any more down there?' 'Yes, I saw another,' I answered. 'Well what are you waiting for? Get back down there!' somebody yelled and I went down again. When Charlie pointed out the second bar, I had them toss over the underwater movie camera and took a picture of it as it lay there. Then one of the boys came down, clothes and all, wearing black-and-white shoes, and he took a picture of me recovering the bar. You saw those movies on the Dave Garroway show.

"This second bar was heavier and after I sent it up, Charlie looked down through the glass-bottomed bucket and, lip reading, I saw him say, 'It's gold!' I had been down a long time that day and he was really saying, 'Are you cold?' but I lip-read wrong. I thought, the first bar was silver, the second was heavier and I saw Charlie say it was gold. Then I got the third bar and it was heavier yet and I thought—if this is platinum, we're made. Just goes to show that a person is never satisfied!"

The three silver bars weighed 60, 70 and 75 pounds individually. The 70-pound bar was purchased by the National Museum (Smithsonian Institution) in Washington, which announced that it was their outstanding acquisition for that year. The 60- and 75-pound bars are in McKee's Fortress of Sunken Treasure on exhibit.

A similar silver bar weighing 72 pounds, dated 1652 and cast in the foundry at Santa Fé de Bogotá, Colombia, was found by Howard Lightbourne and Roscoe Thompson off Great Abaco Island in the Bahamas. It is in very clean and uncorroded condition. It was acquired from the finders by a public-spirited citizen, Albert Edward Worswick, who presented it to the Bahama Development Board. It is on exhibit in Nassau. A. J. S. McNickle, a famous numismatist, appraised this bar as worth about $1,150 in 1652, a purchasing power of $20,000 based on today's values. (See photo section.)

When I asked McKee when he expected to bring up his first million in gold, he laughed:

"Who knows? I may move over a few feet on one of these 1733 wrecks and uncover a ton or so of gold. Only Davy Jones has full knowledge of the exact spots where it lies. Of the billions in treasure on the sea bottom, only a small part has been recovered. I am working slowly and carefully to save valuable historical relics for future generations, and adding to man's knowledge in a new field—marine archeology. We have tons of coral-covered material on shore to crack open for valuables, and more tons on the bottom to be raised. I just think of William Phips and keep diving—who knows when or what treasure may show up next?"

There are many sunken galleons outside of McKee's area. If you wish to try for one during your spare time, all you need is a motor cruiser, a trustworthy crew, a few thousand dollars' worth of electrical gadgets, tackle to raise a cargo of gold ingots and silver bars, a couple of experienced divers, and *plenty of patience*. If this equipment is too costly for you, try a glass-bottomed bucket and a rowboat. That's all the equipment Charlie Brookfield had when he spotted the silver bars. Teddy Tucker of Bermuda got his gold by digging in the sand with his fingers. Of course you have to be in the right place. Do not become discouraged if you fail on your first—or tenth—try. The treasure is there and if you miss it you will have a good time, get a fine Florida tan, and have some wonderful tales to tell your friends.

What are we waiting for? Grab your diving helmet and let's shove off for the golden galleons of the Florida Keys.

CHAPTER 3

Captain William Kidd—Pirate?

"Our trusty and well beloved Captain William Kidd."

—*King William*

"This fellow was a fool as well as a rogue."
—*Sir Edward Seymour*

"This worthy, honest hearted, steadfast, much enduring sailor."

—*Sir Cornelius Dalton*

"At best Kidd was a third-rate pirate and a fourth-rate gentleman."

—*Dr. Frank Monaghan*

"One of God's finest gentlemen."
—*Robert W. Chambers*

"There was never a greater liar or thief in the world than this Kidd."

—*The Earl of Bellomont*

"My lord, it is a very hard sentence. For my part, I am the innocentest person of them all."
—*Captain William Kidd*

IF YOU GO by tradition, Captain Kidd was one of the most noted pirates of his era, a murderer and a scoundrel. He was reputed to have ravaged shipping from the Indian Ocean to the Atlantic Coast and to have buried vast treasures in jewels, gold, and pieces-of-eight in coves, inlets, islands beyond number—and beyond discovery. If the old wives' tales were true, Kidd buried loot in more places than George Washington slept.

By historical record he was an honest sea captain who had fought against the French in the West Indies, and was respected in New York City, where he owned a fine home and had loaned tackle to help erect Trinity Church. He made plenty of mistakes in judgment, the most serious of which was to become entangled with some shrewd nobles and politicians, who left Kidd holding the bag when things went wrong with their plans.

In this period of colonial history, New York and East Coast ports were receiving privateers regularly. They posed as honest merchants engaged in what was termed "the Red Sea Trade." So-called merchant ships went out carrying, for merchantmen, oddly mixed cargoes, the main quantities being arms and gunpowder and cannon balls and lead, and strong spirits, and provisions and sea-stores. Setting a course to the southeastward, they would slip around the Cape of Good Hope to some convenient meeting place in the Indian Ocean, usually Madagascar. There they would find other ships, whereof the lading was Eastern stuff and spices and precious stones, and a great deal of yellow-red Arabian gold. From the rough and tumble, daredevil, bushy-bearded set of men no information was volunteered as to where these commodities came from and neither did the New Yorkers manifest any indiscreet curiosity. When the exchange had been effected the parties separated. The late vendors of Oriental goods, gloriously drunk on their purchases of West-India rum, went off to parts unknown while the New Yorkers sailed for home with their fine new cargos.

It is difficult to tell where privateering and trading

stopped and smuggling and piracy began. Reports from ye king's men in the colonies were full of complaints to the Lords of Trade in London.

We have a parcell of pirates in these parts which people call the Red Sea men, who often get great bootys of Arabian gold. His Excellency [Governor Fletcher of New York] gives all due encouragement to these men, because they make all due acknowledgement to him; one Coats, a captain of this honourable order presented His Excellency with his ship, which his Excellency sold for 800 pounds and every one of the crew made him a suitable present of Arabian gold for his protection; one Captain Twoo who is gone to the Red Sea upon the same errand was before his departure highly caressed by his Excellency in his coach and six horses and presented with a gold watch to engage him to make New York his port at his return. Twoo retaliated the kindness with a present of jewels; but I can't learn how much further the bargain proceeded; time only must show that.

So wrote Peter de la Noy. These were the great days of piracy when Henry Avery and Captains Tew, Mason, Glover, Wake, Hore, and others were creating havoc around Madagascar, the East Indies, and the Red Sea. The British East India Company complained regularly and often about piracy in their trading area. The pirates were welcomed in colonial American harbors. They brought money into the country. They brought needed goods. Profits of as much as 3,000 per cent were realized by ship owners, who built up great fortunes and broad estates on the trade. Although the king issued proclamations against pirates, they had many friends in high standing in the colonies who gave them protection.

It was a prominent New York merchant, Robert Livingston, who had the idea which entrapped Captain Kidd into the plan to pirate against pirates and which started the captain on his way to Execution Dock.

Livingston was a shrewd and wealthy politician and

trader, and during a trip to London in 1695 to try to collect debts owed to him by the New York Government, Livingston's path crossed Kidd's and a plan was hatched. They were friends and fellow Scotsmen who had sided politically in earlier days in New York.

The idea was to place Captain Kidd in command of a ship to catch pirates and make a huge profit on their stolen goods. The booty was to be divided among five great Whig politicians, with Livingston and Captain Kidd getting their share. The chief backers were Sir Edward Russell, First Lord of the Admiralty; Sir John Somers, Lord Keeper of the Great Seal; the Duke of Shrewsbury, Secretary of State; and the Earl of Romney, Master-General of Ordnance. Richard Coote, Earl of Bellomont, who had been appointed Governor of New York, but had not left London, was the prime promoter who enlisted the backers. Their names appeared in the agreements under aliases and it was whispered that King William III had a share in the expedition and was to receive 10 per cent of the take.

The contracts were drawn up, signed, and sealed, the money and bonds were raised, and Captain Kidd received his royal commission under the Great Seal of the Crown of England to head the project. A letter of marque was also issued to him giving him authority to capture ships sailing under the French flag. The *Adventure Galley* was purchased and outfitted and was ready by February 20, 1696.

> How then, you ask, has Kidd attained
> This reputation as a pirate?
> The fact is readily explained.
> When friends of his got really irate
> And cried 'These pirates, if we let 'em,
> Will steal the ocean drop by drop,'
> Kidd volunteered to go and get 'em,
> And so became a pirate cop.
>
> —Richard J. Walsh

Captain Kidd sailed from New York in September 1696 for the pirate hunting grounds in the Red Sea. He had enlisted a tough crew on a "no prey, no pay" basis with some difficulty before leaving port.

For a year he caught up with no pirates and made prizes of no French ships. With his crew in a mutinous state and out of control Kidd's nerve weakened and he started plundering the very ships he had been sent to protect.

Captain Kidd kills Moore, his gunner, with a bucket. Kidd's first trial was for this murder. (From a 19th-century woodcut.)

He unsuccessfully attacked the Mocha fleet in August 1697, but in September succeeded in taking several small trading vessels of no great value. On January 30, 1697/8, he captured his most valuable prize, an Armenian merchantman, the *Quedah*. He looted and burned another after taking her cargo. The *Adventure* was by that time leaky, worm-eaten, and unseaworthy and Kidd transferred his flag to the *Quedah* and abandoned the *Adventure* on the Madagascar coast. Out of his captures he took nearly a half-million dollars' worth of gold, jewels, silver, silk, and merchandise. The crew jumped ship and took the greater share of the treasure with them, leaving Kidd with some one hundred thousand dollars' worth.

Kidd was later accused of consorting and drinking with one of the pirates whom he had been sent to capture, Captain Culliford. Kidd did visit and drink with him in his cabin. He drank a cup or two of "bomboo," a soft drink of lime juice, sugar, and water. Kidd was hardly in a position to attack Culliford, as ninety-five of his crew had deserted and the remainder were paying slight attention to his orders.

News of Kidd's attacks on Moorish ships traveled fast. On November 18, 1698, the East India Company reported to the Lords Justices in London that he had turned pirate. A week later, orders went to all the Colonial governors to arrest Kidd on sight and an English squadron put to sea on his trail.

Kidd, with the remainder of his crew, sailed in the *Quedah* to the West Indies and landed at Anguilla. Here he heard that he had been proclaimed pirate. He then stopped at St. Thomas in the Virgin Islands, where the Danish governor refused to allow him to land. Five of the crew deserted and Samuel Bradley, the brother of Kidd's wife, was put ashore. Bradley was sick and probably glad to get ashore. Kidd then sailed to Mona Island (where treasure hunters have since dug), and met Henry Bolton, a merchant, who was trading among the islands. Through Bolton, Kidd sold goods out of his prize to the value of 11,200 pieces-of-eight. With part of this he bought a sloop, the *San Antonio,* or *St. Anthony.*

The *Quedah* was left in care of Bolton and the last eighteen of Kidd's crew in the river Higuey at the island of Hispaniola. Kidd sailed north in the *San Antonio* with his money and some cargo. Bolton testified later that Kidd's men plundered the *Quedah* and after five weeks left for parts unknown, telling Bolton to "stay in the ship and be damned for they would stay no longer." Most of the crew had "three or four hundred pounds a man." Bolton claimed that from sales of the cargo he only grossed 380 pieces-of-eight, which did not cover his charges and left him in debt.

Everybody except Captain Kidd seemed to be cashing in on his troubles, and as time passed the noose around his neck began to tighten.

When Kidd sailed north in the *San Antonio*, his first stop was at Lewes, in Delaware Bay, where he purchased provisions. The few men that were on board went ashore with their money. A number of the local merchants were arrested for trading with the pirates as the town had only a few days earlier been visited by another pirate. Captain Giles Shelley, a well-known Red Sea "trader," had appeared on the coast and landed twenty of Kidd's former crew at Lewes and sixteen more at Cape May. These men had come back from Madagascar as passengers with Shelley and the law was hot after them. Colonel Robert Quarry of Philadelphia reported that his sheriffs had succeeded in arresting only two with a measly two thousand pieces-of-eight between them.

From Lewes, Kidd made for Oyster Bay on Long Island Sound where he wrote to a famous lawyer, James Emmot, and to Mrs. Kidd, in New York. They met the captain and sailed with him to Narragansett Bay. Here Emmot, who agreed to represent Kidd, traveled overland to Boston to see Lord Bellomont and explain Kidd's case. The captain did not realize what a furore he had caused in the world and was simple enough to believe that Bellomont and his prominent associates would protect him against the charges of piracy.

Times had changed, however, since Governor Fletcher's era as Kidd soon found out. His partner in crime, Bellomont, laid his trap carefully to entice Kidd into his hands at Boston.

After seeing Bellomont and giving him Kidd's story and two French passes which Kidd had taken from the captured ships, Emmot returned. With him was Duncan Campbell, the postmaster of Boston, and a carefully worded letter from Bellomont saying that Kidd would receive fair treatment and his story would be given consideration. Kidd did not trust the governor's honeyed words, but he would go to Boston, and he replied, "The clamorous and false stories that have been reported of me made me fearful of writing or coming into any harbor till I could hear from your Lordship." Kidd then anchored at Gardiner's Island and in the words of John Gardiner, the proprietor, this is what took place.

Narrative of John Gardiner of Gardiner's Island, or Isle of Wight, Relating to Captain William Kidd

"That about Twenty Days ago, Mr. Emot of New York came to the Narrator's House, and desired a Boat to go for New York; telling the Narrator he came from My Lord at Boston; Whereupon the Narrator furnished the said Emot with a Boat; and he went for New York: And that Evening the Narrator saw a Sloop with Six Guns riding at Anchor off Gardiner's Island: and Two Days afterwards, in the Evening, the Narrator went aboard the said Sloop to inquire what she was; and, so soon as he came aboard, Captain Kidd, then unknown to the Narrator, asked him how Himself and Family did; telling him, That he, the said Kidd, was going to My Lord at Boston; and desired

the Narrator to take Three Negroes, Two Boys and a Girl,
ashore, to keep till he, the said Kidd, or his Order should
call for them: which the Narrator accordingly did. That,
about Two Hours after the Narrator had got the said
Negroes ashore, Captain Kidd sent his Boat ashore with
Two Bales of Goods and a Negro Boy: And the Morning
after, the said Kidd desired the Narrator to come immediately on board, and bring Six Sheep with him, for his,
the said Kidd's, Voyage to Boston; which the Narrator
did, when Kidd asked him to spare a Barrel of Cyder;
which the Narrator, with great Importunity, consented to;
and sent Two of his Men for it, who brought the Cyder on
board the said Sloop; But whilst the Men were gone for
the Cyder, Captain Kidd offered the Narrator several
Pieces of Damnified Muslins and Bengals, as a present to
his wife; which the said Kidd put in a Bag, and gave the
Narrator; and about a Quarter of an Hour afterwards,
the said Kidd took up Two or Three Pieces of Damnified
Muslin, and gave the Narrator for his proper use: And
the Narrator's Men then coming on board with the said
Barrel of Cyder, as aforesaid, the said Kidd gave them
Four Pieces of Arabian Gold for their Trouble, and also
for bringing him Wood; Then the said Kidd, ready to
sail, told the Narrator he would pay for his Cyder; to
which the Narrator answered, That he was already satisfied for it by the Present to his Wife. And this Narrator
observed, That some of Kidd's Men gave to the Narrator's
Men some inconsiderable Things of small value, which,
this Narrator believes, were Muslins for Neckcloths.

"And then the Narrator took leave of the said Kidd, and
went ashore; and at parting, the said Kidd fired Four
Guns, and stood for Block Island. About Three Days afterwards, the said Kidd sent the Master of the Sloop and one
Clark, in his Boat, for the Narrator, who went on board
with them; And the said Kidd desired this Narrator to

take on shore with him, and keep for him, the said Kidd and Order, a Chest, and a Box of Gold, and a Bundle of Quilts, and Four Bales of Goods; which Box of Gold, the said Kidd told the Narrator, was intended for My Lord [Bellomont]; and the Narrator complied with the said Kidd's request, and took on shore the said Chest, Box of Gold, Quilts, and Bales of Goods.

"And the Narrator further saith, That Two of Kidd's Crew, who went by the names of Cook and Parrot, delivered to him, the Narrator, Two Bags of Silver; which, they told the Narrator, weighed Thirty Pound Weight; for which he gave Receipt: And that another of Kidd's Men delivered to the Narrator a small Bundle of Gold and Gold Dust, of about a Pound Weight, to keep for him; and did also present the Narrator with a Sash, and a Pair of Worsted Stockings; And just before the Sloop sailed, Captain Kidd presented the Narrator with a Bag of Sugar; and then took Leave, and sailed for Boston.

"And the Narrator further saith, That he knew nothing of Kidd's being proclaimed a Pirate; and if he had, he durst not have acted otherwise than he has done, having no force to oppose them; and for that he hath formerly been threatened to be killed by Privateers, if he should carry unkindly of them.

[signed] John Gardiner

"The within-named Narrator further saith, That whilst Captain Kidd lay with his Sloop at Gardiner's Island, there was a New York Sloop, whereof one Coster is Master, and his Mate is a little black Man, unknown to the Narrator by name; who, as it is said, had been formerly Captain Kidd's Quarter-Master; and another Sloop belonging to New York, Jacob Ferrick Master; both which lay near to Kidd's Sloop Three Days together: And whilst the Narrator was on board with Captain Kidd, there was several

Bales of Goods and other Things, put on board the other
Two Sloops aforesaid; and the said Two Sloops sailed up
the Sound: After which Kidd sailed with his Sloop for
Block Island; and being absent for the space of Three
Days, returned to Gardiner's Island again, in company
of another Sloop belonging to New York, Cornelius Quick
Master; on board of which was one Thomas Clark of
Setauket, commonly called Whisking Clark, and one Har-
rison of Jamaica, Father to a boy that was with Captain
Kidd; and Captain Kidd's Wife was then on board his
own Sloop: and Quick remained with his Sloop there from
Noon till the Evening of the same Day, and took on board
Two Chests, that came out of the said Kidd's Sloop, under
the observance of this Narrator; and he believes several
Goods more; and they sailed up the Sound: Kidd remained
there with his Sloop next morning, and then set sail; in-
tending, as he said, for Boston.

"Further the Narrator saith, That the next Day after
Quick sailed with his Sloop from Gardiner's Island, he
saw him turning out of a Bay called Oyster-pan Bay,
although the Wind was all the time fair to carry him up
to the Sound. The Narrator supposes he went thither to
land some goods.

[signed] John Gardiner"

So ends John Gardiner's account.

When Kidd arrived in Boston and reported to Bellomont, he was free for a few days but soon landed in jail,
loaded with chains, or as Bellomont reported, "He has
without doubt a great deal of Gold, which is apt to tempt
men that have not principles of honour: I have therefore,
to try the power of dull Iron against Gold, put him in to
Irons that weigh 16 Pound."

Bellomont, in an attempt to collect any loose treasure,
then went after everybody who had been near Captain

Kidd. John Gardiner had the largest part at his island and carried all but the baled fabrics to Boston in person. When he returned home he found that one diamond had fallen from a package and lodged in the bottom of his bag. Mrs. Gardiner kept it, and it was later given to her daughter, Elizabeth. It was this treasure left with Gardiner on the island that probably started the buried-treasure stories but Gardiner in his sworn statement says nothing of it being buried, in fact he does not mention that Captain Kidd even set foot on the island.

The cargo had been carried away and could not be recovered. Whisking Clark was arrested and charged with depositing 10,000 pounds' worth of Kidd's goods with a Stamford, Connecticut, trader. Captain Paine, an ex-pirate of Newport, turned in seven small gold bars weighing one and three-quarter pounds to sheriff John Knott on Mrs. Kidd's order, but Knott reported that "upon the road homeward, the weight of the Gold broke his pocket, and he lost one of the bars." Mrs. Kidd's personal money and silver was seized, but later returned, on her protest. Bellomont even seized a waistcoat thought to have diamond buttons from Kidd. Seven buttons were missing, and the rest were glass. Duncan Campbell gave up the valuables which Kidd had entrusted to him. The *San Antonio* was sent to the West Indies to recover Kidd's loot, but returned empty-handed except for a report that the *Quedah* had been rifled and burned by a few of her crew.

When Bellomont and his trusted assistants finally collected all of Kidd's treasure on which they could lay hands, the list would make anyone's mouth water. (See first photo section.)

Lord Bellomont had seized Kidd on July 6, 1699, and H.M.S. *Advice*, which was sent to Boston to pick up Kidd and a load of pirates, did not arrive back in London until April 6, 1700. Kidd was held in Newgate prison until May 8, 1701, before being brought to trial at the Old Bailey, nearly two years after his arrest. Before trial Parliament ordered that the Admiralty produce all papers relating to Kidd, but when they were presented they were so mixed up with other documents that it was necessary to appoint a Special Committee to sort them out, a three-week job. When Kidd requested his papers on April 16, 1701, to prepare his defense, the French passes taken from his prize ships were missing, although they had been delivered to Bellomont in New York. These documents on which Kidd largely based his innocence of piracy were never produced at the trial. They did not come to light until Ralph D. Paine uncovered them in the Public Record Office about 1910, over two centuries too late to save Kidd.

Six judges sat at Kidd's trials, one of whom, Powell, was well known from having presided at the trial of Jane Wenham, accused of witchcraft. It was alleged at her trial that Jane could fly through the air and Powell beamed down on the prisoner and exclaimed, "You may—there is no law against flying."

Kidd was to be tried on six indictments: 1. The murder of William Moore, his gunner; 2. Piracy against the *Quedah* merchant; 3, 4, 5, & 6. Piracy against various ships in September, November, December, 1697, and January, 1698, by Kidd and nine of his crew.

A prisoner could not give evidence in his own defense and Kidd's men were charged with the same crimes as himself, which prevented his calling them to testify in his own behalf. The rules also deprived prisoners of having the services of counsel for cross-examinations.

The trials were run off in two days, May 8 and 9, 1701. The judges ordered the juries to bring in verdicts of guilty on each indictment. Kidd's innocence or guilt has been argued ever since and opinion is still divided as to whether he had a fair trial or was railroaded to the gibbet. One thing seems sure: the Admiralty, Parliament, Kidd's backers, the public, and the judges had all made up their minds that Kidd should hang.

Narcissus Luttrell, a famous diarist, noted:

Thursday, 8 May 1701. This afternoon, Captain Kidd was found guilty of murther, for killing a seaman on board a ship, also one of pyracy, and will be tried upon four others.

Saturday, 10 May 1701. Capt Kidd is found guilty upon 6 indictments of pyracy, and 8 other pyrates are condemned.

Kidd was hanged on May 23, 1701, at Execution Dock in Wapping, with three of his crew. The hangman received one pound per pirate, which was more than Kidd's backers received from their investment. To the great delight of the mob, the rope broke and Kidd was assisted up the scaffold for a second hanging. His body was then hanged in chains at Tilbury Point in the Thames estuary, where it swung in the breeze for years.

That is how he became the famous—or infamous—great Captain Kidd the pirate. He was six times found guilty and three times hanged. His money and jewels were sold at public auction on November 13, 1701, and brought £6,472/1s., which Queen Anne granted to the Royal Naval Hospital at Greenwich for disabled seamen.

Was Kidd a pirate? Did he bury his treasure? Your guess is as good as mine.

Moral

To win a Bradstreet reputation
'Tis not enough that you be pure,
Avoid the very implication
Of knowing any evil-doer.
Seek not his mischief to undo,
Nor separate him from his pelf,
Or fame may mix him up with you,

And you with him.
Don't Kidd yourself.

—Richard J. Walsh

Digging for Captain Kidd's money became a popular pastime even before his hanging. His reputed treasure-burying grounds include almost every beach or island on the Atlantic seaboard from Maine to Florida and the West Indies, Nova Scotia, the Indian Ocean, the China Seas, and the South Pacific. Maybe some of the old salts, beachcombers, hermits, or clam diggers of bygone days have unearthed some of Kidd's loot. If they did, they wisely kept their mouths shut and spent the money a little at a time and so warily that their friends and neighbors did not suspect their sudden wealth.

But tales of Kidd's treasure have been told for centuries and his name has for so long been associated with buried pirate treasure that Kidd and Treasure are synonymous in the minds of many.

From an advertisement in the New York *Mercury* in May 1762, it would seem that treasure hunters were becoming a nuisance in Manhattan. That solid citizen, Nicholas Bayard, offered a reward of five pounds for information concerning persons unknown who invaded his property by night and dug holes in his farmland. If they were money diggers, the advertisement read, Bayard would permit them to dig by daylight, provided they would refill their excavations. He also offered to return two spades and a pick left behind on their night expedition. It may be presumed they were after Captain Kidd's treasure.

An original essay on "The Art of Digging Money," which made front-page news in *The Herald of Freedom and The Federal Advertiser,* a Boston newspaper, in November 1788, explained the background of pirate treasure tales:

Towards the close of the sixteenth century and early

in the seventeenth, large numbers of pirates infested the European seas, and committed great robberies upon the property of all nations, under circumstances of unparalleled barbarity. To rid the world of these lawless freebooters, the maritime powers joined forces and "pursued the black flag" with great zeal. Many pirates were captured, condemned, and executed and those who escaped hid in various harbors and creeks in the American colonies. These retreats afforded only temporary shelter from "the extended sword of public justice . . . for although they had fled before the bursting tempest of transatlantic vengeance, to . . . havens of fancied security," proclamations soon followed them, describing their persons and their vessels, and documenting their atrocities. Great numbers of them were arrested, tried, and found guilty, which "satisfied the cries of murdered innocence, with blood for blood." The apparent poverty of some held up their punishment for a while; but the conclusion that they had secreted their wealth brought down "the stroke with double force." One or two declared at the place of execution that they were willing to purchase pardon by producing amazing treasure, concealed on various islands, but these confessions received little regard as being due to "the love of life, and the dread of death."

The public had opinions which prevented any search for the hidden treasures—as the tales circulated "that a human being was buried upon every pile"; and the superstitious believed that the blood of this victim not only formed a potent charm but also transferred the treasure to Satan who held it against any mortal hand. "Thus, for nearly half a century, these ghost-guarded, devil-watched abodes, remained undisturbed" by crowbars or spades.

The Boston author, after diligent research, could not find that his great-grandfathers had picked out any one spot, or island, as a sure hiding place of the plunder. And although several ignorant fishermen and illiterate lobstermen seriously affirmed that they had "seen gigantick apparitions on top of *Nick's Mate,* the ghosts of well-known departed pirates on *Deer Island,* and sulphur breathing genii on the *Bluff of Nantasket,*" these reports were believed the figments of disturbed imaginations and ignored. However, in process of time, stories pregnant with horror became more frequent and every month added to the growing budget of terrors. These reached the ears of half a dozen "venerable, second-sighted old women who held a weekly, winter evening's club, to frighten themselves and their neighbors with all the wild ideas of a gloomy mind."

This society pronounced every idle fiction to be the solemn truth, and invented fifty new-fangled tales to add to the pile of nonsense. They asserted *"that undiscovered millions were emboweled in such and such particular places."* With the restless curiosity of antiquated females they exhorted their male friends to raise the ghosts and demand exact answers to the treasure spots. Their endeavors met with little success, and, worn out with fruitless entreaties, they at last gathered their daughters and made them swear by the ashes of their ancestors to transmit their mothers' creed to the next generation, "wishing them all the wealth in the Chest at the bottom of the Common, and the two Pots of Gold back of the present Powder-House." These dying orders were carried out; grandames treasured up the wondrous tales and delivered the whole to their descendants.

The author (in 1788) concludes his first chapter with: "From hence it is proved, beyond the possibility of a doubt, that the present Deer Island Money-Digging Society, has the honour to deduce their origin from the eternal loquacity of six great grandmothers, the unsatisfied desires of twelve grandames, and the inflamed curiosity of 100 silly old women, of the third generation."

Chapter II of "The Art of Digging Money" appeared on December 1, 1788, and took a crack at the money-digging fraternity. It stated that "the faithful historic page, shall infallibly rescue their names from the genius of oblivion; and consecrate the trophies of superstition in the temple of ignorance." The author then went on to explain the history of digging:

A.D. 1750, produced the first attempt of any consequence, for recovery of those supposititious treasures, which common fame had buryed somewhere or other; but the expedition . . . unhappily miscarried. This did not deter a set of zealous adventurers, from prosecuting similar operations, early the following spring; and in spite of repeated disappointments, annually renewing them, for the term of twenty succeeding summers.

When a chest of massy silver, after being weighed from its dark abode, 12 feet depth, suddenly broke from the grasp of thirteen stout men, and plunged, with wonderful celerity, at least a hundred fathoms beneath the ground—not to mention a large iron pot, filled with double Johannes's, that underwent a horrid transmutation, in its passage upwards; and presented the astonished beholders, with a small quantum of red sand—or, the memorable box, two yards square, replete with the best of plate and jewels, which at the identical moment of its gaining the surface, was seized upon by a rascally set of barge men, thought to be part of Captain Avery's deceased crew, who rowed the spirit of their mouldered boat, manned with ghosts, directly into the hole, and clapping the helm suddenly up, forced a passage for the boat, skiff, and apparitions through the frog pond.

The Lynn Witch and a strolling conjurer explained that these disappointments came from a lack of knowledge. "The chest having sunk, as the result of someone saying 'here it comes,' which would forever be the case if anyone spoke. The gold was transmuted into red sand by one of the devil's alchymists because the magic circles were drawn from West to East—and that Avery's barge men carried off the box, when the left foot was foremost in the pit."

The author ends his original essay with the rules of the Deer Island Money-Digging Society, "in commemoration of forty thousand pounds sterling, deposited on said island, recoverable to and for the use of this fraternity, at the good pleasure of his Satanic Majesty, and the spirits of four murdered sailors who guard it watch and watch."

Rules and regulations are listed. Members were never to exceed 7 times 7 in number; meetings were to begin at 7 minutes past 7 P.M. and to close at 7 seconds before 7 A.M.; on the 7th of March 7 officers were to be elected, etc. Article 5 reads: "Every member shall be always furnished with an iron crow-bar, spade and pick axe, together with a gun, small sword, bible, and steel chains, 7 essential instruments, to be ready at a moments warning." At the June meeting all members "shall pay down 7 s. and 7 d. to furnish indigent brothers with 7 rounds of cartridge, charged with silver ball, for the purpose of shooting departed spirits, frequently hovering round treasure in the shape of goats, bulls, cows, etc. . . . and to pay the funeral expenses of any poor member who may be frightened to death by the appearance of the above mentioned."

The rules were signed on March 7, 1770, 7 seconds before 7 A.M.

That the editors of the Boston newspaper, *The Herald of Freedom and The Federal Advertiser*, saw fit to devote front pages to this essay by an unknown author shows how popular digging for pirate treasure was in 1788 and to what extent it had reached. The author's explanation of how the fad began probably contains more truth than fiction but the basic idea—that all pirates buried their money—has been so firmly planted in the historic sagas of America that it will never die.

Treasure hunting seemed to run in cycles. Sometimes it would boom suddenly for a few years following the publication of news that pirate treasure had been discovered or again when an author published a book or pamphlet on the subject. Of course the treasure did not have to be Kidd's; any pirate cache would do, and dirt would be thrown up almost anywhere by eager hunters.

The treasure fiction of Washington Irving, J. Fenimore Cooper, and Robert Louis Stevenson, plus old sailors' yarns, all helped to keep the public treasure-conscious. There were tales of digging at night, in which the Devil, ghosts, dogs with blazing eyes, and sulfurous fumes guarded the money.

A pamphlet published in 1844 with the story of a sunken ship in the Hudson River at the base of Dunderbergh had a Kidd text, as the vessel supposedly was his. Called "An Account of Some of the Traditions and Experiments Respecting Captain Kidd's Piratical Vessel," it sold readily. The traditions assert that Kidd's vessel was chased up the Hudson River by English men-of-war. In order to prevent her capture, those on board set fire to her, and escaped to the shore with as much money as they could carry. They left the largest portion of the gold and silver on board the wreck, which sank at the entrance to the Highlands. Kidd and his men went further up the river in boats and crossing over the land reached Boston.

This story was followed in 1846 with 'A Wonderful Mesmeric Revelation, giving an account of the discovery and description of a sunken vessel, near Caldwell's Landing, supposed to be that of the pirate Kidd, includ-

ing an account of his character and death, at a distance
of nearly three hundred miles from the place."

These old tales are garnished with weird incidents,
such as Kidd running his sword through a child which
had been left by its mother in a log house in the woods;
and an old Indian coming from Michigan to point out
to a young brave the place where the vessel had sunk.
The revelations by mesmerism were the most remarkable.
Mrs. Chester of Lynn, Massachusetts, declared that she
had never heard of the sunken ship, that she had never
been on the Hudson River, and that she had no knowledge of Kidd's history. But when put into a "magnetic
state," she revealed the sunken ship at the right spot,
and discovered through some strange power that a pirate
had been its captain. She *saw* a large stout man—not
tall—with a large chest, broad shoulders, stout neck, a
Roman nose, piercing eyes, with a character of cautious-
ness, combativeness, and destructiveness—a bloodthirsty
filibuster. She also *saw* the vessel with chests full of
gold bars, heaps of precious stones, including diamonds,
in decayed shot bags; "gold watches like duck's eggs in
a pond of water," a diamond necklace, and near it, the
remains of a beautiful young woman.

"This revelation," wrote an editor of the period, tongue
in cheek, "as it is corroborated by traditions, presents
us with another triumph of animal magnetism, and must
serve not only to advance that science, but to demon-
strate how much safer it is to rely upon tradition, than
upon written evidence made in courts of justice, held
contemporaneously with the events, or official documents
preserved in public archives."

The nickel and dime novels, so popular during 1850-
1920, built up Kidd's reputation along with those of Buffalo Bill, Frank Reid, and the Merriwell boys. There were
pirate stories like the Red Raven Library, with Captain

Kidd's Sea Swoop, Captain Kidd's Buried Treasure, Captain Kidd's Revenge, his Stratagem, his Long Chase, his Drag-Net, Kidd at Bay and Kidd in New Orleans. There were Haunted Islands, Golden Skulls, Ogres of the Ocean, Greybeard, Blackbeard and Red Beard; there were Death Ships, Sea Fiends, Pirate Doctors, and Demons of the Deep. It was a very poor writer indeed who could not get a pirate and his treasure into print. And Kidd led them all in popularity.

As recently as 1951, Kidd hit the headlines, because of the demise of one of his stanchest boosters, Hubert Palmer, of Eastbourne, England. For many years Palmer gathered pirate relics of his favorite hero, Captain Kidd. It would seem that almost everything (except treasure) that had ever touched Kidd's hands gravitated to Palmer's Kidd Museum. When Harold T. Wilkins, an expert on pirate lore and a friend of Palmer's, wrote *Captain Kidd and His Skeleton Island* in 1937, the Kidd relics were described and illustrated. Palmer owned a piece of Kidd's black flag, an oil portrait of Kidd, and a plaster skull-and-bible on which Kidd's crew supposedly swore allegiance—but the most valuable of the Kidd mementos were a number of chests and a desk. Each of these items was carved and initialed "W.K." or lettered "William Kidd, His Chest," and, believe it or not, in each was hidden, in a false bottom or hollowed-out secret spot, a manuscript map of an island where Kidd buried his booty.

When Hubert Palmer passed on to join his friends Kidd and company, he willed his collection to his housekeeper, who had loyally dusted the leg-irons, polished the pistols and waxed the chests in the Museum. When the relics were publicly auctioned, the Kidd treasure maps were held at a value of $8,400, and the highest bid being only a paltry $70, they were withdrawn from the sale. Soon after, eager treasure hunters sought out the owner, Mrs. Elizabeth Dick, with plans to sail to the spot "X" and recover the treasure.

The first attempt to organize an expedition by members of a Rye, England, boat yard seemed a good idea. The originators of the plan advertised for twelve people who would be carefully selected to form the party, and who were to put up enough cash to finance the expenses. If no treasure was found, the party would get their money's worth in adventure on a long sea voyage. The Palmer map presumably located Kidd's hoard on an island a few hundred miles off Singapore, in the South China Sea. How Kidd came to visit an island in that part of the world was not explained. The history of his exploits does not seem to place him in the area during his career. This expedition died from what was reported as "legal troubles," a common complaint among treasure-trove addicts.

Late in 1951, another group was formed consisting of fourteen amateur seamen with Captain A. Coumandareas, a fifty-seven-year-old Greek ex-freighter captain. Coumandareas owned the schooner-rigged racing yacht *Lamorna,* and was willing to carry the treasure party. They armed themselves with elephant guns and revolvers as protection against Chinese pirates. The yacht was palatially equipped with a salon, baths, and modern conveniences, and a pleasant trip seemed assured. In high spirits, with the skull and crossbones of the Jolly Roger flying from her masthead, the *Lamorna* sailed from Gosport. Photographers and reporters cheered the adventurers on their merry way in the search for Kidd's booty, forgetting the curse on pirate gold.

Four days out they ran into a full gale. Heavy seas swept the racing yacht's deck. The mainsail ripped to shreds. The foremast snapped and crashed down taking the mainmast with it. The Royal Navy frigate *Redpole* picked up the *Lamorna's* distress signals and sped to the helpless yacht. At great danger, the frigate's crew rescued the treasure hunters in life boats and the *Lamorna* ran ashore, a total wreck. Another unsuccessful treasure hunt was added to the lengthening list of failures.

The numerous tales of Kidd and his treasure would easily fill a five-foot shelf, and one of the most famous is here reprinted in full. This yarn was first told in 1894 and has been in more or less private circulation for over sixty years, with an occasional, and sometimes garbled, rewrite in the daily press. Since it is the very stuff of romance and high adventure, the entire document is included.

A Notable Lawsuit *

by
Franklin H. Head.

Magna est veritas et prevalebit

"*The inquiry of truth, which is the love-making or wooing of it; the knowledge of truth, which is the presence of it; and the belief of truth, which is the enjoying of it—is the sovereign good of human nature.*"

—*Francis Bacon*

"The suit commenced some three years since by Mr. Frederic Law Olmsted against the various members of the Astor family in the New York Superior Court, attracted considerable attention at the time, both from the prominence of the parties to the litigation, and the large amount claimed by Mr. Olmsted, something over $5,000,000. As the case has not come to a hearing, owing to the delays

* From *Studies in Early American History*, Chicago, privately printed, 1897.

in the proceedings at law, the matter has, in a measure, passed from notice, scarcely anything connected with it having appeared in the public prints since the commencement of the action.

"Through the courtesy of Mr. Olmsted, I spent several days during the summer of 1895, as a guest at his summer residence on Deer Isle, which lies in Penobscot Bay, off the mouth of the Penobscot River, on the coast of Maine; and having heard quite in detail the history of the cause of action, which seemed to me a most forcible illustration of the maxim that truth is stranger than fiction, I take pleasure in giving the story as told me by Mr. Olmsted and the members of his family.

"An ancester, seven generations back, of Mr. Olmsted, whose name was Cotton Mather Olmsted, was an Indian trader, and spent a part of each year from 1696 to 1705, in what is now the State of Maine. His treatment of the Indians was always fair and honourable, whereby he won their confidence and esteem. Winnepesaukee, then the head sachem of the Penobscot tribe, was at one time severely wounded by a bear, and Mr. Olmsted having cared for him, dressed his wounds, and aided greatly in his recovery, the chief, as a token of gratitude, presented to him the Deer Isle before named, a portion of which has ever since remained in the possession of his descendants, and is now the property and summer home of Mr. Frederic Law Olmsted. The original deed of gift, written on a piece of birch-bark, and bearing date January 24, 1699, is still in the possession of Mr. Olmsted, and after the independence of the United States was acknowledged, the validity of the transfer was recognized and affirmed, and a formal patent issued by the Secretary of the Treasury during the second term of President Washington's administration.

"Upon the rocky shore near the residence of Mr. Olm-

sted, and at the extreme south end of the island, is a
cave, the opening of which is upon the sea. The cave is
about ten feet wide and high, of irregular shape, and
extends back into the rock formation some twenty-five
feet. It has evidently been excavated by the ceaseless
action of the waves upon a portion of the rock somewhat
softer than its surroundings. At high tide the entire cave
is under water, but at low tide it can be entered dry-shod,
being entirely above the sea-level. The bottom of the cave
is covered with coarse sand, five or six inches deep, below
which is a compact bed of hard blue clay. At low tide the
cave is often visited by the family of Mr. Olmsted, and
the other residents of the island. In 1892, Mr. Olmsted
observed upon the rock at the inner end of the cave some
marks or indentations, something in the form of a rude
cross, which seemed to him possibly of artificial origin. If
so, it was of ancient date, as its edges were not well
defined—were rounded and worn, as by the action of the
waves and ice. Still, it appeared more regular in form
than the other markings upon the walls of the cave, and
Mr. Olmsted one day suggested to his family, when in the
cave, that as stories of Captain Kidd's buried treasures had
sometimes located such treasures upon the Maine coast,
they should dig at the place below the cross for such hidden wealth. Purely as a matter of sport, the excavation
was commenced: the sand was cleared away, and, to their
surprise, a rectangular hole in the clay was discovered,
about fifteen by thirty inches on the surface and about
fifteen inches deep. This was filled with sand, and upon
the sand being carefully removed, there was plainly to be
seen upon the bottom of the hole the marks of a row of
bolt heads some three or four inches apart, and extending
around the bottom about one inch from its edge. The
appearance was precisely as if an iron box heavily bolted
at its joints had been buried in the compact clay for a

period long enough to have left a perfect impress of itself in the clay, and after its removal, the excavation having been filled with sand, the impression had been perfectly preserved. After a perfect facsimile of the bottom of the hole had been taken in plaster of Paris, the excavation was again filled with sand. The clay was so hard that the taking of the cast did not mar its surface. The bottom of the hole and such portions of the sides as had not been marred by the removal of the box were heavily coated with iron-rust, so that everything indicated the former presence of an iron box which had remained buried in the clay long enough at least to become thoroughly rusted on its surface and firmly imbedded in the clay matrix. As there were various legends relative to the presence of Captain Kidd upon the Maine coast, the discovery of the excavation was sufficient to awaken eager interest in the question of the iron box and the person who carried it away.

"About the year 1801 a French-Canadian, named Jacques Cartier, who was one of the employees of John Jacob Astor in his fur trade, and who had for several winters traded with the Indians and hunters along the upper waters of the Penobscot River, returned from New York, where he had been to deliver the season's collection of furs, and expressed a desire to purchase from Oliver Cromwell Olmsted, who was then the owner, by inheritance, of Deer Isle, either the whole island or the south end, where the cave before described was located. Mr. Olmsted refused both requests, but finally sold him a few acres near the center of the island, where he built a log house and lived for many years with an Indian wife, hunting and fishing occasionally as a diversion, but giving up entirely his former method of gaining a livelihood. This trader had for several years previous to 1801 camped upon the south end of Deer Isle when collecting his furs, passing up the Penobscot River and its tributaries in a small canoe, and storing his furs in a hut at his camping-place until the end of his season, when he sailed with his little cargo for New York. He had always seemed extremely poor, having but a meager salary from Mr. Astor, but when he purchased a portion of the island he seemed to have an abundance of money, sufficient in fact to meet his wants for many years. Occasionally, when under the influence of whiskey, he would speak vaguely of some sudden good fortune which had befallen him, but when sober he always denied ever having made the statement, and seemed much disturbed when asked about the source of his wealth, which led to various suspicions among the few inhabitants of the island as to the honesty of his methods in acquiring it. These suspicions ultimately became so pointed that he suddenly disappeared from the island and never returned. On searching his cabin some fragments of papers were found, torn and partially burned, so that no connected meaning could be determined from them. On one fragment was the signature of John Jacob Astor, and on another, in the same handwriting, the words: 'absolute secrecy must be observed because.' These fragments were preserved, however, and are now in the possession of Mr. Frederic Law Olmsted. From the story of the trader and from the fragmentary papers, Mr. Olmsted fancied that there might be some connection between the mysterious box and the newly acquired wealth of the trader, and that the secret, if one there was, was shared by Mr. Astor. As the trader for many years previous to his sudden good fortune had camped upon the end of the island immediately adjoining the cave, it might readily be conceived that a heavy storm had washed the sand away so as to make the top of the box visible, and that he had found it and taken it with him to New York to Mr. Astor, with his boatload of furs. His desire to purchase this particular location in the island harmonized with this suggestion.

"Various questions presented themselves regarding this theory. Had the box contained the long-lost treasures of Captain Kidd? If so, to whom did the box and its contents belong? Mr. William M. Evarts, to whom Mr. Olmsted applied for an opinion as to the legal phase of this question, after careful examination of the evidence, gave his views, in substance, as follows:

1. That Captain Kidd, in the year 1700, had acquired, by pillage, vast treasures of gold and gems, which he had somewhere concealed prior to his execution in 1701.
2. That if such treasure was concealed upon Deer Island, that island was the absolute property, at that time, of Cotton Mather Olmsted; for while the record title to the island bore date in President Washington's administration in 1794, yet this, as appeared by its tenor, was in affirmation of the title made in 1699, when the island was given to Cotton Mather Olmsted by the Indian chief, Winnepesaukee, and established the ownership of the island in Mr. Olmsted when the box, if concealed by Captain Kidd, was buried, and that Frederic Law Olmsted, by inheritance and purchase, had acquired all the rights originally held by his ancestor in that part of the island where the treasure was concealed.
3. That, as owner of such real estate, the treasure would belong to him, as affixed to the land, as against the whole world, except possibly the lineal descendants of Captain Kidd, if any there were.

"Mr. Olmsted learned that, in his early life, Mr. Astor kept for many years his first and only bank account with the Manhattan Bank, and as the books of the bank are all preserved, he was enabled, by a plausible pretext, to secure an examination of Mr. Astor's financial transactions from the beginning. His idea, in this search, was to learn if Mr. Astor's fortune had increased at the same time as that of the French-Canadian. The business of both Mr. Astor and the bank was small in those early days, and the entries of the customers' accounts were much more in detail than in our time, when, as a rule, only amounts are recorded. The account commenced in 1798, being one of the first accounts opened after the picturesque organization of the bank of Aaron Burr, and for several years the total deposits for an entire year did not exceed $4,000. He shipped some of his furs abroad, and others were sold to dealers and manufacturers, and whenever he drew on a customer with a bill of lading, the books of the bank show virtually the whole transaction. Entries like the following are of frequent occurrence:

Cr. J. J. Astor, $33. proceeds draft for sale of 40 Muskrat, 4 Bear, 3 Deer and 12 Mink Skins.

Credit John J. Astor $49.50, proceeds of draft for sale of 400 Skunk Skins.

Cr. John Jacob Astor $131. proceeds of draft on London for £26/10s. for sale 87 Otter Skins, 46 Mink and 30 Beaver Pelts.

"Each year showed a modest increase in the volume of business of the thrifty furrier, but the aggregates were only moderate until the year 1801, being the same year the Canadian trader bought of Mr. Olmsted a portion of Deer Isle, when the volume of bank transactions reached, for the time, enormous dimensions, springing from an aggregate for the year 1799 of $4,011 to over $500,000 for the year 1801. Among the entries in the latter year are two of the same date for cheques to Jacques Cartier, the French-Canadian: one of $133.50, drawn 'In settlement fur account,' and one for $5,000, 'In settlement to date.' Inasmuch as in each previous year the aggregate fur transactions with Mr. Cartier had never exceeded $500, the entry of $5,000 seemed inexplicable on any ordinary grounds.

"The enormous growth of Mr. Astor's own transactions

also seemed equally mysterious. Mr. Astor had evidently
visited England in the year 1801, as the bank entries are
filled with credits to him of drafts remitted by him from
Roderick Streeter, varying from £10,000 to £40,000, and
aggregating, during the year, nearly $495,000. Credits of
the same Streeter drafts are made also during the two
following years to the amount of over $800,000 more, or a
total of over $1,300,000, when the Streeter remittances
abruptly cease. Edwin W. Streeter of London is at the
present time one of the largest dealers in precious stones
in the world, and as in England the same business is often
continued in a family for many generations, it occurred to
Mr. Frederic Law Olmsted, who, from the facts already
given, had become greatly interested in following the
matter to a conclusion, that the Streeter who had made
the vast remittances to Mr. Astor might be an ancestor of
the present London merchant. An inquiry by mail developed the fact that the present Mr. Streeter was a great-
grandson of Roderick Streeter, and that the business had
been continued in the family for five generations. Mr. Olmsted thereupon sent a confidential agent to London, who
succeeded in getting access to the books of the Streeter
firm for the years 1798 to 1802, inclusive. Here was found
a detailed statement of the transactions with Mr. Astor.
The first item was for £40,000 entered as 'Advances on
ancient French and Spanish Gold Coins' deposited by
Mr. Astor, and later another of £4,213/8s. for 'Balance
due for the French and Spanish gold coins.' All other
entries were for the sale of precious stones, mostly diamonds, rubies and pearls, which, in all, with the sums
paid for the French and Spanish gold, reached the enormous aggregate heretofore given. Certain of the gems
were purchased outright by Mr. Streeter and the others
were sold by him, as a broker, for the account of Mr. Astor,
and the proceeds duly remitted during the years 1801-

1802. The whole account corresponded exactly, item for item, with the various entries of Streeter remittances shown on the books of the Manhattan Bank.

"The facts gathered thus far enabled Mr. Olmsted to formulate a theory in substance as follows: That Jacques Cartier had found the box containing the buried treasures of Captain Kidd; that he had taken it to New York and delivered it to Mr. Astor; that Mr. Astor had bought the contents of the box, or his interest in them, for the cheque of $5,000; that he had taken the contents to England, and had, from their sale, realized the vast sums paid him by Mr. Streeter. Many links in the chain of evidence, however, were still missing, and a great point would be gained if the mysterious box could be traced to the custody of Mr. Astor. It seemed reasonable that this box, if ever in the possession of Mr. Astor, and if its contents were of such great value, would be retained by him with scrupulous care, and that, if he had imparted the secret to his children, it would still be in their possession. If not, it might have been sold and lost sight of, as a piece of worthless scrap-iron, after the death of the first Mr. Astor. Mr. Olmsted learned that the last house in which the original John Jacob Astor had lived had been torn down in the year 1893, to be replaced by a superb modern building, and that the old building had been sold to a well-known house wrecking firm for an insignificant sum, as the material was worth but little above the cost of tearing down and removal. In the hope that the rusty box had been sold with other rubbish about the premises, Mr. Olmsted inserted the following advertisement in the New York *Tribune:*

> A rusty iron box, strongly made and bolted, was by mistake sold in 1893 to a dealer in junk, supposedly in New York or Brooklyn. The dimensions were 15 X 30 X 15 inches. A person, for sentimental reasons, wishes to reclaim this box, and will pay

to its present owner for the same several times its value as scrap-iron. Address F. L. Box 74, N.Y. *Tribune*.

"Within a few days, Mr. Olmsted received a letter from Mr. Bronson B. Tuttle of Naugatuck, Connecticut, an iron manufacturer, stating that, in a car of scrap-iron bought by him from Melchisedec Jacobs of Brooklyn, was an iron box answering the description given in the *Tribune;* that if it was of any value to the advertiser, it would be forwarded on receipt of eighty cents, which was its cost to him at $11 per ton, the price paid for the carload of scrap. Mr. Olmsted at once procured the box and shipped it to Deer Isle, where the bolts upon its bottom and the box itself, were found to fit perfectly the print in the clay bottom of the cave. The plaster cast of the bottom of the cavity, taken when it was first discovered, matched the bottom of the box as perfectly as ever a casting fitted the mold in which it was made. Every peculiarity in the shape of a bolthead, every hammer-mark made in riveting the bolts, as shown in the clay, was reproduced in the iron box. There was no possible question that the box was the identical one which had been long before buried in the cave. On the top of the box, too, was distinguishable despite the heavy coating of rust, in rude and irregularly formed characters, as if made by strokes of a cold chisel or some similar tool, the letters W.K., the initials of the veritable and eminent pirate, Captain William Kidd. Further inquiry developed the fact that Melchisedec Jacobs, the Brooklyn junk dealer, had purchased the box in a large dray-load of scrap-iron, mostly made up of a cooking-range, sash weights, gas, steam and water pipes, etc. from the wrecking firm of Jones & Co., and that Jones & Co., had taken much material from the family mansion occupied by the original John Jacob Astor at the time of his death, when tearing it down to make room for the new buildings. The indications thickened that the mysterious box contained the long-lost and widely sought treasures of Captain Kidd. One peculiarity of the box was, that there had apparently been no way of opening it except by cutting it apart. The top had been firmly riveted in its place, and this fact possibly indicated the reason of its purchase by Mr. Astor at the moderate price of $5,000, as the trader who found it had been unable to open it before his arrival in New York. As, however, we have no information of the contract between Mr. Astor and Jacques Cartier, the amount named, $5,000, may have been precisely the percentage agreed upon, which he received upon the profits of his season's business in addition to a salary.

"Mr. Olmsted had an accurate copy made of all entries in the books of the Manhattan Bank as to the transactions of Mr. Astor shown by such books, from 1798 to 1803, and his English agent had similar copies made of all entries in the books of Roderick Streeter for the same period, also copies of many letters passing between the parties. The agent also looked up and reported everything available relative to the career of Captain Kidd, the substance of which was as follows:—

"Captain Kidd had won an enviable reputation in the English and American merchant marine, as a brave and intelligent officer. For many years the English merchant vessels had been preyed upon by pirates, numerous vessels were captured and destroyed, and others robbed of all their treasure. These depredations were largely along the coast of Madagascar and Mozambique, on the route of the English vessels in the India trade, and off the coast of South America, where the Spanish galleons bore great treasure from the Peruvian gold-fields. The depredations of the pirates became so great that the English merchants finally bought and equipped a stanch war-vessel, placed the same under the command of Captain Kidd, and sent him out expressly to chastise and destroy the pirates. As these pirates were known to have secured vast amounts of gold and gems, it was expected that Captain Kidd might not only clear the infested seas of the piratical craft, but capture from them enough treasure to make the operation a profitable one. After reaching the coast of East Africa, news was received of the destruction by him of sundry piratical vessels containing much treasure, but the capture of this treasure seemed to excite his own cupidity, and he decided to himself engage in the occupation of being a malefactor. For some two years thereafter he was literally the scourge of the seas. He plundered alike other pirates, and the merchant vessels of every nation. Finally, after a cruise along the eastern coast of the United States, as far north as the port of Halifax, he, for some reason, decided to boldly make an entry at the port of Boston as an English merchant vessel, under the papers originally furnished him in England. Before entering Boston harbor, he put ashore and concealed on Gardiner's Island a considerable quantity of merchandise, consisting largely of bales of valuable silks and velvets, with a small amount of gold and silver and precious stones. These articles were afterwards discovered and reclaimed by the owners of the vessel, and sold for some £14,000, which was divided among them. From the great number of vessels which he had destroyed and plundered, with their ascertained cargoes, it was known that the treasure thus discovered was but an insignificant fraction of what he had captured,— was known that gold and gems of vast value were somewhere concealed,—and thence came the endless searches from Key West, and Jekyl Island to Halifax for the treasure, which had thus far seemingly escaped human vision and utterly disappeared. In fact, from the little care taken by Captain Kidd as to the plunder hidden on Gardiner's Island, the owners of his ship concluded that to be merely a blind to divert their attention from the vastly greater wealth he had appropriated. A short time after his arrival in Boston he was arrested and sent to England, and at once put on trial for piracy. In two days he was tried, convicted, and hanged. This illustrates the great progress in civilization since that benighted age, for now the most red-handed and popular murderers are allowed months for preparation and trial, are feted, garlanded, and made the heroes of the day, and assigned, with all priestly assurance, to the mansions of the blest. His wife was not allowed to see him, except for a half-hour after the death sentence had been pronounced.

"They held a whispered conference, and at its close he was seen to hand her a card, upon which he had written the figures 44106818. This card was taken from her by the guards and never restored, and every effort was made to induce her to tell the meaning of the figure, but she utterly refused, and even claimed not herself to know. The paper was preserved among the proceedings of the trial, and a photographed copy secured by Mr. Olmsted. From the records of the trial, it appeared that Captain Kidd was the only child of his parents; that he had been married for several years; that two children had been born to him, a daughter, who died while yet a child and before the trial, and a son, who survived both his father and his mother. It also appeared that this son, ten years after his father's execution, enlisted as a private soldier in the English Army and was killed in the battle near Sterling in 1715. The records of the English War-Office showed that the widow of this son applied for a pension under the then existing law, that her affidavit and marriage certificate showed her to have been married to the son of Captain Kidd, and that no child had been born to them, and the usual pension was awarded her and paid until her death in 1744. These facts settled the question as to any claim upon the treasure by descendants of Captain Kidd. The records of the trial also contained a report by experts upon the card given by Kidd to his wife, to the effect that they had applied to the figures upon it the usual tests for the reading of cipher-writings, without avail, and if the figures ever had a meaning, it was undiscoverable. The same conclusion was reached by several people to whom Mr. Olmsted showed the copy of the card.

"In the summer of 1894, when Prof. David P. Todd, the astronomer of Amherst College, was visiting the family of Mr. Olmsted at Deer Isle, he one day amused himself by calculating the latitude and longitude of the home, near the cave, and gave the results to Miss Marion Olmsted. As she was entering the results in her journal, she was struck by the fact that the figures for the latitude, 44°10', were the same as the first four figures on the card, 4410, and that the other four figures, 6818, were almost the exact longitude west from Greenwich, which was 68°13', a difference easily accounted for by a moderate variation in Capt. Kidd's chronometer. The latitude, taken by observation of the pole-star, was absolutely accurate. It appeared as though Capt. Kidd had told his wife in this manner where to find the hidden treasure, but that, inasmuch as the government authorities had seized the card, she preferred silence toward those who had pursued her husband to his death, and the total loss to everyone of the treasure, rather than, by a confession, to give it into the hands of his enemies. The very simplicity of the supposed cipher-writing had been its safeguard, since all the experts had sought for some abstruse and occult meaning in the combination of figures.

"By a happy thought of Miss Olmsted, another link was thus added to the chain of evidence. With the facts given, the only point seemingly needed to show that the Kidd treasure had come into the possession of Mr. Astor, was to show that some of the money or gems sold by him had been actually seized by Captain Kidd. Even this, by a happy chance, became possible through the correspondence secured from Mr. Streeter of London.

"It appeared that, in the year 1700, Lord and Lady Dunmore were returning to England from India, when the vessel upon which they had taken passage was fired upon and captured by Capt. Kidd. His first order was that every person on board should walk the plank into the sea, but several ladies who were passengers pleaded so earnestly for their lives, that Kidd finally decided to plunder the cargo and passengers and let the vessel proceed on her voyage. The ladies were compelled, on peril of their lives, to surrender all their jewelry, and among the articles taken from Lady Dunmore was a pair of superb pearl bracelets, the pearls being set in a somewhat peculiar fashion. Another pair, an exact duplicate of those possessed by Lady Dunmore, had been purchased by Lord Dunmore as a wedding gift to his sister, and the story of the two pairs of bracelets and the loss of Lady Dunmore's pearls, which were of great value, and of her pleading for her life to Capt. Kidd, is a matter of history, as well as one of the cherished family traditions. In 1801, Roderick Streeter writes to Mr. Astor that the then Lady Dunmore, in looking over some gems which he was offering her, had seen a pair of exquisite pearl bracelets which were a part of the Astor consignment, and had at once recognized them as the identical pair taken by Kidd nearly one hundred years before. She returned the following day, with the family solicitor, bringing the duplicate bracelets; told and verified the story of the loss of one pair by Lady Dunmore; compared the two pairs, showing their almost perfect identity, showing certain private marks upon each, and demonstrating beyond question that the pearls offered by Mr. Streeter were the identical gems seized by Captain Kidd. The solicitor demanded their surrender to Lady Dunmore on the ground that, having been stolen, no property in them could pass even to an innocent purchaser. Mr. Streeter then stated that he had asked for delay until he could communicate with the owner of the gems, and asked Mr. Astor for instructions. Mr. Astor replied, authorizing the delivery of the bracelets to Lady Dunmore, and asking Mr. Streeter to assure her that the supposed owner was guiltless of wrong in the matter, and was an entirely innocent holder. He repeated the caution, given also in sundry other letters, that to no one was the ownership of the gems sold by Mr. Streeter to be revealed. They were to be sold as the property of Streeter, acquired in the regular course of business. Lady Dunmore afterward sat to Sir Thomas Lawrence for her portrait, and was painted wearing upon her arms the pearl bracelets thus curiously reclaimed. This portrait is considered one of the masterpieces of Lawrence and is now in the collection of Mr. Hall McCormick of Chicago.

"By the discovery of the hole in a cave in Maine, after a lapse of nearly two hundred years, was thus curiously brought to light the apparent origin of the colossal Astor fortune. Prior to the acquisition of the Kidd treasures by the first American Astor, he was simply a modest trader, earning each year, by frugality and thrift, two or three hundred dollars above his living expenses, with a fair prospect of accumulating, by an industrious life, a fortune of twenty or thirty thousand dollars. When he became possessed of the Kidd plunder, he handled it with the skill of a great general. He expanded his fur trade until it embraced the continent. The record of his cheques given during the three years when he received the one million, three hundred thousand dollars shows that he expended over seven hundred thousand dollars of the amount in the purchase of real estate in the City of New York. The entries of the various cheques are recorded as 'Payment for the Wall Street property,' the 'Bond Street land,' the 'Broadway corner,' etc. the descriptions being sufficiently accurate, when verified by comparison with the titles of record, to locate at this date every parcel of land bought, and all of which is still in the possession of the Astor family. Some twenty different tracts of land in what is now the very heart of the business and residence portion of Manhattan were thus purchased, each one of which is now probably of more value than the price originally paid for the whole. In obtaining a knowledge of the various details already given, over two years had been spent by Mr. Olmsted and his agents. The results seemingly reached may be summarized as follows:—

1. Captain Kidd had sailed along the Maine coast shortly before his arrest, and an iron box, marked with his initials, was afterward taken from the cave upon the land of Mr. Olmsted, and this box afterward came into Mr. Astor's possession.

2. Jacques Cartier had camped for many years, while employed by Mr. Astor, immediately adjoining the cave where the box was concealed, and his rapid increase in wealth and that of Mr. Astor were simultaneous.

3. Mr. Astor's great wealth came from the sale, through Mr. Streeter, of ancient Spanish and French gold, and of gems, some of which were proved to have been part of the spoils of Captain Kidd, which made it a reasonable presumption that all of such property was of the same character.

4. Captain Kidd was known to have captured and somewhere concealed gold and gems of vast value, and the card given to his wife just before his execution indicated, by a plausible reading, the cave upon Mr. Olmsted's land as a place of concealment.

5. The family of Captain Kidd had long been extinct, and no one could successfully contest with Mr. Olmsted the ownership of the property concealed upon his land.

"Having his evidence thus formulated, Mr. Olmsted called upon the descendants of Mr. Astor, accompanied by his attorney, Mr. Wm. M. Evarts, and demanded of them:—

1. A payment by them to him of the sum of $1,300,000. The amount received of Mr. Streeter, with interest from the date of its receipt. The total amount, computed according to the laws of New York in force since 1796, was $5,112,234.80; and Mr. Olmsted offered, on condition of immediate cash payment, to deduct the item of $34.80. This demand was refused.

2. Mr. Olmsted then demanded that the Astor family should convey to him all the real estate in New York City purchased by their ancestor with the money received from Mr. Streeter, with the accrued rents and profits from the date of its purchase, and this demand was likewise refused.

"These refusals left Mr. Olmsted no other alternative except to resort to the courts for the establishment of his rights, and an action was accordingly commenced. The declaration filed by his attorneys, Joseph Choate, Stewart L. Woodford, and Frederick W. Holls, sets out in full the history of the claim from the beginning, as has been detailed herein, and petitions the Court for alternative relief; either that the descendants of John Jacob Astor pay to Mr. Olmsted the sum of $1,300,000, with interest from the time of its receipt by Mr. Astor; or, failing in this, that Mr. Astor be adjudged a trustee for the rightful owner of the money thus received, and that the property purchased with such funds be ordered conveyed to Mr. Olmsted. To this declaration the Astor family, by their solicitors, Elihu Root and Edward Isham, answered, denying all liability, upon the ground that the cause of action, if ever valid, was barred by the statute of limitations. To this answer the plaintiffs demurred, alleging for grounds thereof that it appeared clearly from the pleadings that Mr. Olmsted had been vigilant in the assertion of his claim as soon as reasonable proof of its existence came to his knowledge, and further, that the statute of limitations did not run as against a trust. The demurrer was sustained by the Court upon both grounds, the Court intimating, however, that when the case came to a hearing the plaintiff must select and rest his case on one or the other form of relief demanded, and could not, in the same action, secure the alternative relief sought. After this decision the defendants filed a general denial of all the claims of Mr. Olmsted.

"This is the present status of the litigation, and it is expected that the case will be brought to final trial during the present year.

"Should the judgment upon the trial be in favor of Mr. Olmsted, or even against him upon some technical ground, it would, in either event, be a great boon to the people along our Atlantic seaboard, in that it will reveal the actual fate of the Kidd treasures. The publicity upon this point will stop the ceaseless and fruitless expenditure of money in digging for such hidden wealth, as well as the exactions of clairvoyants, Indian spiritual mediums, rappers, professional ghosts, and witch-hazel experts, who have yearly preyed upon the credulity of their victims in locating the Kidd deposits.

"From the dramatic character of the claim, from the eminent ability of the counsel for each contestant, and from the large amount involved, it is needless to add that the trial will be watched with intense interest, and that it will stand as the *cause célèbre* of our century."

This tale was written for amusement in 1894 by Franklin H. Head, a prominent Chicago manufacturer and a friend of the Olmsteds who owned a summer home at Deer Isle, Maine. So many people were taken in by the story that the Olmsteds were called upon for years with an almost endless chain of inquiries from friends, acquaintances, and total strangers, asking for full details and explanations. Frederic L. Olmsted, in self-defense, finally sent out a circular to newspapers and public libraries, in which he explained that the story was written purely for the amusement of the author and his friends. Mr. Head, he wrote, had also produced a monograph called "Shakespeare's Insomnia"; while it had been amusing to explain the Kidd-Astor fabrication to friends, after more than thirty years it was becoming a bore.

It has now been well over half a century since Franklin Head and the Olmsted family laughed over the tale, which is one of the best and most successful hoaxes ever perpetrated. When reprinted in *Forum* in July 1931, the editors hoped "to lay this ghost for all time" as the story had no foundation in fact whatsoever; they ended their exposé with the observation "the truth which is stranger than fiction *is* fiction."

CHAPTER 4

The Treasures of Silver Shoals and the Isle of Mystery

The tale of two great hoards still waiting to be brought to light; the Spanish galleons that Sir William Phips missed and a great pirate treasure that defied two years' efforts on the island where pirate headquarters was established. The story of a skilled treasure hunter who went after the loot, and who tells why it is still there.

IN THE YEAR 1683 the British Admiralty sent two naval ships, the *Faulcon* and the *Bonetta*, to chase pirates and try to locate the Spanish fleet of galleons from Mexico to Spain that went to the ocean bottom on November 14, 1643. Old sailors of the West Indies, even those with firsthand knowledge of the wrecks, disagreed as to where the galleons had been lost. About eighteen leagues southeast of Turks Islands and north of Santo Domingo lay what the English called Handkerchief Shoal, known to the French as Mouchoir Carré and to the Spanish as Los Abrojos, and called by the English Abroxes or Ambroses. To the southeast of these lay Am-

90

brosia Bank and the North and South Riffs, and it was
on one of these that the wrecks were suspected to have
struck.

Captain George Churchill was in charge of the expedition on the *Faulcon,* and under him was Captain
Edward Stanley on the *Bonetta.* Serving on the *Bonetta*
at the time was that old buccaneer Bartholomew Sharp
of South Seas fame, who had quit pirating and gone into
naval service. Churchill had with him, as the expedition's guide, a Dutch captain named Harman, who
was presumed to know the location of the sunken Spanish ships. They cruised around the area for months and
finally gave up the hunt.

Churchill was later made Commissioner of the Admiralty and was serving in that capacity when Captain
Kidd was hanged in 1701. In 1702 he was made Admiral
of the Blue. Sir Winston Churchill, his present-day
kinsman, refers to Captain George as "virtually, in modern terms, 'First Sea Lord,'" and elsewhere quotes him
as having used, on a notable occasion, a fine old piratical aphorism which he may well have picked up in the
West Indies: "Dead men tell no tales." Captain George
Churchill in my records is just "The Man Who Missed
the Boat," as it was to the honor, fame, and wealth of
William Phips that the galleon treasure accrued.

Captain Phips, one of a New England family of
twenty-six children, heard about the Spanish wrecks and
stuck to the search until, after three cruises that were
marred by mutinies, disappointments, and competition,
he hit the jackpot. With native skin divers Phips recovered 65,466 pounds' weight of gold and silver from one
wreck. A hired assistant, Captain Adderley, brought up
six tons with another boat. They also gathered gold,
pearls, and jewels, and Phips honestly carried the loot
back to England where it was divided. Adderley retired

to Bermuda and drank himself to death, while Phips was knighted by King James II and made Governor of the New England Colony. He died in 1694, and the story of his success is chiseled on his gravestone: ". . . by his great industry, [he] discovered among the rocks near the Banks of Bahama on the north side of Hispaniola a Spanish plate-ship which had been under water 44 years, out of which he took in gold and silver to the value of £300,000 Sterling: and with a fidelity equal to his conduct, brought it all to London, where it was divided between himself and the rest of the adventurers. . . ."

The light-green combers broke on the offshore reef and foamed up onto the South Florida beach. The stiff inshore wind from the east made the palm fronds sing like wind-harps. That weird coppery light across the Gulf Stream toward Spain threatened the coming of the hurricane season and I could almost see the galleon fleet rolling homeward in the deep blue distance.

"You know," said Logan, "it is this sort of weather that has sent many a treasure expedition racing for its home port. This is no time of year to be anchored over Silver Shoals. I tried it and I know. Right now I would be making for Puerto Plata and a safe anchorage. We really had it on that Silver Shoals trip."

This was what I wanted to hear. I had been lucky to catch up with my friend, Waldo Logan, and get him to talk. Logan was one of the few men I have known in a lifetime of meeting treasure hunters who have really dug into the subject—mentally and physically. He was a big man . . . a hulking cross between buccaneer and college professor. In Sir Henry Morgan's attire, Logan would not only look the part but could talk it—he had trod Morgan's path and a few spots that even the great

Sir Henry never saw. He spent years in research, dug, dived on, or just visited scores of historically noted treasure sites, and during his spare time compiled a list of over two thousand pirates, their haunts, and their time of action.

While the wind rattled the palms, I listened and Logan talked. . . .

"Under the scientific aegis of Beloit College Museum, I financed and headed an assault on Silver Shoals in 1936. We first made an aerial survey using a plane supplied by President Trujillo of Santo Domingo and based our operations on Puerto Plata. All I wanted to do was to thoroughly study the possibilities of salvaging treasure there, not to actually go after it then. I had laid out a five-year plan for myself in the Caribbean, and the Shoals represented only one of eighty-three sites that I planned to visit. These treasure locations were divided about equally above and below water and I managed to get to seventy-six of them before the war intervened. If we had tripped over any treasure on these surveys we wouldn't have kicked it out of the way, but we were not equipped for salvage at this time.

"In the party were Captain John D. Craig, the noted diver and movie photographer; Dr. Edgar End of Marquette University, who was studying the effects of helium gas on divers; Tommy Larkin, an Akron photographer; René Dussaq; a couple of others and a native crew.

"One of the most relentlessly dangerous areas in any ocean of the world lies eighty-five miles off the coast of Santo Domingo, formerly Hispaniola. It is composed of strange coral growths which rise from the deep to spread like monstrous lily pads a half mile or so across. They are just barely awash when the sea is still and a roaring caldron of destruction when wild water smashes into the more than five-hundred-square-mile area of jagged teeth and unpredictable currents. The area is not accurately charted, to this day.

"It was straight into this watery inferno that the great West Indian hurricane drove the Spanish flota of 1643, carrying one of the richest treasures ever to join the water-soaked wealth of Davy Jones.

"The Spanish galleon fleet of that year was deeply laden with treasure from the New World. Even the ballast of rocks in six of the ships had been replaced with rough chunks of gold-bearing ore that assayed well over $100,000 to the ton. Twenty-six ships carried a combined value (as of 1643) of $112,500,000 in gold, silver and merchandise.

"The fleet sailed straight to destruction. Only a handful of wretches, who managed to bind heavy timbers into a raft onto which they lashed a keg of water and three silver bars, survived. Days later they washed ashore on the Santo Domingo coast, more dead than alive, and reported the disaster.

"In the dim past, the man who was to become famous as Sir William Phips took $1,322,000 from one wreck alone, using native divers from the Indian Ocean and long-handled rakes and grapnels. By the ingenious use of large wooden tubs inverted to hold air in storage for the divers to gulp, they were able to stay under for more than twenty minutes at a time. Later, the local fishermen and natives raised another million or more, after Phips sailed for home.

"That was the background of Silver Shoals, to which we headed with modern equipment. As I look back, my admiration grows for tough old New Englander Phips and his divers. He deserved his fame and honor and wealth.

"After careful preparation, including the aerial photography, which helped us chart reefs, shoals, and wrecks not visible from sea level, we left Puerto Plata in the *Isabella*, a salt lugger turned sponger. She was sixty-two feet over-all, with fourteen-foot beam, and drew about seven feet—ideal as far as vermin and insect life were concerned, as the salt-impregnated wood repels them.

"Going out of the harbor we lost the log line to a shark; our chronometer was my Ingersoll. The skipper and crew did not know our destination or they would not have sailed, as the place has a bad name among the superstitious natives. The Shoals are mischarted eighteen miles in one direction and a good twenty in another. The best time to work there, strange to say, is the hurricane season, for that's the only time you get calms. You need constant radio weather reports, as even in a chop the place becomes a maelstrom.

"Thanks to our air pix and research, we eventually found the wrecks. We anchored in a fairly clear area about a quarter of a mile away, and went to work. It was a strange place. The great expanse of lily-padlike heads of coral creates an optical illusion so amazing that you would swear the longboat was below the level of the surrounding sea. Everybody got the same feeling. We were all unaccountably nervous for the first two days, till we figured it out. The Doc and Larkin were both in bad shape and pretty miserable; in fact, Doc was so sick at one time that I thought he was going to pass out.

"We did a lot of diving with Craig's equipment—a forerunner of the self-contained diving apparatus of masks with rebreathing gadgets. We also used a complete suit and helium-oxygen. We had a couple of close calls, with gear failing at a critical point, but those things are always a possibility on any diving job. We shot some of the first successful sixteen-millimeter undersea color film and incidentally discovered that the first twenty to twenty-five feet of water filters out all the reds.

"Picture yourself standing on the bottom. Fading off into the distance on all sides are strange vistas formed by hundreds, even thousands, of huge, toadstoollike pillars, in weird conformations, rising and spreading out at the surface above you into vast irregularly rounded platforms. The sides of these pillars and the bottom are thick with various coral growths (we brought back eleven previously unknown varieties) laced with kelp and all kinds of entangling plants swaying and waving in the ever-changing currents. We did a lot of exploring and brought up plenty of corroborating stuff. The wrecks we found will yield if handled right. There is much coral incrustation and silting over them. It would be *very* costly.

"The peculiar conditions on top are the biggest problem, which of course would govern actual salvage. Several times, black squalls came up on a serene day in as little as twelve minutes. You need a couple of rabbit's feet, a mother's prayer, and a good radio—our receiver conked out the first week.

"One of the native crew was among the strangest guys I ever met. He was white, to begin with, but you'd never know it and he never let on. He was known to have killed at least two men but was usually very pleasant. The strangest part—and all of us will swear to it—was that at first light of day, he closed his right eye and kept it closed all day. At night, he opened it and could see fine. We never could figure it out. But he was the best damn seaman I ever saw. I'll tell you why.

"There was no question but that we were pressing our luck. Then we got a taste of a real blow and had to get the heck out of there fast. I wanted to measure the height of the waves and went a little way into the rigging. They were running about fifty-two feet high. Coming down, a sea caught me and slammed me onto the deck, breaking two of my small ribs. The boat was so wild there was a chance of getting a punctured lung or something. I asked this character when he thought we would sight the lighthouse outside Puerto Plata. It was about 10 P.M. and he answered (as always, in bad Spanish), 'About 2:30.' In a nasty blow, with a compass gone haywire, completely dead reckoning, and a leaking hull thick with growths, he hit it almost right on the nose at 2:25. The distance was nearly a hundred miles when we started. I was mighty glad to see the light. After I got taped up, he and I went on a binge. That's when I learned he was white and could speak excellent English.

"After we got back, we fritzed around Santo Domingo for a while, then went to Mona, but not before poor Doc landed in the hospital and I got bit by a tarantula at sea. It was about six and a half inches across and damn near killed me. Wow!

"Say, did I ever tell you how to cut banana stalks so they will ripen consecutively? It sure comes in handy at sea."

"Never mind the bananas," I said, "you had me right along with you on Silver Shoals. What a movie that underwater jungle would make. Of course you should have a school of octopussies or bloodsucking wampuses attack Craig, while you filmed his struggles to bring up the gold."

Twilight had changed the light on the ocean to silver and pink pastels. The humid wind had lessened and for a while we sat silent. My companion was a real student of pirate and treasure lore and I was reluctant to have him stop talking. "You told me you had outlined around eighty spots to survey," I said. "Where, if you had to pick one location, would you really go to work and stay with it until you brought up the treasure?" I asked.

"That's not tough to answer," said Logan, and he went on—

"Let's call it Isle of Mystery or The Great Treasure or something. You will understand when you hear about the place why I am reluctant to spill the name or location. Maybe I will get back there someday and finish up the job I started just before the war. I have $87,000 and twenty-two months' hard work invested in the place. Of course that sum represents various expenses over the years such as travel and other activities directly laid out on this one project. More than half was actually spent on the island itself.

"I first learned about this great treasure just twenty-five years ago. Bit by bit and piece by piece the information collected in years of research, study, and travel finally fell into place and facts began to emerge.

"This island in the Caribbean could be called the Cross-roads of the Buccaneers. In my examination of seventy-six good locations, the most important was this Isle of Mystery. Properly approached, I believed it would yield rich treasure. I still do. With an all-out assault any participant would be richly rewarded. The treasure, at the time of its concealment, was estimated at a value of $110,000,000.

"Forgive me if I sound like a stock-selling prospectus. There are at least two other treasure hoards on the island. One is possibly the remains of the cache from which a beachcomber digging in the sand took $40,000 in 1935. Another is believed to have been discovered a while before, but the finder went insane. He was removed to the mainland but never gave out any sensible information on his strike—a true case of gold madness.

"The island has been largely barren since an earthquake in the 1700's but is partly covered with dense jungle growth. It resembles a gigantic jigsaw piece, upended in some titanic upheaval and honeycombed with caves, some of which are enormous. The beaches are wide and were used in pirate days for careening and carousing—the place was the favorite haunt of many famous pirates and their women.

"Before the earthquake shook the island to its core and in the days when the Caribbean was overrun by the Brethren of the Coast, this spot was a popular hide-out. Pirates came and went, huge camps were set up and tended by slaves ministering to every wish of their wild masters, while others tended livestock and field crops. There were streams of fresh water on the island then, and although the water is now gone, the island still shelters wild goats and hogs which hide in the caves by day and forage by night. I have often thought of capturing some of these wild animals and holding them for a short while without water . . . they could be then given a shot of some harmless radioactive isotope, released, and tracked to their fresh-water supply with a Geiger counter.

"More unadulterated deviltry and rapine was launched here than from any other Caribbean pirate island. The Spaniards, realizing the danger from this pirate nest, started building a fort to guard it and the sea route it threatened. The pirates watched its progress until completion, then swooped down in a murderous tide and took it for their own. It offered many conveniences they had hitherto been denied, a good anchorage and privacy to gather, refit, and plan. From the island they ranged the far corners of the world, returning to revel, split their loot, or lick their wounds. It was natural that some would use the place as a safe deposit for the tons of heavy gold and silver accumulated from many captures.

"One of the boldest and shrewdest of the pirates was a certain captain, well known in history. Not only did he lead many raids on the seas but towns and islands either surrendered to him or went up in flames so his men could pillage and search the ruins. He was not above lifting the hard-won spoils of a fellow pirate. He was hated, feared, and despised, except by his own crew, who swore by—and at—him. Before one rendezvous with other pirate chiefs for an expedition against a rich but strongly fortified town, our captain thought of his vast hoard piled away in caves. Suppose some of his rivals cleaned him out while he was away—he might be gone for months—whom could he trust?—only himself. And he made a plan.

"The single cave that formed the entrance to an inner treasure-filled cavern, he blocked with dirt, and he covered the doorway with a huge flat stone, cunningly fitted. He then detonated heavy charges of gunpowder in the cliff over the entrance until tons of earth covered the area. It would take fifty slaves working a month to uncover even the face of the entrance cave, and his men from a nearby island could report any activity in the vicinity. Even if the outer cave was reached, the dirt with which it was filled would have to be emptied before the inner connecting caves and his treasure would be in danger.

"He sailed with the pirate fleet, and they attempted their raid, but they found they had blundered into an ambush. The Spaniards blew most of their vessels out of the water or sent them down in flames. The pirates that were not killed in action soon died at the hands of their captors. Of the bare handful that escaped, our captain was one. Badly wounded, he managed after many hardships to reach his own country, where he died in bed—one of the few pirates in history to cheat the gallows."

"Waldo, my friend, are you sure you are not giving me the 'Tiger of the Seas' of Beadle's Dime Library, No. 1507?" I asked.

A large orange moon had risen over the Gulf Stream and I wondered if the romance of the tropic evening had not carried my friend into the realms of fancy.

"I was never more serious," he answered soberly. "Do

you think I would have spent over $80,000 of my own money on a dream? Let the Cocos Island diggers do that, not me. I carefully documented my facts before I tackled the place."

"I apologize," said I, "but for a minute I thought you were going to tell me that you fell into a hole in a cave and found the skeletons of twelve pirates playing fan-tan around a table of solid gold."

"I'll tell you as much as I can release about this great treasure," said Logan, "and what happened when I went there." And he continued his tale.

"That famous pirate—I am deliberately withholding his name—was a wise and canny scoundrel. He took great precautions that only one person should have certain clues to the exact location of the entrance. He then added the precaution that some of those clues should be written in the now long-dead patois of the pirate colony of the island of Madagascar. A ray of light appeared rather early in my research because of a chance interpretation of a word in Arabic, which in turn led me to study the artificial language referred to.

"Putting all my records together, sorting, arranging, and discarding, I gradually found that the true picture of this great treasure was meeting the acid tests of treasure hunting. I have evolved, over the years, two basic questions.

"They are: 1. Was the treasure actually in existence at the particular time involved?

"2. Was it disposed of in the manner you believe?

"If both can properly and truthfully be answered Yes, and the treasure has not been found, you are a long way toward its recovery, if you know how to go about getting it, going after it, and bringing it back.

"After many blind alleys, wrong leads, and interruptions, some very important facts were established, so I could answer the two questions with Yes. Now I must go to the island in person, for I was the only one who knew what to look for, and where.

"I went to the island and was happy to find that the site of the treasure was undisturbed. Returning to the United States, I outfitted a complete expedition, returned to the island, and began work. It was slow and tedious. The obstacles that had to be overcome were tough but not insurmountable.

"The project on which I spent almost two years consumed over two tons of high explosives. I also used powerful hydraulic jets of sea water. I was told that it would be impossible to set the crated pump engine, weighing 726 pounds, in a fourteen-foot rowboat and ferry it more than a mile to shore through a lagoon, to say nothing of hauling it up a sheer cliff thirteen feet high and then carrying it about seven hundred feet through practically impassable brush.

"We had about two inches of freeboard after we got the engine into the boat. Now we waited three days for the right tide and conditions. It got through all right, was hoisted up the cliff, set onto a sled with corrugated iron runners, and dragged through a path that took twelve good machete men six days to hack out. It worked like a charm for months and we sometimes threw water as high as a hundred and fifty feet up the cliffs with one-hundred-pounds-per-square-inch pressure. We were really hydraulic mining and if we had been working in pay dirt would have cleaned up a fortune.

"Did I get the treasure? No. I was reluctantly forced to discontinue operations and withdraw at the express wish of the governor of that group of islands because of the imminence of war. A little later, a German sub surfaced off shore and fired more than twenty shells into the old workings, apparently thinking they were a part of some army installation.

"Before leaving I had altered the landscape enough to make the correct location impossible to detect, and I have a complete plan of attack in case I find it possible to return to the island again.

"Since that day, much more than two centuries ago, when the man-made landslide roared down to cover the spot, nothing but an earthquake has moved those piles of thick golden coins and blackened pieces-of-eight. They lie there in their massed thousands, with blood-red rubies from the mines of Mogok, great glowing emeralds, and pearls beyond price, while against the walls are piled the wealth of Spanish galleons, rich cathedral crosses, and the loot of three towns—the Great Treasure of that Isle of Mystery."

CHAPTER 5

The Pirate's Skull

A weird tale told on a windy, stormy night on Cape Cod

"Why Bluebeard had only one wife at a time, although he murdered five of them, whereas Blackbeard had seldom fewer than a dozen, and he was never known to murder above three. . . . He never wore anything but a full-dress purple velvet coat, under which bristled three brace of pistols, and two naked stilettos, only eighteen inches long, and he generally had a lighted match fizzing in the bow of his cocked scraper, whereat he lighted his pipe, or fired off a cannon, as pleased him . . . he died where he fell, like a hero—'his face to the sky, and his feet to the foe', leaving eleven forlorn widows, being the fourteen wives, minus the three that he had throttled."

—*Michael Scott, "Tom Cringle's Log,"*
Blackwood's Magazine, *1829*

THE SKULL before us on the table stared at me with empty eye sockets. Outside, the gale rattled the windows. The three of us—the skull, my host, and myself—kept cozy company together before the blazing driftwood fire. Here, on Cape Cod, in an old New England house, it was hard for me to believe that, a few

104

hours before, I had been in my office in noisy New York.

The telegram from my old friend, Ed Snow, reached me just before lunch. It had read, "Come today to stay overnight. Will meet you South Station," and I had locked my office and taken the next train to Boston. On the way, I had wondered why Snow wanted to see me and I thought of the time I had missed his treasure discovery on Cape Cod because I was out of town when he sent for me.

Edward Rowe Snow is an interesting and amazing man. He has dug for—and found—buried treasure; does four weekly radio broadcasts; writes one book a year on shipwrecks and storms; knows every lighthouse keeper on the Atlantic coast; and, as the flying Santa Claus, drops them Christmas bundles from a plane. He has tramped almost every foot of the Atlantic coast line, solved the mystery of the heart buried on Nantucket Island, traced down a confession of the Borden ax murders signed by Lizzie herself, and owns not one but a whole collection of pirate treasure chests. When he has a new discovery and says "Come!" it is something worth seeing and hearing. You can understand why I dashed for Boston when his wire arrived.

We met at South Station and drove to the Snow residence through torrents of rain. On the drive down I tried, with no results, to find out what Ed had to show or tell me.

"Wait till after supper and you'll find out. I didn't get you up here for a wild-goose chase."

After Mrs. Snow had stuffed us with Boston baked beans and ham, I followed Ed upstairs to his den. Here, surrounded with pirate relics, with a warm fire roaring, we could talk all night. Ed is a teetotaler, but he hospitably brought out the Medford rum and, when I had poured myself a mug, said: "I won't hold out on you any longer—I have found the skull of Blackbeard!"

He placed a small iron-banded box on the table, unfastened the catch, lifted the lid, and said, "See for yourself."

Inside the lid a silver plate was fastened on which was engraved in antique style:

Captain Edward Teach or Thatch

"Blackbeard"

Killed in battle by Lieut. Maynard

21 November 1718

Reaching into the box, my friend carefully lifted out a rounded object wrapped in tissue paper, closed the lid, unwrapped the tissue, and laid a human skull on the table before me. I had expected to see a gruesome yellowed and dirty cranium and was surprised to see that this one was silver-coated. The fire's flames played strange tricks with the lighting, and I could almost imagine that the jaw, a few of its teeth missing, moved a little.

I laughed nervously, took a quick drink of my rum, and asked: "Is it the real thing, and why the silver finish? Is it really Blackbeard's? Where did you get it? Where has it been all these years? I hope you haven't been taken in by some scheming antique dealer."

"My friend," answered Snow, "I love you like a brother, but you talk too much. Pipe down, take another swig of rum, and relax. This is my tale and I can assure you that *that skull is Blackbeard's.*"

As I relaxed, the skull staring steadfast at me, Ed told his story.

"As you know," Ed said, "the worst of the pirates that ever sailed the Atlantic coast in the 1700's was this villain, Captain Teach, or Thatch, or Blackbeard. A more ferocious, evil-looking, and more devilish rogue never existed. He sailed into Charleston harbor and held the whole town at bay until the Governor raised a ransom for an important citizen he had captured. Teach called his crew into his cabin one night, touched off a pot of sulfur, and shouted, 'Let's make a little Hell of our own and see who can stay longest.' While his gang ran on deck choking and blinded with the fumes, Blackbeard roared with laughter and outstayed them all. One night he fired his pistol under the table and blew away the knee of his mate, Israel Hands, crippling him for life. A fine joke! He buried treasure along the coast and stated before he died, 'Nobody but me and the Devil knows where my money is buried and the one what lives longest will get it all!' He had many wives, and reports were that he did away with most of them. He—"

"Pardon my interruption, Ed, but that's all in the history books. As to wives, I understand that one of Blackbeard's chests was dug up along the Virginia Capes. The finders were surprised when they pried up the lid and instead of gold doubloons, found the skeleton of Blackbeard's seventh wife, badly water-soaked. Tell me how and where you found that silver-painted bonehead and how you can prove it was the one Blackbeard inhabited."

Snow got down to business and I listened.

"Blackbeard was killed in a fight with Lieutenant Maynard, his head cut off, tied to the bowsprit, and taken into port. It was obtained by one of the influential men of Bathtown, who had the skull lined with silver, inside and out, after which the boldest of the owner's family and friends would challenge each other to drink

toasts from it. It later became the property of a college
fraternity, was resilvered, and initiates were obliged to
drink a pint of wine from Blackbeard's skull to qualify.

"When the fraternity dissolved, about the time of the
American Revolution, the skull's owner bought a tavern
on the Potomac River. At his death his son continued
the tavern and exhibited the skull from time to time."

On a trip to Virginia to solve some historical mystery,
Snow visited a ninety-year-old historian and a chance
remark led to the rediscovery of the pirate's skull in a
small nearby village. After considerable discussion, examination, and appraisal, the skull became Snow's property. That was the substance of his tale of the skull's
history.

"So far," said I, "it's a darn good yarn and well
documented as to where it has been for all these years.
But I wonder—couldn't that be any old skull from some
medical student or surgeon? Maybe the owner told so
many people that it was Blackbeard's that after a while
he believed his own story."

"I *know* it is the skull of Blackbeard," said Snow
positively. "I'll tell you what finally proved it to me. I
have not told this to anyone; in fact, I don't dare to. You
know that I am a sensible, sober man. You know that I
would not try to fool you. I *know* that is Blackbeard's
skull because he talked to me. Right here. Last night.
Right where I am sitting now." And while the rain beat
on the windows and the firelight flickered, Ed talked
on as I stared at the skull and it stared back at me.

"Last night I was trying to finish a chapter in my next
book. I was tired and not in the mood. The first part of my
tale had almost written itself, but I now found myself unable to concentrate. It was a wild night outside. The wind

Blackbeard (left) killed in a fight with Lieut. Maynard. (From a 19th-century woodcut.)

had come up and was howling around the chimney and the eaves. A shutter was loose and banging. It was a terrible night and I thought of the lighthouse keepers in their lonely towers and the fishermen off this dangerous shore. It was on such a night that the pirate Bellamy and his crew went ashore on Cape Cod, and, except for the season, the same kind of storm in which the steamer *Portland*

went down with all souls. I threw down my pen and, plac-
ing one elbow on the desk, rested my cheek in my palm. A
distant rumble of thunder rolled and torrents of rain beat
against the dormer windows. The wind rose almost to
screams.

"I had remained in that position for perhaps three minutes when I heard a voice—a low but distinct voice—
saying—

" ' 'Tis a dirty night to be off a lee shore—get to the
pumps, you dogs—'

"I instantly turned around, expecting to see someone
standing behind me, though in the very act of turning I
thought how impossible it was for a visitor to come upstairs at that time of night. There was nobody visible. I
glanced toward the door leading to the stairs. It was un-
likely that the door could have been opened and closed
without my hearing it, and the family was asleep.

"Again I heard the voice distinctly, 'Get a reef in that
sail, you lubbers—do yer want your bones to bleach on
the beach?'

" 'I am dashing around on a wild nightmare,' I said to
myself. 'Clearly this is a result of overwork.' My next
impression was that I was being made the victim of some
practical joker who had ingeniously put a recording on
my machine and timed it to play at a late hour. But I
recalled that my tape recorder was out of gear and needed
a new tube. The voice had certainly come from somewhere
in this room. The skull was sitting on the window sill,
behind me. Could the voice have come from the skull? It
seemed like nonsense, but since the thing was unexplain-
able I decided to accept it.

"I turned and looked steadily at the skull and said, 'Are
you the person who just spoke to me?'

" 'I am not a person,' replied the voice, slowly, as if with
difficulty. 'Formerly I was a person—a person of impor-

tance. Possibly you have heard of me—I was Captain Teach.'

"Mechanically I threw a sheet of paper over the last page of my manuscript. Not ten minutes before, I had written the following:

" 'When Blackbeard was pardoned by Governor Eden's court, he acquired another woman as his wife and with her sailed north to the Isle of Shoals, off the New Hampshire coast. There he lived happily with his bride for several weeks while supposedly burying a treasure of silver bars and gold coins on the two islands of Smuttynose and Londoner. Just as he finished, his men reported a British fleet in the offing and Blackbeard was forced to flee. Mrs. Blackbeard (Number Six) was left on Smuttynose Island to await the return of her husband. Blackbeard never returned, and tradition tells us that the woman lived for many years at the Isle of Shoals, until her death in 1735. It is said that her ghost still haunts the lonely place.'

"I have never been a believer in spirit manifestations, perhaps because I was never fortunate enough to witness any. But here was a mystery that demanded consideration—something that could not be explained away on the theory that my senses had deceived me. What is strictly supernatural is not always to be taken too seriously. Perhaps it was my immense curiosity rather than any spirit of scientific investigation that steadied my nerves; for I was now as cool and collected as I am right now with you visiting me. I settled back in my chair and crossed my legs.

" 'Did I understand you to say,' I asked, 'that you were the great Captain Teach, who was called Blackbeard?'

" 'Indeed I was,' said the skull.

" 'Blackbeard, who held the whole coast in fear and was not afraid of man or the Devil?'

" 'Ah, you know me! I was certain of it when I was carried here and heard the waves and the moaning of the wind. I thought for a few minutes we were going ashore on this dangerous coast, where my pal Bellamy and his crew met their end.'

" 'Almost everybody knows you, Captain. You have been the subject of much discussion, many books, articles, and pamphlets. Your treasure has been hunted for over two hundred years. Even Hollywood made a movie of you last year.'

" 'Hollywood? I know not what you blab about Hollywood—nor have I ever seen the name on any chart. But they have written books about me; well, well, I should have furnished news for many a tale by some lousy scrivener to peddle on the streets.'

" 'Were you not aware of it? That you were famous?'

" 'Yes, mate, I was famous in my day but, alas, I know nothing that has happened since that evil day in 1718 when the tide left us grounded in Ocracoke Inlet. I would have shown those British my stern, if we had not grounded. That crew of mine were a scurvy lot, but had they the guts to fight like men, we would have won that skirmish. I hope they swung for their weakhearted surrender. At least I cheated them from making a show of me on the gallows. Hell's fire! 'tis better to stand up and die like a man, says I, and I did. Some dog cut me down from behind, curse him, while I was engaged face to face with that navy Leftenant.'

" 'If it makes you feel better, Captain, I can tell you that you have always been credited with being a devil both in fighting and with the women. It is written you had seven wives.'

" 'Such slander—what belittling fool wrote that? It was Bluebeard he meant, not me. I, Blackbeard, had no less than thirteen wenches who were proud to be called Mistress Teach—for a short time each, to be truthful. What happened to the wife I left on Smuttynose? If she found another man with my guts she was lucky.'

" 'Well, Captain, most of the talk about you turns to your treasure. Nobody, so far, has been able to locate it. I have even tried myself. A friend of mine, Jafar Clarke, claims that you never buried any loot, that you were swindled out of it—what you didn't spend on rum and women.'

Blackbeard's head hanging from the bowsprit. (From a 19th-century woodcut.)

" 'Damn my eyes, I spent plenty and the wenches got a lot of it, but there was more than enough. It will rust underground till Doomsday and no one but me and the Devil knows where I planted it.'

" 'Why don't you fool the Devil . . . you fooled every-body else . . . and give me a clue? I can make you more famous in my next book with a lead to work on, and I will not belittle your genius, I can assure you.'

"The storm outside had become worse and the wind was howling in gale force.

" 'Well,' said the voice, 'I wouldn't mind if you dug up a little—say about two pecks of doubloons and some nice jeweled sword hilts and such. Are you familiar with the coast along by Hatteras? Well—it might be somewhere along there—some of it. It's been a long time and I planted more than one lot. The Hatteras chest had two of the starboard watch, who was good diggers but bad hands, planted on top with holes in their heads. I had to push the sand in on 'em myself. They'll hold that pot o' gold down for me and the Devil.'

" 'Captain,' said I, 'that's not much help. How about an-other spot without the bones holding down the loot?'

" 'Well, matey,' said the skull, 'I can recollect putting a small keg down on the beach above high-water mark about three leagues north from Nahant. Take a bead from that egg-shaped rock and line up three big oaks on a crescent-shaped beach, then go ashore, walk northwest for fifteen—'

"A terrible flash and thunderclap came together. The room was illuminated for an instant and in the flash I saw the skull topple from the shelf and all was black. Our lights had gone out. Groping around, I found my flashlight and picked up the skull. It had sustained a fracture of the jaw and two teeth had fallen out. You will note that some of the silver is knocked off.

"And that," said Ed, "is why I know for sure that I really own the pirate Blackbeard's skull."

If you don't believe this, you can see the skull any-time at Snow's house, unless, as a little while ago, it was on exhibit in Goodspeed's Book Store, on Cornhill, in Bos-

ton. It's Blackbeard's, all right. Because nobody else but
Blackbeard and the Devil knows where his treasures
are buried and I am very sure that Ed was not chatting
with the Devil on that stormy night on Cape Cod.

CHAPTER 6

Oak Island's Secret

1795-1957

> *The facts relating to the efforts made to recover an*
> *alleged cache of fabulous wealth buried over a*
> *hundred and fifty feet deep in the soil of a small*
> *island in Mahone Bay, Nova Scotia. Is it the treasure*
> *of the Vikings? Is it Louis XVI's riches? Is it pirate*
> *loot? Is treasure there?*

WHEN SPRING COMES to Nova Scotia the diggers return to Oak Island as regularly as the swallows return to Capistrano. The treasure digging began in 1795 and will no doubt continue until the riddle is solved by modern science.

Oak Island is one of three hundred islands in Mahone Bay. A narrow channel separates it from the mainland, at Western Shore, about four miles from the town of Chester. It is about a mile in length and half as broad. The formation is a hard, tough clay. The eastern end of the island was originally covered with oak trees but few remain today.

Near the close of the eighteenth century this part of Nova Scotia was very sparsely populated and Oak Island had no inhabitants. In 1795, three young men— Jack Smith, Daniel McGinnis, and Anthony Vaughn— visited the island and, rambling over the eastern part of

116

it, came to a spot where unusual conditions caught their attention. Vaughn, only sixteen at the time of their visit, later told the story. The spot had every appearance of having been cleared many years before. Red clover and other plants altogether foreign to the area were growing there. Near the center of the clearing stood a large oak tree with marks and figures on its trunk. One of the lower and larger branches, the outer end of which had been sawed off, projected directly over the center of a deep circular depression in the ground about thirteen feet in diameter. These and other "signs" shortly after led the three men to investigate.

After digging a few feet, they found that they were working in a well-defined shaft, the walls of which were hard and solid; and in some places old pick marks could be seen. Within these walls, the earth was so loose that picks were not needed. On reaching a depth of ten feet they came to a covering of oak plank. They kept on digging until they had reached a depth of thirty feet, finding marks at each ten-foot level. At this point the work proved to be too heavy for them. Superstition was rampant in those days and they were unable to get help to continue the work. Finally they abandoned their digging.

Nothing more was done for six or seven years. About 1801 or '02, Dr. Lynds, a young physician of Truro, Nova Scotia, visited the island and talked to Smith, Vaughn, and McGinnis. He then returned to Truro and organized a company for further search. In this company were several prominent men, among them Colonel Robert Archibald, Captain David Archibald, and Sheriff Harris. Work was resumed and the shaft was excavated to a depth of 95 feet. Marks were found every ten feet, as before. At the 90-foot mark was a flat stone about three feet long and sixteen inches wide. Reportedly, the stone had some undecipherable marks or characters cut on it. The stone when removed was placed in the jamb of a fireplace in a house Mr. Smith was building on the island. It was seen by thousands of visitors. Years later, the house was demolished and the stone was removed from the chimney and taken to Halifax to have, if possible, the characters deciphered.

A rumor that grew over the years has it that the inscription read, "Ten feet below are two million pounds buried." Another rumor says, "Forty feet below . . ." Why was not the stone preserved by the treasure company, or Smith? It was last reported to be in the possession of a book binder who used it to beat skins on.

The crew had dug to a depth of 95 feet without encountering water or any sand or gravel through which water could seep. At this depth they met a wooden platform which, soundings revealed, extended over the entire surface of the shaft. It was on a Saturday evening and the crew stopped work over the Sabbath.

Monday, when the men returned, the shaft was filled with water to within twenty-five feet of the top. They attempted to bail out the water and continued day and night until they found it was a hopeless task. It was then decided to sink a new shaft a few feet to the east of the original hole or "money pit" as it was called. The plan was to go down with shaft No. 2 to 110 feet and tunnel under the "money pit" to take out the treasure from below. This shaft was dug and a tunnel started to connect with the money pit. Just before reaching it, the water suddenly burst through on the workers, who barely escaped with their lives. Water soon filled both shafts and ended the operations of the first company.

Nothing more was done until 1849, when a new company was formed and work again commenced. Two of the original "old diggers," Dr. Lynds of Truro and Mr.

Vaughn of Western Shore, were still alive and gave the new company their information on the old diggings and expressed their firm belief in the existence of the treasure. Vaughn soon located the site of the money pit, although it had filled up. Digging was started and reached a depth of 86 feet. Once again water appeared and the men were driven out of the pit.

After an unsuccessful attempt to bail out the water, work was suspended and the men returned to their homes. Shortly after, men with primitive boring apparatus used to prospect for coal were sent to the island. A platform was rigged in the money pit thirty feet below the surface and just above the water level. The boring started and J.B. McCully of Truro, who was manager of the group, reported:

> The platform was struck at 98 feet, just as the old diggers found it when sounding with an iron bar. After boring through this platform, which was 5 inches thick, and proved to be spruce, the auger dropped 12 inches and then went through 4 inches of oak; then it went through 22 inches of metal in pieces, but the auger failed to take any of it in except three small gold links, resembling part of an ancient watch chain. It then went through 8 inches of oak, which was thought to be the bottom of the first box and top of the next; then 22 inches of metal, the same as before; then 4 inches of oak and 6 inches of spruce; then into clay 7 feet without striking anything else. In the next boring the platform was struck as before at 98 feet; passing through this, the auger fell about 18 inches and came in contact with, as supposed, the side of a cask. The flat chisel revolving close to the side of the cask gave it a jerky and irregular motion. On withdrawing the auger several splinters of oak, such as might come from the side of an oak stave, and a small quantity of a brown fibrous substance, closely resembling the husk of a coconut, were brought up. The distance between the upper and lower platforms was found to be 6 feet.

Another crew under James Pitblado, as foreman, bored and found, as far as the wood at the bottom of the shaft was concerned, the same conditions. John Gammell, a large stockholder who was present, stated that he saw Pitblado take something out of the auger, wash and examine it closely, then put it in his pocket. When asked by Gammell to show his find, he declined, and said he would show it at a director's meeting, but at the meeting Pitblado failed to appear. It was reported later that he had made "certain revelations" to the manager of the Acadia Iron Works at Londonderry, Nova Scotia, which led that gentleman to make a determined but unsuccessful effort to get possession of the land where the money pit lay. He was later called to England and Pitblado was accidentally killed in a gold mine. It has never been discovered what he got from the auger.

In 1850 a new shaft, No. 3, was sunk at the west side of the money pit and about ten feet from it. This shaft was 109 feet deep and was through the hardest kind of red clay. Again, as from shaft No. 2, a tunnel was driven from the bottom toward the money pit. Again water broke through and filled shaft No. 3—to a depth of 45 feet in twenty minutes. Bailing was started with two sets of horse-driven equipment working in both pits. For a week, by day and by night, the bailing continued but the water, while lowered more than before, still filled the shafts. About this time somebody finally made the discovery that the water was salt and they had been trying to pump the ocean out through the pits. The tide rose and fell about eighteen inches in each shaft.

Someone then deduced that if the water was coming through a natural channel, it would have prevented the original diggers (supposed to be pirates) from doing their work when the treasure was planted. On this theory a search was made to find the inlet. Smith's Cove, on the extreme eastern end of the island and about thirty rods from the money pit, was examined. Near the center of the cove, water was seen running out of the sand at low tide. A few minutes' shoveling proved that they had found the place they were looking for. After removing the sand and gravel on the beach, they came to a covering or bed of a brown, fibrous plant, the fiber resembling the husk of a coconut. This was tested and proved to be a tropical fiber at one time used as "dunnage" in stowing ship's cargo. The area covered with this fiber extended 145 feet along the shore line, and from a little above low to high-water mark. The fiber was about two inches thick. Underlying this and over the same area was some four or five inches of decayed eelgrass, and under this, a compact mass of beach rocks free from sand or gravel.

To investigate this area, a cofferdam was built around part of the cove to keep the tide back, and the rocks nearest low water were removed. It was found that the clay (which with the sand and gravel originally formed the beach) had been dug out and removed and replaced with beach rocks. Resting on the bottom of this excavation were five well-constructed drains formed by laying parallel lines of rocks about eight inches apart and covering them with flat stones. These drains near the ocean were a considerable distance apart and converged, like fingers on a hand, at the inland side of the cove, where they connected with one drain or tunnel. When the tide came in it soaked through the fiber as through a giant sponge and drained the sea water into the money pit as from a reservoir.

Work on the beach continued until half of the rocks had been removed where the clay banks showed to a depth of five feet, at which depth a partially burned piece of oak was found. About this time an unusually high tide overflowed the dam. This had not been designed to resist pressure from the inside, and when the tide receded, it carried the dam away. To rebuild it would be costly; there still remained many rocks to remove. Since there could be no reasonable doubt that this spot was the starting point of a tunnel by which water was conveyed to the money pit, it was decided to abandon the work and to sink a shaft a short distance inland to intercept the tunnel. A spot was selected and a shaft was sunk to a depth of 75 feet in hard clay. It missed the tunnel. Another shaft was sunk. When a depth of 35 feet was reached and a large boulder pried up, a rush of water filled the shaft. The water was salt and it seemed to prove that the tunnel theory was correct. Attempts to block off the tunnel with piling failed.

A short time later another shaft, No. 4, was sunk on the south side of the money pit to a depth of 118 feet. This and the three others were in close proximity and could be included in a circle of fifty-foot diameter. This shaft was eight feet deeper than the others. A tunnel was driven toward the money pit and reached a point under it. The workmen stopped for dinner and a great crash was heard. Rushing back to the pit, they found that the bottom had fallen out of the money pit into the tunnel and that the new shaft was filling with water. Twelve feet of mud had been driven by the force of water from the old into the new shaft.

The funds of this company having been exhausted, nothing was done until 1863. In that year a new effort was made to overcome the water and secure the long-searched-for treasure. At this time a powerful engine and pump were erected. The pump was placed in the 118-foot shaft and started. The object was to clear out both the No. 4 pit and the tunnel between it and the money pit where the treasure was thought to have fallen when the cave-in took place. The flow of water was so heavy that it could only be kept below the 100-foot level. While pumping was continued, the water in the pit by the shore was kept at a lower level than before or after, thus proving the existence of a subterranean water course.

About this time the men engaged in the underground work had an idea that the shaft was in danger of caving in and some refused to work in it. An examination was made and it was found to be very unsafe and was condemned. The pump was withdrawn and work was stopped. Nobody knew what to try next.

A syndicate of Halifax capitalists had meanwhile been organized and entered into an agreement with the old company to clean out the original money pit and recover the treasure for a share of the amount discovered. This syndicate spent a large amount of money in sinking another shaft, No. 5, and made heroic but vain efforts to overcome the water, and it, too, was forced to abandon work.

About 1880, the owner of the island was plowing with oxen. When about eighty feet from the pit and over the tunnel to the cove, both oxen suddenly went down into a hole some eight feet in diameter and ten to fifteen feet deep. It is supposed that this cave-in had something to do with the tunnel but no further investigations at the spot were made.

A report of the finding of a copper coin on the island dated 1317 and weighing 1½ ounces and bearing strange designs, together with the discovery of a boatswain's whistle of ancient pattern, had no relation to the pits. Numismatists would like to see the coin. It was more likely dated 1713. The whistle was said to be bone or stone.

In 1894, the Oak Island Treasure Company was formed with $60,000 capital in shares of $5 each. Of this, $30,000 was to be spent to continue the work. The other $30,000 was used by the promoters to secure a three years' lease on that part of the island where the treasure was supposed to be buried and the rights to any treasure recovered.

This company believed that the big mistake of previous workers was in attempting to bail out the ocean through the pits. They planned instead to cut off the water near the shore before attempting to empty the pits. They drilled holes near the beach and exploded charges of dynamite at a depth of 70 feet. This caused a vast amount of earth movement but had no apparent success in shutting off the flow. They then began boring with a 2½-inch drill inside a 3-inch pipe. Wood was struck at various levels below 100 feet. When 130 feet were drilled, the hole produced a flow of water amounting to 400 gallons a minute. At 153 feet they struck what appeared to be cement, then wood, and then a space and more cement. Here again, this seemed to suggest a concrete chamber. When red dye was pumped into the shaft, it came out on the south side of the island and not at Smith's Cove. This would seem to prove the existence of a second water tunnel.

It was during this year's work in 1895 that the core drill brought up a small fragment of parchment on which was written a script *v* or *r* and *i*. This and the small links of chain that came up on the auger in 1849 are all the tangible evidence that has been found.

The late Frederick L. Blair of Amherst, Nova Scotia, became interested in the Oak Island treasure after reading about the 1865 and 1874 syndicates. He took over the rights when the money ran out in 1897 and preserved the relics carefully. Blair's faith in Oak Island never wavered and he continued backing and boosting the treasure hunt until his death in 1953. His contract with the Canadian government gave him the rights from 1894 to 1944, a fifty-year period. In 1903 Blair's money ran out and it was not until 1909 that a new syndicate made arrangements to have a try at the elusive treasure of Oak Island.

In that year, Franklin D. Roosevelt, a young lawyer, whose summers were spent on Campobello Island, New Brunswick, with a few friends raised $5,000 for a summer's sport. When F.D.R., in his later days as President, put in at Cocos Island on a U. S. Navy cruiser, he turned the gobs loose for a day's treasure hunting on that famous spot. They met with the same lack of success as his 1909 Oak Island attempt.

Captain H. L. Bowdoin, a famous deep-sea diver and inventor of salvage apparatus, commanded the 1909 Oak Island hunt. The idea was to send divers down into the money pit, as water seemed to be the great obstacle. This plan was abandoned as too dangerous and again the hole was attacked with drills. Nothing came up but the bits of so-called cement, which had been previously analyzed as "man-made." The searchers believed that they were on the trail of the lost crown jewels and wealth of Louis XVI, which have never been found. Rumor is that these were carried to Louisburg by a lady in waiting, who escaped the French mob when Marie Antoinette and Louis XVI were captured at Varennes.

When this expedition ended, Captain Bowdoin claimed to have solved the mystery of Oak Island, contending that there was no treasure on the island. This was based on his belief that no one would have buried a treasure so deep in the earth; that no tunnel from Smith's Cove existed because if such an engineering job had been planned it would have been constructed from the nearer shore; that the drain from a sea beach would not have stayed open; that the water seeped in from the shore; that no borings brought up the parchment fragment or the gold links, unless they had been accidentally dropped in the pit by some early workers, and that there were no characters on the rock taken from the shaft.

To all treasure fans this was rank heresy and Mr.

Blair came to the defense of believers in Oak Island's mystery by refuting Bowdoin's statements. Blair said that neither he nor Bowdoin could possibly prove or disprove the absence of treasure on the island since neither of them had explored it completely. As to depth, Blair had found that the soil below 130 feet was not natural formation. When he dynamited to cut the flow from the tunnel, the water boiled up in the money pit, proving the connection with the beach. He also said that Bowdoin did not understand that the tunnel ended on the beach at a point between high and low water. He pointed out the beach had partially washed away in past years and that water would not seep into the pit as fast as four hundred gallons per minute. He also said that Mr. Putnam, who brought the scrap of parchment to Truro, was the largest stockholder in the company and when the parchment was dried and examined, Putnam invested everything in the project and died bankrupt. It would be ridiculous to believe that Putnam would "discover" a clue deliberately to bankrupt himself. Mr. Blair also restated that the cement from the money pit had been examined by experts and reported "as worked by man" and that the funds raised to search for and find the treasure had been largely raised among those who knew most about the island and its history. He concluded, "The knowledge I have obtained in respect to Oak Island has made me a firm believer in the existence of buried treasure in the so-called money pit thereon. That it will be recovered some day is also my opinion, and I trust that I may live to see such a result and the mystery solved."

Another stanch supporter of the treasure on Oak Island was William Chappell, a contractor, of Sydney, Nova Scotia. He first dug on the island with the 1895 company and was also with the 1922 hunt. In 1931,

Chappell, then over eighty years of age, made one more try. With a crew of workmen and a steam hoisting engine, a twelve-foot-square shaft was sunk to a depth of 160 feet, near the original pit. They ran through blue clay and no water entered the shaft. As the spot at the bottom of the money pit is in mud, it would seem that they missed the treasure by a few feet. A son of Mr. Chappell continues the contracting business in Sydney and has furnished equipment and men for various excavations since his father's days. He was the last reported owner of that section of the island.

In 1932, a Mrs. Mary Steward of New York financed a short and unsuccessful hunt with her nephew, Montgomery Robbins, and with the help of a Brooklyn engineer, John Talbot. Under a contract from Mr. Blair they drilled, and drilled with difficulty. They reached, only once, a depth of 150 feet. Oak chips showed up at various levels between 113 and 150 feet. That was all.

By 1935, Oak Island had a new believer and worker. A New Jersey engineer, Gilbert D. Hedden, caught the fever in 1928 when he read an article in the New York *Times* and planned a new attack with modern machinery. An electric pump of 1,000-gallons-per-minute capacity drawing from a 165-foot shaft beside and below the money pit was to keep the water under control. Powerful electric drills that fanned out from a center with 20-foot spokes were to probe a large area for the concrete treasure vault. The money pit was opened up and re-timbered down to 155 feet but the ground had been so dug over and disturbed that the treasure could be anywhere in a 100-foot radius at an indeterminate depth in mud. Hedden spent the summer of 1936 sinking a shaft more than double the size of the money pit and beside it. By the end of 1937, the shaft was down 125 feet and the first intake tunnel was cut through to the money pit. Water was diverted to an old shaft for the pumps to take to the surface.

During his research, Mr. Hedden came upon a reproduction of the so-called Kidd map owned by Hubert Palmer of England. The similarity in shape between the Palmer-Kidd island and Oak Island was so striking Mr. Hedden made a trip to England to see Palmer. It turned out to be lost effort. Although similar in shape, the latitude and longitude of the island on the Kidd-Palmer map placed it in the China Sea, about as far from Oak Island as it is possible to go. But, as he was checking on the maps and surveying Oak Island, in an effort to fit their similarity together, two far-distant boulders in which holes had been drilled were discovered. At the time it was believed that these fell in line with certain stones on the beach and that the angles pointed toward the money pit. It is interesting to note that in fourteenth-century Norway holes were drilled in rocks near the shore to hold wooden plugs to which boats could be moored. Did the Norsemen who visited the coasts of America spend some time at Oak Island?

Early explorers of Oak Island included two brothers from Michigan who were working on a historical incident. They claimed that while Pizarro was on a three-year visit to Spain, some of his men took Inca treasures on board a ship which was driven by gales north to the Nova Scotia coast.

Mr. Hedden finally gave up his quest and Colonel H. A. Gardner of Arlington, Virginia, tried out a new metal-finding device which reacted strongly near the site of the money pit. Gardner made a contract to buy Hedden's rights but died in 1949 before the transaction had been completed.

In 1950 the island had a new prospector, Mr. John

Whitney Lewis, a New York mining engineer. Lewis moved in with a 12-ton steam shovel and in one of the existing pits really started to move dirt. The 12-ton shovel was found inadequate and a 20-ton machine was shipped from Halifax. Here, the guardians of all buried treasure stepped in. The dredge was lost over-

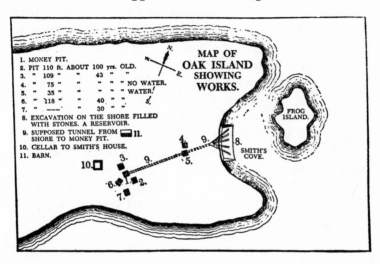

1. MONEY PIT.
2. PIT 110 ft. ABOUT 100 yrs. OLD.
3. " 109 " " 43 " "
4. " 75 " " " " " NO WATER.
5. " 35 " " " " " WATER.
6. " 118 " " 40 " "
7. " ——— " " 30 " "
8. EXCAVATION ON THE SHORE FILLED WITH STONES. A RESERVOIR.
9. SUPPOSED TUNNEL FROM SHORE TO MONEY PIT.
10. CELLAR TO SMITH'S HOUSE.
11. BARN.

MAP OF
OAK ISLAND
SHOWING
WORKS.

FROG ISLAND.

SMITH'S COVE.

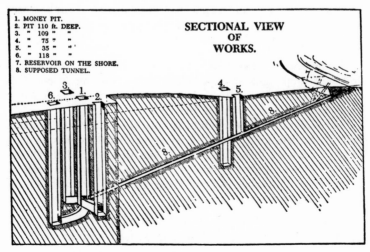

1. MONEY PIT.
2. PIT 110 ft. DEEP.
3. " 109 " "
4. " 75 " "
5. " 35 " "
6. " 118 "
7. RESERVOIR ON THE SHORE.
8. SUPPOSED TUNNEL.

SECTIONAL VIEW
OF
WORKS.

board from a scow near Smith's Cove and had to be salvaged by a Halifax ship. All that remains today of the Lewis digging is a miniature lake, produced by T. Huntley of Ontario and Arthur Freda of Chester who were in charge of the work.

A drill truck was reported at work in 1951 on the southeast slope of a hill about two hundred feet from the original pit. The outfit belonged to contractor Parker Kennedy of Bridgetown and the work was under the supervision of Harry Leighton of Windsor. They drilled test holes about sixty feet deep around the area, which brought up a mixture that looked like wet concrete. When the water was drained off it proved to be sand, gravel, and small stones.

By October 1955, the newspapers carried the story of the latest Oak Island attempt to prove or disprove the treasure saga. Mr. George J. Greene of Corpus Christi, Texas, representative of five Texas oil companies, went to work with a core drill. For four weeks the drilling crew confined their work to the site of the original money pit, now a deep excavation filled with 70 feet of water. In four borings, platforms of wood were struck every 10 feet from the surface to the 111-foot level. On October 26, Greene said:

Below the 111-foot level there is nothing but cavity. The drills just drop right through. We went to 180 feet in one hole before we found the bottom of the cavity. All we have found is wood and we are after some of that cement.

Some folks are silly enough to say that there can't be a concrete vault at the bottom of this pit. They argue that there was no such thing as concrete in early days, but the Romans had it. Others say that there's nothing here at all. Well, either someone went to an awful lot of trouble to plant those platforms or there are an awful lot of liars in the world.

Texas drill crews have a long history of not giving up. If they sink a dry hole they move over and keep drilling until they hit the black gold, and my money is on George Greene to come up with the answer to the mystery of Oak Island. When he gets through pushing his core drill the island may look like a sponge but if the crown jewels of Louis XVI, the doubloons of Captain Kidd, the Peruvian Incas' riches, or anything else is planted on that mysterious island, he will know it.

In Greene's words, "The game's not over yet."

CHAPTER 7

Lutine Gold

The story of Simon Lake, the Connecticut Yankee, submarine inventor, and treasure hunter, whose undersea salvage equipment really worked but whose plans to salvage the Lutine *gold and the Frigate* Hussar's *red-taped treasure was foiled by war, mud, and tides, while others were successful.*

IF SIMON LAKE were alive today he might see some of his dreams of recovering fortunes from the sea realized. Lake, a pioneer in submarine invention but an unsuccessful treasure hunter, is being honored by a new undersea treasure syndicate.

The *Simon Lake,* a fifty-five-foot salvage tug commanded by Captain William Baum and fitted with every modern device known to navigation and deep-sea diving, will act as mother ship. From her davits, ready to cruise along the sea bottom, will hang a two-man submarine capable of descending one thousand feet. The tiny sub is equipped with M-scope, searchlights, underwater TV camera, and robot arms to pick up and raise objects from the sea bottom. It is self-contained and electrically driven, and can stay down on a dive for six hours. It should be named the *Argonaut* after Simon Lake's first submarine to operate successfully in the open sea.

Lake loved to tell of his first trial run from Norfolk,

Virginia, to New York in the *Argonaut* in 1897. While
near the Virginia coast the sub surfaced. Black smoke
spouted from her exhaust pipe. Lake, his face smeared
with grease and soot, opened the conning tower hatch
and shouted to a local fisherman, "Where are we?" The
horror-struck native without answering rowed for shore
with all his strength, and took off through the woods.
Racing for town, he dashed panting into the crossroads
general store and breathlessly described how the devil
himself had popped up from the sea in a cloud of smoke
and flame and yelled at him. What Old Nick wanted, he
did not wait to find out.

Simon Lake's boyhood dreams were about Jules
Verne's *Twenty Thousand Leagues Under the Sea,* and
in spite of his success with his inventions, patents, and
war-submarines, Lake always believed in the possibility
of commercially recovering the natural products of the
sea and sunken treasure. Like many another inventor he
struggled for recognition and was cursed with financial
difficulties. Between wars, when government contracts
for war subs were canceled and the Lake Torpedo Company plant at Bridgeport, Connecticut, was closed and
later sold for 5 per cent of its value, Lake turned to his
commercial submarine ideas.

In 1920 he organized "The Submarine Exploration
and Recovery Company" to "build boats for pleasure or
exploration purposes with the right to charge passenger
fees, or to rent out such vessels for scientific investigation; taking underseas photographs and moving pictures
of underseas life, also for the purpose of building vessels
to recover material products of the seas—such as coral,
sponges, mother of pearl shells, pearls, all kinds of edible
shell fish, the phosphate producing submarine vegetables
such as the loggerhead or giant sponges, kelp, etc., also
for the conduct of submarine mining operations in the

recovery of gold and diamondiferous gravels and all other metals or gems where natural deposits extend out under the seas, also coal, asphalt or other submarine carbon deposits."

Dreams? Yes, the dreams of a man like Fulton, the Wright Brothers, and Marconi. Lake died a poor man at seventy-eight, but he spent his last dollars (and the money of many investors who believed as he did) to prove that commercial submarines were practical. Many a practical invention is a financial failure to its discoverer. So it was with Simon Lake.

Lake did something besides dream. He begged and borrowed all he could get to prove he was right.

For years his plan was to construct a combined surface and submarine boat in which the propelling, navigating, air compressing and most of the other machinery could be carried in the surface boat, leaving the submarine boat itself free of machinery and thus able to carry passengers. In 1919 he built such a combination boat called the *Argosy & Argonaut III* and tested it out in Long Island Sound. Representatives of the press and motion picture companies were taken down in the submarine. Men and women who went into the diving compartment sat at an open door and speared fish, netted crabs, and other crustacea; took off their shoes and stockings and walked on the bottom of the hard sands, picked up oysters, clams, and scallops with their naked hands, sixty feet below the surface in the murky waters of Long Island Sound. It was possible to stay for hours in the diver's compartment watching the changing conditions on the seabed as the submarine was propelled along a foot or so above it.

The company bought the old submarine torpedo boat *Defender*, 92 feet over-all, with a diver's compartment and bottom wheels, which had been successfully oper-

ated at a depth of 137 feet. She was obsolete for naval purposes as her speed was only about eight knots but Lake proposed to use her in his new underseas exploration method. The sub was to be connected to the surface craft by a hollow steel access tube about six feet in diameter and long enough to reach the maximum depth required when the tube was inclined at an angle of 60°. When navigating on the surface the sub and tube were pushed ahead of the surface boat. Flexible ball-and-socket and hinge joints permitted the two vessels to roll and pitch independently of one another; passengers could view the scenery from windows and strong lights illuminated the undersea area. A diver's compartment in the bow of the sub would allow the gathering of treasure, sponges, pearls or anything else from the sea bottom.

This plan did not get far financially, as carrying passengers and picking up lobsters and clams from the ocean bottom was not romantic enough to appeal to many of the share-buying public. Lake, however, did a lot of surveying on the bottom of Long Island Sound and located many sunken coal barges. He hooked up pumps with his tube and raised many tons of coal, which were sold to help pay for further experiment.

In 1929 the Deep Sea Submarine Salvage Corporation was incorporated under the Laws of the State of Maine and granted a license to operate under Lake Submarine and Argonaut Salvage Corporation patents. This was to extend the operations to salvaging sunken vessels and cargoes in any part of the world, where there were "over twenty millions of tons and over six billions of dollars worth of ships and cargoes lost during the World War and the annual loss in peace times exceeds $100,000,000." The equipment was to be enlarged to operate in depths up to one hundred feet to recover about one hundred tons of anthracite coal an hour, for less than fifty cents a ton. Lake's deep-sea salvage equipment was to be extended to operate at a depth of two hundred feet. Lake had also located and recovered cargoes of pig iron, scrap iron, hides, and copper matte.

By 1933 a new Lake Submarine Salvage Corporation was operating. This was more romantically and popularly aimed at putting undersea treasure hunts on a business basis. A fascinating list of famous treasure ships was mentioned, enough to arouse excitement in the most apathetic individual.

There was the steamship *Islander,* which sank on August 15, 1901, in Stevens Passage, nine miles from Juneau, Alaska, with $3,000,000 in gold dust and nuggets aboard. The *Islander* had been the subject of conversation among contractors and salvage men of the Pacific Coast for years. Seventy-two of the 145 persons aboard were lost when the ill-fated ship struck an iceberg and went down in five minutes. The gold was being shipped at the time of the gold rush in Alaska and the Klondike territory.

In the Mediterranean lay the Japanese ship *Yasaka Maru* with $12,000,000 in gold and a maharajah's gems appraised at another $4,000,000.

There were the *Arabic* with $5,000,000 and the *Lusitania,* the *Black Prince* lost in Balaklava Bay in 1854, the *Merida,* on which several salvage parties were working, and the Vigo Bay galleons. It was suggested that when Lake's company had recovered a few thousand tons of coal from various depths along the Atlantic coast, an attempt would be made by the corporation on the *Lusitania,* sunk off Old Kinsdale, Ireland, in 1915.

These rumors brought a flood of letters to Lake's mail box. Divers wrote asking for jobs and telling of other treasure hordes which they "had seen with their own eyes, but which certain reasons of their own had prevented them from recovering." A letter from the West coast told of the discovery of Noah's Ark on an isolated mountaintop in Asia Minor and asked for a contribution of $10,000 to continue research on it. A message from a woman of apparent wealth and breeding who declared she had lost a $100,000 diamond necklace in the wreck of the *Lusitania* pleaded, "Will you please get it for me? It will be a simple matter. I left it in stateroom 357—B deck—under the pillow in my berth."

As a boy, Lake lived at Ocean City, New Jersey, and at that time efforts were being made to locate the hull of H.M. sloop of war *De Braak.* A cousin of Lake's father, a civil engineer, was engaged to plot her location from old records.

The *De Braak,* built in 1797, was originally a Dutch naval vessel, constructed of oak and teak. She came into the possession of the British and was commissioned on June 3, 1797, under the command of Captain James Drew and manned by a crew of eighty-six officers and men. She carried sixteen brass cannon.

Captain Drew was ordered to join the British West India Squadron and take part in the war against Spain. In the spring of 1798 the *De Braak* was reported to have captured a large Spanish ship sailing from La Plata for Spain with a valuable cargo of gold and silver bars and precious stones. She then captured another Spanish treasure ship, the *St. Francis Xavier,* and later, another off the Delaware Capes. With the treasure from these three ships on board, together with many prisoners, Captain Drew decided to put in at Delaware Bay to replenish his stores and water before sailing for England.

According to the *Porcupine Gazette* of May 28, 1798, published in Philadelphia, she was reported as having arrived off Cape Henlopen on the twenty-fifth of May and was about to anchor about a mile off the lightship when a sudden squall hit and she capsized and filled. She carried down with her Captain Drew, the First Lieutenant, thirty-eight officers, seamen, and marines, and two hundred Spanish prisoners who were in irons below decks. The rest of the crew escaped in the ship's boats and the Philadelphia *Gazette* of May 30 reported that "the survivors of the English sloop of war *Braak* arrived at this port yesterday" and further that she had captured five Spanish ships all of which had treasure aboard. A Halifax news account of her loss states: "H.M.S. *Braak* we are informed, was capsized off the Capes of Delaware returning from a successful cruise on the Spanish main; she had on board seventy tons of copper and an immense amount of treasure consisting of gold and silver bars and precious stones, also eighty thousand pounds in English gold taken on board at Jamaica for transportation to England."

In 1920 Simon Lake remembered that Captain Jeff Townsend of Somers Point, New Jersey, was attempting to locate the *De Braak* with his steamer the *Tamasee,* under the auspices of a Philadelphia syndicate headed by a Dr. Pancoast. In Lake's records was an unsigned letter reading:

Lewes, Delaware
April 25, 1889.

I had a talk with Capt. Townsend yesterday in regard to the chain he found embedded in the sand; he said it was within one hundred and fifty yards of the place where Dr. Pancoast claimed to have found the *De Braak* last year.

Capt. Townsend tackled the chain the second time, the last time he took Ross, the diver, and he went down with a sand pump and blew the sand out from around the chain until he was afraid to go any deeper for fear of it coming in on him. And still the

Tamasee could not start it with all her power. They hove her down as low as she would bear, and still could not release the chain, which appeared to be under something that was deep under the sand.

I asked him what kind of a chain it was? He said it was about fifteen fathoms long and large and heavy. I asked him if it was such a chain as he would use in raising a vessel? He said it was just such a chain as he used on their pontoons for raising vessels. I told him he ought to buoy it for fear the sand would cover the chain, and it would not be [re]found. I see he is there on the place this morning, I suppose for the purpose of buoying it.

An old pilot by the name of John Saunders who was living while I was a boy, said that the British government sent two large vessels here to raise the *De Braak* and they put chains under her and raised her some distance from the bottom, when the chains broke and she went down again and they gave up the job; so I really think that this chain that is found under the *De Braak* is one of those placed under her to raise her. Ross found no wood as undoubtedly the top had all rotted off and gone long ago.

As his opinion, Lake wrote: "It would appear that the *De Braak* really did carry a large amount of treasure on board, but I can hardly conceive of such a large amount as 10 million dollars, let alone 25 millions, being risked in one ship at that time, and I am inclined to believe that the promoters of the company in their enthusiasm allowed their imagination too free play in making up their estimate of the treasure she really carried. I know of only one ship that has been lost in our recent war that carried an amount as large as 25 millions of dollars. It does not seem like good business to risk such enormous sums in a single ship. . . . As years go by I have no doubt but these sums will be greatly magnified in the minds of treasure hunters of the future; there is no way to check the losses that actually occur at sea as far as I am aware—even seeing the ship's manifest would not be a guarantee that the treasure was still on board."

In 1930 the Baltimore Derrick and Salvage Corporation located a wreck supposed to be the *De Braak*. They ran into hard luck when their wrecking launch *Katie Burn* caught fire and burned, and although they surveyed the site and planned to salvage, the winter storms and other difficulties blocked their efforts.

The *De Braak* appears frequently in the news, and the most recent idea has been developed by an Atlantic City company. They offer a combined vacation and treasure trip to skin divers who care to charter a boat to the *De Braak* site, under an agreement that any treasure recovered will be divided between the company and the divers.

As far back as 1907, while Lake was operating with European nations which were buying his plans and submarines, he built the submarine portion of an apparatus to raise the treasure from the *Lutine*. Lake in later years compared himself to Mark Twain, who in *Roughing It* said he was once a millionaire. Twain (or Clemens) had staked out with his partner, Higbie, a valuable claim and then lost it by neglecting to work it, as the law required, inside of ten days. Each had gone off for ten days leaving a note for the other to work the claim, neither knew the other was going away and neither received the other's note until the time had expired. Twain and his partner thus lost their rights, which would have made them millionaires. Lake had invested thousands of dollars on his *Lutine* salvage tube and sub, but had to leave for the United States after he had obtained a contract from Lloyd's of London paying him 50 per cent of any treasure he recovered. The contract was for two years and Lake never got back to England to finish his work and the contract lapsed.

While working on salvage apparatus Lake had his technical offices at 11 Regent Street, London, and put en-

gineers and research men on the history of the *Lutine* and
her gold, to authenticate her history. Here is the story of
perhaps the most noted treasure ship in the world from
Lake's own records:

"I have in my possession a book bound in oak from one
of the timbers of the *Lutine,* and which contains a most

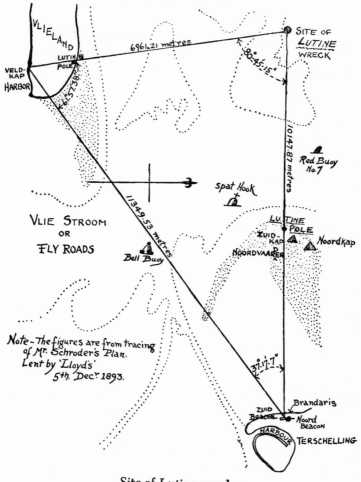

Site of *Lutine* wreck.

complete record of her loss and the numerous attempts to
recover her treasure. This book represents years of research on the part of its compilers. In the Committee Room
at Lloyd's are a huge table, highly polished, of dark wood,
a magnificently carved arm chair, and a ship's bell. The
table bears a silver plate inscribed as follows:

H.B.M. Ship *La Lutine*
32-Gun Frigate
Commanded by Captain Lancelot Skynner, R.N.
Sailed from Yarmouth Roads
On the morning of the 9th of October, 1799 with a large
amount of specie on board,
And was wrecked off the Island of Vlieland the same night,
When all on board were lost except one man."

The rudder and bell of the *Lutine* were raised from
the wreck in 1859. From the wood of the rudder the
table and chair were made. The *Lutine's* bell is suspended in the rostrum in the Underwriting Room and
is rung whenever a ship is lost, or an overdue vessel
is reported to have reached port.

Lake continues:

"The *Lutine* originally belonged to the French but the
Royalists of Toulon turned her with other ships over to
the English in command of Lord Hood in 1793 to prevent
them from falling into the hands of the Republicans. She
was afterwards a tender at Woolwich and was probably
repaired there and resheathed with copper.

"In the fall of 1799 there was a commercial crisis in
Hamburg much in the nature of our modern panics
which caused a run on the banks. Many London merchants and private bankers were associated with them
and decided to rush funds in silver and gold coin and bars
to back up their Hamburg affiliates and stop the panic.
France, Holland, and England were involved in war and

the London bankers requested the use of a fast and well-armed naval vessel to transport the treasure. The *Lutine* was assigned to the duty.

"The treasure was put aboard the *Lutine* and she sailed from Yarmouth on the morning of October 9, 1799. The book I have contains many records of public documents and news items published at the time. The treasure is computed to have been worth $5,750,000, the greater part of which was insured by Lloyd's.

"The *Lutine's* course seems to have deviated that night, and led her close to the islands off the coast of Holland. During a heavy northwest gale she struck on the edge of one of the many treacherous sand banks which abound in this locality and was lost with all hands except two men who were picked up adrift on oars. One of these survivors died after reaching shore.

"In the morning no sight of the ship was seen as she had capsized and slid off the bank into deep water. She had struck on a sandbank off the Island of Terschelling near the entrance to Vlie Stroom, or Fly Roads, and as Holland was an ally of France and France and England were at war, the King of Holland claimed the ship as a prize of war.

"The Secretary of Lloyd's wrote to the Secretary of the Admiralty under the date of October 22, 1799, stating, 'A sum of money equal to that unfortunately lost in the *Lutine* is going off tonight for Hamburg and we trust their Lordships will direct such steps as they may deem expedient for its protection, etc.' The Admiralty replied that they had ordered Admiral Duncan to provide a convoy but that Lloyd's must not expect that the packets can again be convoyed.

"Lloyd's has never abandoned their rights to the salvage of the treasure. They watched over the wreck and collected evidence for years to protect their interests.

First Salvage Attempts

"Conducted under the strict control of the Strandvon-derij (Official Wreck Receivers), the daily proceedings are recorded with extreme minuteness.

"The means employed were very simple—the art of diving as practiced in modern days was then unknown, and all that could be done was carried out from the surface. The ship appears to have been lying on her side upon the edge of a bank in shallow water (20 feet at low water). Her stern was broken, and the treasure recovered was obtained with 'knippers,' tongs, and iron nets, fastened to the ends of poles. In many cases the tongs which clasped gold and silver bars among the broken wreckage, slipped, and the bars fell back into the sea. Casks of coin also were broken and their contents scattered. This first attempt at salvage terminated in 1801 owing to the wreck settling down into the sand and fresh sand gathering on the bank until the wreck was covered.

"Recovered were 58 bars of gold, 323 kilos; 35 bars of silver, 879 kilos; and a number of gold and silver Spanish and French coins, together with 4 guineas and 2 half-guineas—the total value of the whole salvage being £55,770.

"The covering up of the wreck with sand, and the war which lasted until Napoleon's banishment to Elba in 1814 prevented any further search after the treasure in the *Lutine*. But with the establishment of peace, the Heer Pierre Eschauzier, then official Wreck Receiver, began to entertain hopes of further salvage. This official, a gentleman of French descent, had formed an ingenious theory as to the amount of the treasure in the *Lutine* based upon the marks and numbers stamped on the gold and silver bars which had been recovered in the 1800-01 salvage. Although his hypothesis places perhaps a too high value on the treasure, it has received some degree of confirmation in the subsequent findings. His views were adopted by the King of Holland, who in 1814 authorized him to expend the modest sum of 300 guilders, in an attempt to find the position and condition of the *Lutine*. The wreck was located but it was so badly buried in sand that the operators could do nothing.

Second Salvage

"While digging around in the sand near the wreck, the operators found a few pieces of rust, consisting of clots of sand, iron rust, and gunpowder. When broken open these clumps yielded 8 Louis d'ors, 1 gold piastre, and 8 silver piastres. Although he was foiled in his attempts, the Heer Eschauzier kept a constant watch on the wreck and hearing of improvements in the art of diving made in England in 1821, he formed a company bearing the name of the *Onderneming op het Wrak van der Lutine* (or Decretal Salvors). The company had received on Sept. 14, 1821, a royal concession, granting them 50% of any treasure recovered. This syndicate (which is still in existence) expended some £5000 in fruitless attempts at salvage during the next seven years and then abandoned their operations for a time. Their efforts, however, attracted the attention of Lloyd's who considered themselves to be the lawful owners of the wreck, made an application to the Dutch Government to have their rights respected. As a result Lloyd's obtained from the King of Holland a Royal Decree (May 23, 1823) by which the Dutch government resigned to them that half of the treasure recovered in the concession to the Decretal Salvors. It is evident from the wording of the decree that the King of Holland held the view that the amount of treasure was very great but no mention is made by Lloyd's at this time as to what the treasure of the *Lutine* might amount to.

"The only effort made by Lloyd's at this time was to have the site of the wreck examined by a firm of English divers in 1828.

"In 1856, the wreck was accidentally found to be again denuded of sand, by the accident of the chain of a drifting buoy becoming entangled in it. The Decretal Salvors and Lloyd's Agent in Amsterdam speeded efforts and work was begun on July 11, 1857, when the wreckage of the stern was found at a depth of about six fathoms.

Third Salvage

"The Decretal Salvors appointed an engineer and for the first time diving suits were used. Two vessels were employed, a *Blazer,* a small Dutch fishing craft, and a *Bom,* a square shaped boat. Nothing was found by August 15th and the diver was discharged as incompetent. It is probable that the fault was rather with the equipment than the man, for the next day Heer Taurel, the superintendent, went to England to obtain diving gear from the firm of Heinke & Co. The first money found was with tongs on August 31st, and as the divers did not seem to be efficient, a diving bell was tried, but was too difficult to manage and was discontinued.

"In October, a Dutch fisherman attempted to work on the wreck on his own account with tongs and would not stop until a company of Marines from a gunboat and a police officer arrived. He and his boat were searched and he was taken to Hoorn for trial. Later, another fisherman named Van Gelder tried to work on the wreck but was stopped by a naval officer.

"The following year on June 1st, 1858, the diver Wyker picked up a bar of silver. The finds then became frequent and gold and silver bars were recovered until sand again began to cover the wreck.

"In 1859 the work was started in May but the sand

Spanish galleon in Havana harbor, where the fleets gathered annually before sailing for old Spain. (From an early copperplate.)

above: Remains of the Spanish galleon *Capitana,* lost in the hurricane of July 15, 1733. All that remains of the wreck is a large pile of rock ballast covering tons of coral-encrusted relics. Note cannon at top left and timbers uncovered from below sand. *below:* A few of the many artifacts salvaged from the *Capitana* by Arthur McKee, Jr., of Treasure Harbor, Florida. Sword and pewter plate, tankard, cup, inkwell, and candle holder were probably from the captain's cabin. (Photos from McKee's Treasure Fortress.)

above: A small part of the many tons of coral-covered artifacts recovered from the *Capitana* by Arthur McKee, Jr. This lump, when x-rayed *(below),* showed plainly a mass of iron spikes, pieces-of-eight, buckles, buttons, and jewelry. (Photos by Sam Tour & Co., N. Y.)

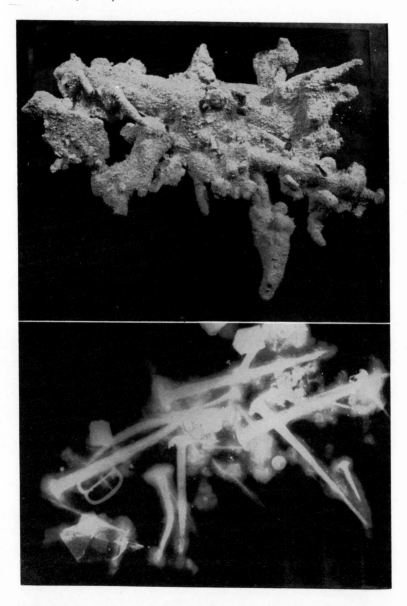

above: Part of the *Crampton* find, washed ashore in a bale of trade goods during a storm at Mantoloking, New Jersey. Belt and shoe buckles, rings, studs, buttons, and counterfeit English gold guineas and half guineas. (Photo by Foul Anchor Archives.) *below:* The Teddy Tucker emerald cross, pearl studs, and gold bars discovered on a Bermuda reef. This was one of the richest underwater discoveries of real 16th-century treasure of our times. (Photo by Frederick L. Hamilton.)

above: Treasure chest of pirate period, showing cut-out steel grille used to cover lock mechanism inside lid. *below:* Handwrought lock mechanism (grille removed). One large key moves center bar and pulls back ten spring locks around edge of lid. When lid is closed, these locks spring back into place. (Photos by Foul Anchor Archives.)

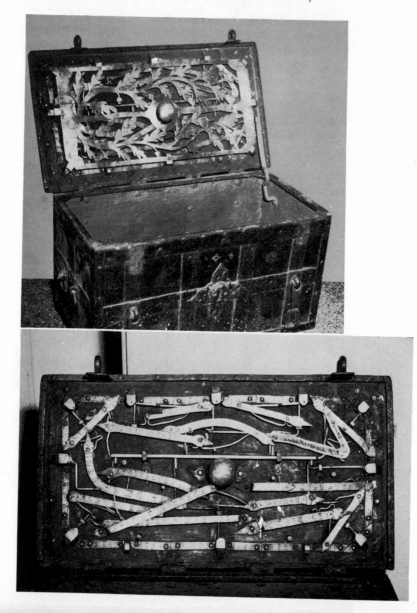

above: One of three silver bars recovered by Charles M. Brookfield and Arthur McKee, Jr., from a reef "east of Key Largo." The bar, weighing 1,280 ounces, assayed 999.1 parts, and 0.17 gold parts, per 1,000. The signs cut into the bar identify it as being the *anata,* or church tax, from the bishopric of Chiapas, Mexico, for the king of Spain, Philip IV; as such, it did not have the royal tax of one fifth deducted by the Royal Treasurer at the Mexican foundry. This bar is in McKee's Fortress of Sunken Treasure. (Photo by Foul Anchor Archives.) *below:* Silver bar found by Howard Lightbourn and Roscoe Thompson off Great Abaco Island in 1950. (Photo by Bahamas Development Board.)

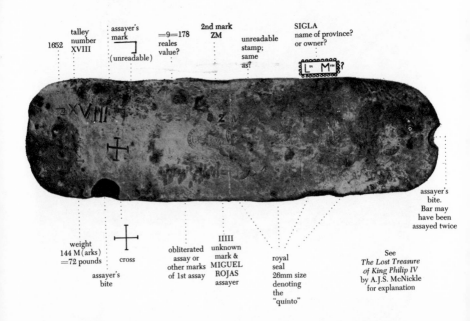

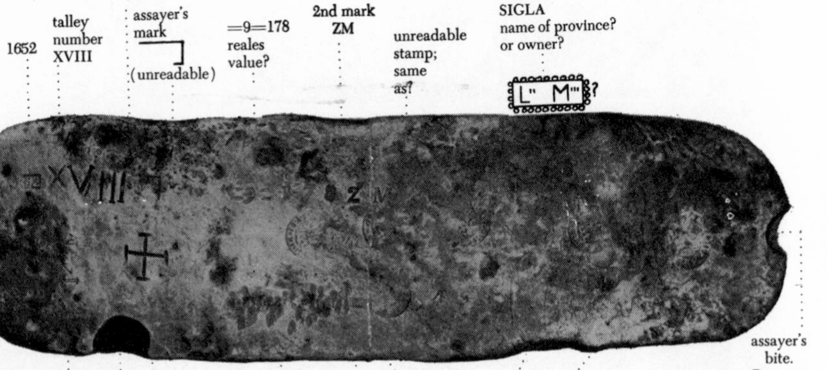
1652
talley number XVIII
assayer's mark
(unreadable)
=9=178 reales value?
2nd mark ZM
unreadable stamp; same as?
SIGLA name of province? or owner?
L" M"' ?
XVIII
Z
assayer's bite. Bar may have been assayed twice
weight 144 M(arks) =72 pounds
cross
assayer's bite
obliterated assay or other marks of 1st assay
IIIII unknown mark & MIGUEL ROJAS assayer
royal seal 26mm size denoting the "quinto"
See *The Lost Treasure of King Philip IV* by A.J.S. McNickle for explanation

List of Captain Kidd's treasures gathered from Gardiner's Island and other places by Lord Bellomont and sent to London, where they are now in the archives of the Public Record Office (Doc. Kidd 64 [xix]. Printed by permission.)

above: Edward Rowe Snow with the silvered skull of the pirate Blackbeard (Edward Teach). (Photo by Foul Anchor Archives.)

below: Bludworth Marine self-propelled "Power Diver," enabling undersea Scuba divers to descend, ascend, bank, roll, and turn at depths down to 180 feet. Developed by Peter Stackpole, photographer, and Link Aviation, it is powered by a 6- or 12-volt aircraft-type rechargeable battery. (Photo by Florida's Silver Springs.)

proved to be an unyielding barrier and only one gold bar was recovered in August. In 1860 further attempts met with but trifling success. The total salvage amounted to 41 bars of gold and 64 bars of silver with some coins—the whole amounting to £44,124 in value.

"The bars were found principally near the rudder. This was removed by diver Swart and lifted on the 18th of Sept. 1858. It was 26 feet high, 7 feet broad and 8 inches thick. From the wood of this rudder the table and chair in Lloyd's were made.

"The Corporation of Lloyd's in order to secure themselves against any possible claimants in England to a share of the '*Lutine* Treasure' obtained an Act of Parliament (34 Victoria C.21) by which they are constituted the heirs to any property recovered from the *Lutine*.

Fourth Salvage

"In 1886 a Mr. Ter Meulen of Bodegraven in Holland, entered into a contract with Lloyd's and the Decretal Salvors for work upon the *Lutine* upon a percentage of the results. For the first time dredges were employed. The site of the wreck had been lost but Mr. Ter Meulen claimed to know where it lay as he had kept a watch on it since 1867. The result of his operations extending over some three years was the recovery of coins valued at £686/10/2 but no bars were raised. In 1893 Mr. Ter Meulen's contract was cancelled and a new contract was made by Lloyd's with the approval of the Decretal Salvors with Mr. W. R. Kinipple of Brighton.

Fifth Salvage

"Mr. John J. Fletcher, the engineer for this 'Lutine Syndicate,' went to Terschelling in 1894 and undertook salvage operations with a suction dredge. They worked on and off for five years with little success as their dredge was of insufficient capacity to keep the sand from filling in the crater as fast as sand was removed. In 1900 this syndicate was liquidated with barely enough money to wind up their affairs. This might have discouraged further tries for the treasure but before the end of 1900, however, Lloyd's had made a new salvage contract with Mr. Kinipple with exclusive rights until Dec. 31, 1904."

This concludes Lake's report of the first five salvage attempts.

Sixth Salvage

The new syndicate formed in 1900 was called the "New Lutine Company, Ltd." capitalized at £6,000. divided into shares of £5. each of which only about £2,800. was subscribed. Mr. John Scott, a resident engineer of the East Indian Railway Co. who had just returned from building the longest bridge yet built in India, was sent to Terschelling in charge of salvage. Mr. Scott produced no treasure but did produce a voluminous 34-page report describing various causes, some avoidable and others beyond control, of the failure of the salvage attempt during 1901. The year 1902 was little better, the weather being exceptionally unfavorable. Nothing was accomplished in the following years but the taking of soundings, although Lloyd's extended the license until Dec. 31, 1907, then until Dec. 31, 1910, and again until Dec. 31, 1911.

This syndicate, through their engineers, learned of Lake's submarine recovery tube, visited him, and suggested that he undertake the recovery. The submarine portion was built and worked perfectly but the surface boats with which the section was supposed to connect were never constructed. Lake was called home to America by additional contracts for submarines for the U.S. Government. Lake stated: "Before I could arrange my business affairs and return to England my contract had expired and I lost half interest in the millions in the 'Sand Bank' off the entrance to the Zuider Zee.

"In November 1910, the New Lutine Company with the consent of the Committee of Lloyd's decided to employ the National Salvage Association. The prospectus of this company issued with the object of raising capital of £79,-800. stated that it had been formed as a salvage and recovery company and it should be clearly understood that it would not engage in 'treasure hunting.' Their manager was Captain Chas. A. P. Gardiner, who had been retained at an annual salary of £720. and was also to be paid an extra £6,800. for the benefit of licenses he had obtained and information he was to supply.

"On November 19, 1910, the salvage vessel, *Lyons,* and the lighter, *Bill O'Malley,* arrived at Terschelling to commence work. The *Lyons* had powerful sand pumps with a capacity said to exceed 2,000 tons per hour. On the night of January 31, 1911, the *Lyons* commenced sucking sand from the *Lutine* site. She worked for 8 hours, after which she had to stop owing to the sudden rise in the wind. This attempt proved that the salvors were in the right location as two small shot about 1½ inches in diameter, a few pieces of wood and two small iron bolts were raised. An exciting time followed with the *Lyons* working on the wreck whenever weather permitted. Copper sheets, copper nails, human bones, cannons, cannon balls, ballast iron, timber and many silver and gold coins were brought up. The two anchors, weighing about 8,000 pounds, were also recovered."

The burgomaster of Terschelling insisted that all articles recovered were to be handed to him in his capacity of wreck receiver. A policeman was stationed on board the *Lyons* and it took the combined action of the Dutch and British authorities with Lloyd's agent calling on the

Governor of the North of Holland and the British Ministry at the Hague to finally overcome the burgomaster's
interference in the operation. The anchors and 3 cannons were exhibited at the Shipping Exhibition at Amsterdam in 1913 and for a time Lloyd's planned to make
a monument with the anchors behind the Royal Exchange. This plan was not carried out but the wooden
stocks bearing the name *Lutine* were sent to the Committee of Lloyd's. Lake continues:

"A man purporting to be Captain Gardiner's aide came
to see me in America, and tried to interest me again in
the *Lutine* Salvage. He told me that he had been down
on the wreck one day and saw through the ribs of the
vessel a pile of gold bars lying under a lot of debris just
out of his reach. Before they could clear the wreckage, a
storm arose and the sand again drifted over the wreck. If
he had stopped there, I might have become interested in
her salvage. When he saw my enthusiasm arise and I
began to discuss the possibility of completing my equipment and taking over the work again, he became very
anxious to sell me his entire stock in the National Salvage
Association at a very low price. He seemed more anxious
to sell his stock than to have the gold bars recovered and
my doubts arose—at least it still remains a mystery hidden beneath the sands of the Zuider Zee as to whether
the treasure of the *Lutine* is partly there or not.

"At the time of the loss of the *Lutine*, Mr. John Mavors
Still, Lloyd's Agent in Amsterdam, made inquiries at Hamburg and London and reported that insurances were
effected for the money, as follows:

Insured by Lloyd's	£900,000
Insured at Hamburg	£160,000"

The National Salvage Association's license was extended from time to time until March 1915 when a year's extension had been agreed upon but World War I interfered with further operations. The *Lyons* was requisitioned by the British Admiralty and the beacons at the Isle of Vlieland and Terschelling, which served as points to locate the *Lutine* site, were removed by order of the Dutch Admiralty.

Seventh Salvage

In 1920, at the request of Lloyd's the marking beacons were re-erected and by 1921 many applications were coming in from interested salvors requesting rights to work the wreck. Lloyd's granted a license in 1924 to Messrs. P. van der Wallen and P. A. van Hecking Colenbrander, who had invented a kind of coal-grab. They believed that with comparatively small cost they could remove what was still left of the *Lutine*. Once the grab reached the wreckage, it would be closed and the contents hauled to the surface. The first disappointment came when the salvors found that the steamer could not anchor in the 5 feet of water at the *Lutine* site, and a seagoing vessel of shallow draft had to be chartered and the equipment transferred. The first attempts were made in August 1924 but the grab would only penetrate to a depth of 36 feet, and the invention had to be altered and improved. Before anything could be recovered the license had expired, but Lloyd's granted a year's extension. A few attempts were made in 1925, but although the grab reached the clay bottom, only some small pieces of rust, timber and cement were hauled up. The contractors ran out of capital and their attempts were abandoned.

Eighth Salvage

After various proposals of applicants had again been considered and rejected, Lloyd's granted in 1928 a five-years' license to the well-known Dutch salvors, Messrs. Stoomboot Maatschappij Texel and Scheepvaart Maatschappij G. Doeksen & Zn. These companies could boast of a long experience in the *Lutine* salvage operations, as they had co-operated with many of the past salvors. They had been wise enough to contract with previous salvors and succeeded in making a profit in an enterprise which resulted in a loss for practically everybody else concerned.

The new salvors proposed to suck away the sand from above the *Lutine,* and recover what was left with divers. There was much more sand on the wreck than expected, in fact the depth at low water on the *Lutine* site was only 12¼ feet, which aggravated the difficulties. During the first years the salvors were unfortunate. There were no long spells of good weather, the suction pipes broke occasionally owing to the swell, and the hopper barges used to catch the sucked-up sand and shell did not work satisfactorily. In 1931 the salvors hired Mr. Victor Hugo Duras of Washington, who with a Radio Metal and Mineral Finding Machine, proposed to indicate exactly where the gold and silver lay. Tests were made but the machine did not operate through the water and mud.

Ninth Salvage

In 1933 the salvors entered into an agreement with a Mr. Beckers, who had designed an iron tower of large dimensions, which was to be lowered on to the wreckage. This tower was fitted with powerful pumps, to move the sand at the bottom of the tower, which would thus work its way down to the clay bottom. The water would then be pumped out of it and the wreckage inside the tower removed. This plan had a certain fascination because it would make the salvors independent of the weather and would enable a thorough research of the wreckage to be made. On the other hand the tower had to be placed at the right spot over the wreckage where gold and silver were most likely to be found. On July 26, 1933, the first part of the salvage tower was placed on the site. Meanwhile the weather was bad and on August 26, 1933, before the tower was completely erected, it collapsed owing to the weakness of its substructure. It was removed and taken to Terschelling where it was found to be not worth repairing. Meanwhile the shell dredgers were working during 1933 and 1934 and brought up large quantities of ballast, copper, cannon balls, etc. Besides that only some copper coins and a guinea dated 1790 and one cannon were recovered with no gold or silver bars or other valuables rewarding the efforts.

Mr. Beckers had a new and much stronger tower constructed, which was placed on the wreck site on September 1, 1934. But, although this tower was indeed so strong that the worst weather did not affect it, it could not be pumped dry, and the examination of the ground covered by the tower was extremely difficult. Only some pieces of rust and cannon balls were collected from the ground in a working period of almost a year.

The shell dredges worked at the same time and divers went down but practically worthless material only was found. The salvors, whose license had been extended until the end of 1936, continued working all those years recovering wreckage which had only scrap value. This scrap was in great demand, and Lloyd's had many inquiries for cannon balls and other souvenirs. In 1935, the Committee of Lloyd's presented King George V with an inkstand made from *Lutine* timber as a Silver Jubilee Gift.

It would seem that all interest in the *Lutine* treasure

would by now have terminated. On the contrary, what little was left of the wreck and her cargo became more desirable than ever. It was soon realized that there was no question of the abandonment of attempts to recover the almost legendary *Lutine* treasures.

Tenth Salvage

In April 1938 the Committee of Lloyd's granted a 5 months' license for working on the *Lutine* to the Billiton Company, one of the wealthiest and largest tin-mining and dredging concerns in the world. This company proposed to attempt to recover what might be left of the *Lutine* with a new sea-going dredger *Karimata*, which had been constructed for tin-dredging in the East Indies. Had there been no *Lutine* she would have been towed from Holland to the island of Billiton directly. She was 246 feet long, with a width of 75½ feet, and displaced 4,200 tons. With a shallow draft of about 10 feet and flat-bottomed she was excellently suited for working on the *Lutine* site. She had 3 Diesel generators supplying current, a 400 H.P. motor driving a bucket chain which could be raised and lowered by motor. The buckets would dredge at any depth down to 98 feet. The material dredged up was carried to a rotating sieve through which the sand and clay was washed by high pressure jets, leaving the salvaged material.

A survey was made which showed that at low tide the wreck was under 13 feet of water. A diver's examination showed that the base of the iron tower left by previous salvors was in the way and, after unsuccessful attempts to cut it up with underwater torches, it finally was dynamited and removed in sections.

The *Karimata* commenced operations on June 9, 1938, skimming the sand from the wreck. During the first few days small copper nails, pieces of copper and part of a copper medal, probably of Frederic-William III of Prussia, were found. On June 12 the first silver piastre was recovered.

Owing to heavy seas and strong winds the dredge had to be towed to Terschelling to repair damage to her wire mooring and windlass. After two weeks, she was back on the wreck in operation on July 14. This second working period became more interesting. About 100 pieces of the *Lutine*'s ballast, four large cannon (all of which were loaded), one small cannon only 23 inches long, several silver and copper coins, uniform buttons, a large copper kettle and an iron stamp bearing the name E. I. T. Porter were recovered.

On July 29, at 2:30 A.M., a gold bar weighing 7 pounds 10 ounces and marked 2 F BB 57 was dredged up. Eleven other bars bearing the same initials had been among the ingots recovered in the past. Four gold pieces were also found and a silver watch with the maker's name Wm. Blew No. 2154, in which was a lock of hair. From July 14 until August 15 the *Karimata* dredged day and night with no interruption. A slight damage to the bucket ladder caused a delay until August 22, when the dredge again began work, which continued until September 12.

The Billiton Company at this time decided to discontinue work on the wreck. Quite a number of coins, even gold ones, were dredged up during these last few weeks, but the absence of pieces of wreckage large enough to give evidence that the *Karimata* was working on some part of the *Lutine,* and the fact that the area marked out at the beginning of the operations had been completely searched, induced the Billiton Company to give up further attempts.

The total quantity of bullion and specie dredged up by the *Karimata* was 1 gold bar; 8 gold coins; 123 silver coins; and 10 copper coins. Apart from the above, about 350 pounds of copper (sheets, nails, clamps, etc.); about 15 tons of iron (pieces of ballast and part of rigging); about 700 pounds of lead (pipes, deep-sea leads, etc.); and about 60 cubic feet of timber were dredged up.

Among the curios recovered were 3 large and 1 small cannon, some 1,000 cannon balls of various diameters, a musket, a bayonet sheath, 13 copper uniform buttons with anchor design, a copper badge, probably part of a soldier's outfit, stamped "G.R. Per Mare et Terram," a small copper medal inscribed "For purifying water 1796, Coventry Street, London"; and a large and well preserved medal, marked: "Academia Bonnensis a Maximiliano Frederico condita a Maximiliano Francisco in Universitatem Erecta XII Cal. Decembr. MDCCLXXXVI.

One fact remains when the history of the salvage operations on the *Lutine* is examined: sea, tide, and sand are the greatest difficulties to overcome even when the treasure lies in shallow water and is known to exist.

CHAPTER **8**

Hell Gate Holds the *Hussar*

ALTHOUGH Lake's plan for salvaging the *Lutine* gold was never executed, he did work for years on the historic wreck of the *Hussar.*

H.M.S. *Hussar* was a 28-gun frigate, 114 feet long with a 30-foot beam and a displacement of about 1,000 tons. She was launched in the Thames in 1763 and was probably copper-sheathed. Her rudder, recovered in 1819, was copper-fastened and -sheathed.

The *Hussar* anchored at New York on Sept. 13, 1780, during the American Revolution and, after taking on money to pay British troops, sailed for Newport. She also carried funds transferred from H.M.S. brig *Mercury.* Altogether, chests containing $4,800,000 were supposed to have been stored in her hold. This amount has probably been greatly exaggerated.

In sailing through Hell Gate, a dangerous passage, the *Hussar* struck on Pot Rock and started to sink. Her captain ran her ashore in an attempt to save the ship, crew, and cargo but the shore was rocky, the tides swift, and the water deep. The crew had time to scram-

ble ashore but reports tell of some fifty American prisoners, shackled in the hold, who went down with the
gold in 75 feet of water.

The British denied at the time that any money was
aboard. This, of course, may have been to prevent the
Americans from recovering the gold. The Boston *Evening Gazette* in 1823 printed a letter from Sir Charles
M. Pole, the *Hussar's* commander. Written on Jan. 24,
1812, it said in part: "It was the *Hussar* which struck
on Pot Rock when I commanded her in 1780. I am
not aware that there was any treasure on board her or
anything but stores belonging to her as a 28-gun ship.
. . . This may perhaps serve to prevent disappointment
for future seekers of treasure trove."

But in 1819, Samuel Bleeker of 81 Water Street, New
York, made a deposition:

In relation to what I heard my father say, in his lifetime, of
there being money put on board of the *Hussar* frigate in this city,
in the year 1780, I state that, on my father's return home, he did say
to my mother, in my presence, that he saw fourteen carts backed
up in front of the British Pay-Office, which now stands in Cherry
Street; that there was a guard of soldiers formed around the
carts, and that there were a number of boxes, containing silver coin,
emptied in an iron chest, one in each cart to the number of ten; that
there were there a number of small kegs, containing gold coins,
emptied in four iron chests—one in each cart; that two British
officers stood by and locked up the chests—after which the carts,
guarded by the soldiers, proceeded to the ship, which lay at Beek-
man's Wharf, and the money was put on board, and that she sailed
immediately. This I have heard my father repeat frequently in his
lifetime.

The reports of treasure on the *Hussar* grew and grew
over the years, from one to four to eight millions. As she
lay so close to the shore of New York City, it was natural that many salvors would try to reach her hull. Samuel Davis is reported to have slipped cables under her

stern and tried to lift her in 1823, but the cables broke and the wreck slipped back into the mud. A British expedition was also reported to have tried to salvage the treasure with a diving bell with no success.

A Worcester, Massachusetts, firm, Pratt and Bancroft, formed the Worcester-Hussar Company and Captain Taylor worked on the wreck on and off from 1840 until 1866. The rights were then sold to the Frigate-Hussar Company. Diving suits were invented during the Pratt and Bancroft time and were used to advantage on the wreck by Capt. Taylor. A traveling exhibition went from town to town in New England showing relics from the *Hussar*. One of its handbills appears on page 161.

This company never succeeded in getting down below the gun deck into the hold, where the treasure was stored. Captain Bancroft always regretted that they could not penetrate the silt that covered the wreck and get to the treasure. His daughters had breastpins made from British gold guineas recovered by their father. Captain George B. Pratt, when work on the wreck ceased, returned to Worcester, where he founded several enterprises and served as Mayor from 1877 to 1879. Some of the relics are in the Worcester Museum.

Simon Lake's boyhood dreams of raising treasure from the sea were always in his mind. In 1920 Lake said:

"As a boy I spent hours watching the old steamer *Chester* pumping the mud of the East River and depositing it on a screen which was expected to catch the golden guineas; even at this early date in my life, I had made plans of a salvaging submarine and I was naturally interested in such a great treasure as the *Hussar* was supposed to have on board.

"When I had built and demonstrated with my *Argonaut* the practicability of my theories, I returned to New York and searched out the man who had spent so many years in the attempt to locate the *Hussar* and learned that he was still alive, that he was Capt. George Thomas and that he lived in New Jersey.

"I went to see Capt. Thomas and introduced myself. He was a venerable, white-haired old gentleman with absolute confidence that an immense treasure was on board the old *Hussar*. He became much interested in my proposed method of searching the bottom, in locating wrecks and was anxious for me to undertake the work under his contract with the United States Treasury Department for its recovery."

(Reports in the U. S. Treasury Department show that Thomas had a contract to work on the *Hussar* from 1880 to 1892. Judge Nelson Cross was Government Receiver. An undated report of 1892 or 1893, made for the purpose of discrediting Thomas, states that he formerly peddled snuff on the New York waterfronts; was a hypocrite who talked about recovering the treasure as the Lord's work and, in raising funds, promised to give the surplus to the Lord; that he was engaged in fraudulent activities in 1884 and that Judge Cross was a party to his acts. Bean and Hartwell took up the contract in 1892 under the name of Treasure Trove, Incorporated. Cross double-crossed Thomas and went in with Treasure Trove, Inc., but the Treasury Department canceled their contract and acting for Francis M. Eppley, a former Thomas associate, double-crossed Cross. The *Hussar* was becoming a political football. When Thomas lost his contract he began to work vigorously on the wreck from an old scow, under a sign "NO ADMITTANCE, GOVERNMENT WORK." He was ordered to desist by the Treasury Department.)

When Simon Lake called on Captain Thomas he saw the documents pertaining to the *Hussar* and listened to the captain's story. Lake reported:

The Sea! The Sea.

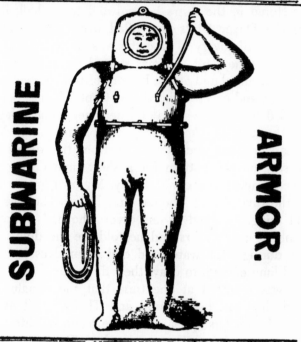

SUBMARINE ARMOR.

NOVEL
EXHIBITION
OF
Submarine Diving Apparatus
AND
NAVAL REVOLUTIONARY RELICS.

From an old circular describing an exhibition of relics from
the *Hussar*.

"The shipment on the *Hussar* of gold had been made in secret for fear that spies might inform the American naval forces. The money was in gold guineas and they were stored in the ship's bottom and then chalk ballast from the Dover Cliffs was piled over the treasure to prevent its discovery in case she was captured.

"By the time Capt. Thomas started work, a deposit of silt had accumulated at the bottom of the river, about 15 feet thick, and covered the wreck. Capt. Thomas believed he had definite knowledge of where her remains lay. He fitted the steamer *Chester* with pumps and pumped mud for years but the currents were so strong that divers could only stay on the bottom for a short time during slack water. Pumping was done blindly. My own impression is that the divers used Thomas and his stockholders as a 'good thing.' I talked to one diver who had worked on the job for some years and he told me the divers went down during slack water and tied themselves fast for a period long enough to draw their day's pay.

"It was reported at one time that the remains of a buried ship had been found and Thomas said another crowd of wreckers appeared on the scene and attempted to jump his claim. That was when Thomas went to Washington and arranged an exclusive contract, signed by John Sherman, Secretary of the Treasury.

"Armed with the contract, Capt. Thomas returned to New York and called on the Coast Guard to drive the wreckers away, but it was a false find and not the *Hussar* that had been located. Some doubt has been expressed that Capt. Thomas had the true facts. I can only say that I do not know whether the treasure is there or not. If it is there, modern engineering methods can readily locate and recover it. It needs only two things, sufficient capital to build proper salvaging appliances backed up by an efficient operating crew to search below the bottom of the comparatively small area in which the *Hussar* presumably lies."

Finding the hull of the *Hussar* turned out to be about as simple as going to Cocos Island and pointing to where the treasure was buried. The shore line had changed. A ferry slip, docks, and other construction had been erected. In 1886, 20,000 tons of rock were blasted out of the channel at Pot Rock. Mud and silt had settled along the shore. In May 1903, a large anchor was recovered while members of the Oak Point Yacht Club were dragging the area for a sunken yacht. It was marked "H.M.S. HUS—" It was turned over to the American Museum of Natural History. Surely the hull of the *Hussar* was somewhere nearby.

Simon Lake's submarine *Salvager* had been raising coal in the nearby waters of Long Island Sound and the Hell Gate area was close enough to work. He asked for and obtained from the Treasury Department the exclusive contract to salvage the *Hussar*. It provided that only 10 per cent of any treasure and any cannons found would go to the government. It also prohibited the use of the contract as a basis for selling stock in the venture. The contract became active in March 1933.

Lake tried to procure capital from New York bankers and brokers to the amount of $750,000 when the Lake Submarine Salvage Corporation was formed in 1930, but the depression was on and he met with no success. In 1934 he had managed to get together a unit comprising an auxiliary schooner, three motor boats, the steam lighter *Lillian,* and the submarine salvager *Laksco I.* The boats *Laksco II, III, IV,* and *V* were also being put in seaworthy condition and fitted with special equipment.

Two salvage outfits were already working on the site of the *Hussar,* under Coast Guard permits—the Empire Marine Salvage and Engineering Corporation and another headed by R. T. Powell, inventor, engineer, and former real-estate man. Powell had spent two years gathering data on the history of the *Hussar*. He claimed that she had $8,000,000 aboard, at present-day prices. His diver, Anton Schacht, uncovered a timber fifty feet long and four feet wide off Stony Point, between 130th Street, the Bronx, and a point just north of Sunken Meadows. In October 1934, Roy Hansen, the diver for Empire Marine, working on the bottom in the 675-pound diving suit "Eleanor" from the tug *Terminal*, found the steamer *Observation* and read her name on the wreck. She had exploded and burned with a loss of life of about one hundred persons in 1932.

Through the years 1935, '36, and '37 the Lake submarine *Salvager* worked as regularly as financing could allow. Frank Crilley, a famous diver of the time, worked with Lake. As the government contract lapsed Lake reported to the Treasury Department that he was narrowing the area in which the *Hussar* must lie and the contract was renewed. Between times, when funds were low, the salvagers raised coal from the many sunken barges they had plotted in the neighborhood. It was demonstrated before newsmen and shareholders that coal could be raised at three hundred tons an hour, and the syndicate knew of fifty barges lying between 138th Street and the Battery.

In April 1935, Lake's equipment was tied up on account of lack of money to pay expenses. Having charted the area in September 1936, he believed the *Hussar* had been located off 135th Street in twelve feet of silt and coated with a residue of tar from a nearby gas plant. The ferries and scows unloading scrap for Japan were in the path of his operations and forced the equipment to move regularly. Lake was ready to bore with a core drill. If he brought up chalk, he could be sure he was getting close to Redcoat gold. The ship carried chalk ballast.

The financing was slowing down and some of the principal shareholders and Lake's staunchest supporters were working hard to raise the capital needed to continue work. In October 1936, the home town of the inventor, Milford, Connecticut, was about to foreclose on his home and property for $4,000 in back taxes. Lake had moved to New York City into small quarters. This seems ironic as the Lake Torpedo Boat Company had spent over $50,000,000 in payrolls in the Milford area in the years they had operated.

Meanwhile, in over a hundred drillings from 134th Street to 136th Street, nothing like chalk or oak from the hull had come up. An area within fifty feet of the 136th Street Pier had not been drilled and as soundings showed 72 feet of water, the right depth, it was possible that the *Hussar* lay in that space. Several hundred thousand dollars had been spent to date on the search.

In the summer and fall of 1937, through the backing of J. S. Jacobs and a few shareholders, capital was raised by the Under Water Recovery Corporation, a survey of sunken barges along the New Jersey coast was made, and 18,000 tons of coal was staked out for salvage.

On September 7, 1937, Simon Lake was interviewed on his seventy-first birthday. He had a little lumbago from the New Jersey coal salvage job but outside of that and one practically blind eye, he was pretty chipper, and said: "Life begins at seventy-one."

"If you want a birthday interview," he continued, "you don't want to see me, but my dad. He was ninety Thursday. My grandfather lived to be ninety-six and his sister kept going till she was a hundred and two or so."

"So you're not going to quit this fussing around in the East River hunting the gold in the *Hussar* and all that claptrap, Cap'n?"

"I won't stop," he said, "till I'm stopped." He had already retired twice. It was no good. "Before I pass out, I want to develop the commercial submarine. I'd have to live to be a hundred to do all I want to do."

Lake's East River hunt for the *Hussar* had brought up odds and ends probably from the wreckage of the *Observation*.

"We found a lot of stuff," the captain said. "Timbers and things of that sort, knives, utensils, part of a watch and eighty-six cents."

Lake was still at it in 1939 probing and pumping along the Bronx shore, finding rivet heads, grate bars, boiler fittings, and crockery. The inventor was still after the *Hussar* and asking the Treasury Department for an extension of his contract. He now believed that the wreck had shifted into the main stream when she was partly lifted in 1818, and he had made improvements in his submarine *Salvager* for another survey. If Lake was not willing to quit, the Treasury Department was, and decided it was a hopeless undertaking, but would renew the contract the next year if Lake was prepared to resume and complete operations.

The concession was not renewed because World War II came along.

Did the *Hussar* have $4,000,000 in gold guineas on board when she sank? Is the treasure there in the mud of Hell Gate? Or is it, as has been suggested, under the foundations of an apartment house on filled-in land? Or does her oak hull hold nothing but chalk ballast and the shackled bones of the American prisoners who drowned like rats when she sank?

Simon Lake, one of America's great inventors and

marine engineers, never found out. With his patience, persistence, and optimism and his submarine *Salvager*, working over a period of years he could not succeed even in locating her hull in the small area near 135th Street, in the Bronx. My guess is that the mystery of whether or not the *Hussar* carried a cargo of Redcoat gold will never be solved.

CHAPTER 9

History Under the Sea

*Scientific expeditions are now at work on the
recovery of historic lost treasures on the sea bottom.
Modern devices and new diving methods and
techniques are enabling research groups backed by
museums to raise from the depths valuable relics of
past civilizations.*

THE PIRATE CAPITAL of the Caribbean, once
the wickedest city in the world, now lies under fifty
feet of water and silt. On June 17, 1692, Port Royal,
Jamaica, was wrecked by a terrific earthquake and tidal
wave and slid into the sea. Even the grave and bones
of the great Sir Henry Morgan vanished beneath the
waves which swallowed swarms of the living.

Measured in time, 265 years is but a few seconds
to an antiquarian trained in the science of archeology.
The museums of the world are filled with rare and
historic discoveries from which the history of where,
when, and how lost civilizations lived has been recon-
structed.

It is one thing to locate and excavate the lost treasures on dry land and another to find and bring them
to the surface from under the sea. Until inventions and
improvements in diving methods were perfected the

168

treasures from the sea bottom were seldom salvaged. Only occasionally did a fishing trawler or a sponge diver accidentally raise the relics by which an ancient ship or sunken city could be identified. In recent years such finds are becoming more and more frequent by the use of free diving techniques.

A skin diver by passing through the waters of the Blue Grotto on the Isle of Capri discovers the grotto where the Emperor Tiberius and his court bathed. By an underwater tunnel he comes upon the remains of steps and man-made architecture dating from Roman times.

A deep-sea diver announces that he has found the ruins of a pre-Inca city submerged in the waters of Lake Titicaca in the Andes. Bolivian archeologists and museums can examine stone implements and objects raised from the ruins ninety-five feet below the surface of the sacred lake. William Mardorf recently announced that he had descended to the lake bottom and photographed the ruins.

An underwater discovery of great historical interest was made when Luis Marden, the National Geographic Society's undersea photographer, found the long-hidden grave of Captain Bligh's *Bounty*.

The famous old ship, taken by Fletcher Christian and the mutineers, vanished on January 23, 1790, when she was burned and scuttled off Pitcairn Island. The nine mutineers, six native men, twelve Tahitian women, and one child went into hiding. A wave of violence and bloodshed took place, and when a vessel finally stopped at the remote volcanic island eighteen years later, only one of the mutineers was found alive.

Tom Christian, twenty-one-year-old great-great-great grandson of Fletcher Christian, and Tom's brother-in-law,

Lew Brown, were trained by Marden in the use of the
Aqua-Lung. They searched six weeks for the *Bounty,*
finally discovering her resting place.

"Every day of reasonable calm we dived," Marden
writes in the December 1957 issue of the *National Geographic Magazine,* "but at first we found nothing."

Marden continues: "Then I came unexpectedly on a
long, sandy trench. I could see little squiggles in the surface of the white limestone, a curious marking that re-
sembled nothing so much as petrified worms.

"I thrust my face closer, almost touching the bottom. My
heart gave a jump. The squiggles were encrusted sheathing nails—*Bounty* nails—dozens of them. We had found
the resting place of the *Bounty.*"

Along the line of the ship's keel they found hull fittings,
an oarlock, and fragments of copper sheathing. Carbonized
wood clung to the metal fastenings. All the objects were
covered with limestone and had to be cut free with a chisel
and hammer.

The rudder of the *Bounty,* worm-eaten and copper-
fastened, had been fished up from six fathoms of water at
Pitcairn in 1933 by Parkin Christian and Robert Young.
It is in the museum at Suva in the Fiji Islands. One of the
Bounty's anchors was discovered by Wilford Fawcett
when Irving Johnson's yacht *Yankee* moored outside Pitcairn in February 1957. Fawcett spotted the anchor in fifty
feet of water on his first dive, well outside Bounty Bay.
Johnson lifted the twelve-foot anchor, and it now rests on
the landing in the bay.

Captain J. Y. Cousteau and his Undersea Research
Group have located and salvaged riches beyond price
from ancient cargo vessels sunk in the Mediterranean
over two thousand years ago. Carved marble columns
and capitals, a lead anchor, scores of wine jars and
amphorae have been recovered from the oldest seagoing

ship ever found. Much of this work has been done in conjunction with the Calypso Oceanographic Expeditions under the auspices of the National Geographic Society. Teams of skilled skin divers worked at a depth of 140 feet on a wine ship of Roman days. The French Navy's *Bathyscaphe* carried men to a depth of 13,281 feet to observe undersea life. Dr. Harold Edgerton's specially built stroboscopic cameras took photographs at 14,000 feet below the surface and a new world was opened to scientists.

Skin divers have much to thank Captain Cousteau for when they dive. He began mask diving in 1936 with Frederick Dumas, "the first of the menfish," and Commandant Philippe Tailliez. Seeking means to stay longer in the sea, Cousteau in 1942 enlisted the aid of the brilliant engineer, Emile Gagnan, in developing an automatic, independent compressed-air breathing apparatus, the now famous Aqua-Lung. The device is used in twelve navies: the American, French, Canadian, Spanish, Japanese, Italian, British, Norwegian, Yugoslavian, Argentinian, Dutch, and Belgian. The Aqua-Lung has lured many marine scientists into the sea, as well as thousands of amateur sportsmen.

These scientific expeditions are after more than mere gold and silver. They are searching back into the ages and reconstructing history drowned in the sea which man has never before been able to study.

But we are concerned with the more recent days of the pirates and the lost treasures of the Spanish galleons.

The sunken city of Port Royal, Jamaica, once known as the "Hellhole of the Caribbean," has recently been explored by an expedition headed by Edwin A. Link in his *Sea Diver*, assisted by Art McKee and Fred Logan. Enthusiastic followers of historic undersea trails,

Link and his party dredged and worked forty feet below the surface in six feet of mud and silt.

They did not walk the streets of the sunken city, as
nothing but rubble remains. They did discover and
raise a section of the old city wall or fort; they found
cannon, bones, clay pipes, jars, bottles, and timbers.
The wall section was presented to Art McKee for his
Sunken Treasure Fortress on the Florida Keys. A 5,200-
pound cannon was given to Bernard Lewis, the historian of the Jamaica Institute. The balance of the relics
are in the Undersea Hall of Archaeology of the Smithsonian Institution endowed by Mr. Link and in the charge
of Curator Mendel L. Peterson.

Edwin A. Link, of Link Aviation fame, has become
America's outstanding patron of marine archeology.
When he first became interested in the subject he used
his boat *Blue Heron* and later purchased the famous
trawler *Sea Diver*. She was originally built for the late
Hugh Matheson, one of the first Floridians to become
interested in sunken wrecks. In 1940, Charles M. Brookfield and Matheson located and salvaged the wreck of
H.M.S. *Winchester* on the Florida Keys. The *Winchester*
was one of three British ships dispatched to harass the
French shipping in the West Indies in the seventeenth
century. Loaded with loot from plundering Cape Haitien,
the ships were returning through the Florida Straits
when the 60-gun *Winchester* struck the Martyrs in a
hurricane and went down with all hands in September
1695. It was not until 245 years later that her resting
place became known when Brookfield and Matheson
raised cannon, coins, silver plate, and other relics; the
markings on the cannon definitely identified their wreck
as the *Winchester*. Not until then did the British Admiralty know the exact location of the ship. In McKee's
Treasure Fortress, among many relics from wrecks, is a

tattered but readable page of a prayer book in Latin from the remains of the *Winchester*. The pages had been preserved by being tightly jammed between two cannon encrusted in a coating of coral.

When Edwin Link purchased the 65-foot *Sea Diver* he equipped her to locate and study historic sites where literally thousands of objects from past centuries lie on the ocean floor. Many of these relics are peculiar to maritime use and would not be found ashore. Such a find was made by Link and Captain P. V. H. Weems in collaboration with the Smithsonian Institution in 1955, when they raised what may prove to be the anchor of Columbus's flagship *Santa Maria*. After two years of study and preparation the expedition searched about ten square miles of sea bottom off Cape Haitien near where the *Santa Maria* was thought to have been lost on Christmas 1492. It was a stormy and difficult undertaking, cursed with accidents and disappointments. When about ready to give up the search, Mrs. Link spotted the anchor in twelve feet of water. It was hand-forged and made of separate pieces of iron, and definitely made in the Columbian era.

"On the basis of the physical condition of the anchor and its shape and workmanship," concluded Mendel Peterson of the Smithsonian, "the anchor could have come from the *Santa Maria*." Link presented the historic 462-year-old relic to the local government and plans to do more undersea research in the area.

Link has sold the *Sea Diver*, and a new *Sea Diver II* is being built to his specifications. She will be larger and roomier, eighty-four feet in length, and equipped with all the latest scientific devices necessary to make her a floating research laboratory.

Sea Diver II will have magnetometers to detect the presence of iron underneath coral and sand several feet in thickness and in depths up to forty feet; electronic detectors which show the presence of any electrical conductor; sonar, with which masses projecting from sea bottom may be discovered; fathometers, which give a constant reading of depth; and navigational aids such as Loran and automatic pilot. All kinds of diving equipment, glass-bottomed launches, cranes to lift heavy cannon, a dredge to suck sand, and an underwater television set will be in use. Air compressors and tanks to provide air for several divers at one time will be built in.

When *Sea Diver II* goes into commission in 1958 the Links with their associated experts in diving, salvaging, and identifying lost ships and treasures will be back in their element searching for hidden history on the sea bottom.

One of the largest and best-equipped treasure expeditions of modern times is now at work out of its home port of Palm Beach, Florida, on the trail of galleon gold and pirate silver. The long and winding route which the leaders of Quest Associates intend to follow has been mapped out by F. L. Coffman, the owner of two companies dealing in various types of marine salvage and underwater recovery equipment.

Mr. Coffman began his research into lost treasures in 1938, and as a publisher of treasure charts and a writer on the subject, has received world-wide fame resulting in his obtaining personal contact with a great many treasure hunters who have contributed their knowledge.

"We will use all the latest scientific instruments," states Mr. Coffman, "and are prepared to work in the air, on the sea, under the sea, and on land. I have investigated over thirty-six thousand reported treasure locations in an attempt to authenticate them as to origin, history, value, and present location. We decided that some fifty sites along the Florida and Gulf Coast and the Caribbean were the best bets to work and the most likely to produce returns."

Associated with Coffman is an imposing staff of experts. With Quest is Captain Ivan H. Vestrem, a pioneer in the development of self-contained diving suits, diving bells, and other undersea equipment. Vestrem has spent a large part of his life underwater as a diver, navy frogman, island navigator, and explorer and in other marine work. He built the first self-contained helium-oxygen diving suit which was used to descend to a depth of 420 feet in Lake Michigan in 1937.

Commander William Baum, ex-electronic engineer of the U.S.S. *Nautilus* submarine, and owner of the diesel-powered tug *Simon Lake,* is also a member of the staff. The tug is equipped with the latest in locators for mineral and metal deposits, enabling it to pinpoint gold and silver loot. An underwater Dage TV camera for observation, a Minneapolis-Honeywell "Sea Scanner" capable of spotting wrecks for a distance of five miles horizontally by sonar, and a vertical depthometer will be carried. A diving bell, Aqua-Lung diving units, deep-water diving gear, and underwater lighting equipment for photography will be used.

The *RX-102,* a two-man submarine robot, will go along. It can descend to a depth of one thousand feet in five minutes and work there for six to eight hours under its own power. The small sub has built-in underwater photo equipment and can flood the ocean floor with 12,000 watts of light. It can swim like a fish with its U.S. Rubber Company bladder. Best of all, the *RX-102* is capable of lifting 3,000 pounds of gold bars from the sea bottom with its detachable claws and arms. If all goes well on the trip Jules Verne's Captain Nemo will look like a piker in treasure-recovery circles.

The *RX-102* is expected to have a test tryout on a fleet of ships, thirty-five in number, lost in deep water off Campos, Brazil, with $121,000,000 in gold dust and nuggets aboard from the Tourinho Placer mines. And if this is not successful, Quest has many more sunken wrecks to search for bullion.

They are after $3,000,000 in silver in three galleons lost on Serinilla Reefs, south of Jamaica; a wreck located in Bermuda waters with silver and gold from Mexico and lost in 1655 with a reputed $2,000,000; a Spanish galleon south of Cartagena, Colombia, in the Isles of Rosario; $5,000,000 in gold and silver coin, bar and plate, lost and lying between islands off the Venezuelan coast; a frigate off the Atlantic coast with $15,000,000 aboard in eighty-four feet of water and covered with mud and sand; and a steamer sunk in a collision in thirty-eight fathoms carrying $3,000,000 of American twenty-dollar gold pieces in kegs.

On the Quest Associates' agenda for the next few years are the following items:

Spanish Treasure Galleon Wrecks

Pedro Bank, August 23, 1730, manifest shows "1,050,000 pieces-of eight, 330 ingots of silver, 88 plates of silver," plus private shipments to Spain. Unrecovered bars	$ 1,000,000
Serinilla Reefs, three galleons, estimated value	3,000,000
Off Venezuela, one galleon, gold and silver	5,000,000
Matanzas Bay, Cuba, galleon, gold and silver	2,000,000
Paita, Peru, galleon, several tons silver bar and plate	3,500,000
Manta Bay, Ecuador, galleon, gold and silver bars	13,000,000
Porto Bello, Panama, galleon, bullion silver	2,000,000
Pte. DuCap, St. Lucia, B.W.I., gold, silver, jewels	20,000,000
Isle of Plate, Ecuador, 45 tons silver bullion	5,000,000
Gulf of Urabá, Colombia, bar and plate	5,000,000

Cape Engaño, Dominican Rep., gold and silver	5,000,000
Bahamas, galleon, silver bullion	3,000,000
Pta. Sta. Elena, Ecuador, one galleon	13,000,000
Pta. Sta. Elena, Ecuador, one galleon	500,000
Maracaibo, Venezuela, lost in 1669, five galleons	11,000,000
Porto Lopez, Venezuela gulf	2,000,000
Off Cuba, one galleon, 300 chests, 1718	3,500,000
Isle of Pines, Cuba, 2 galleons, gold and silver	8,000,000
Tortuga Bay, Cuba, galleon	5,000,000
Off Campeche, Mexico, one galleon with	2,300,000
Off Bragança, Brazil, one galleon, bullion	3,000,000
Silver Bank, off Haiti, 7 galleons	19,000,000
Mona Passage near Puerto Rico, galleon, gold, jewels	7,000,000

Many other galleon locations are on the Quest lists, with no estimate of their treasure, in the Caribbean and along the Gulf shores. Also there are such hoards of buried treasure on land as:

In a cave on an island near the Gulf of Honduras, value	???
On an island south of Haiti, in a cave, value	???
Bar & plate silver on a Virgin Island, unrecovered value $	800,000
West coast of Florida, Lostman's River, hoard value	2,000,000
Buried chests (3) in North Bahama group, gold bars	???
Pirate hoard, Old Providence Island	2,000,000
On a key west of British Honduras, pirate treasure buried in 1680, church ornaments and jewels.	

The total accumulated value at minimum has been estimated by Mr. Coffman as $294 million without including many unidentified ships on their lists and those not valued. He says:

"It is believed that recovery is possible on the majority of these locations by employing the modern equipment and devices available, such as submarine, diving bell, diving gear, helicopter, plane, sonar gear, electronic-magnetic and transistor-type metal locating instruments. In many locations such as the Jardine Rocks, off Cuba, there are many unidentified ships not in our records, any of which may be discovered during our exploration and recovery efforts."

"Our expedition is set for two or three years' hard, carefully planned work," Coffman reports. "We are not going on a pleasure cruise, and are taking along experts in diving, navigation, salvage, marine engineering, TV, still and movie photography, aviation, metallurgy, and medicine. We already have two ships in the Caribbean and are planning to operate from two tropical islands, one in the North and the other in the South Bahama group, where we will have deep anchorages and bases of supply. Treasure hunting is a flourishing American business, and is the backbone of the big skin-diving craze. Everybody dreams of finding treasure but few are willing to go to the expense and trouble of going at it in a businesslike way. Many expeditions have failed because of a lack of factual information on locations and because their equipment and finances were inadequate. We have conquered these shortcomings, and know what we are after and where it is, and we have the means of getting it. How can we lose?"

One of the most successful treasure hunters of recent years lives in Bermuda. His discovery was remarkable for its historical and monetary value.

Edward B. (Teddy) Tucker of Gwelly Hole, Somerset, is a native-born Bermudian. The first Tucker settled in Bermuda in 1620 and Tuckers have been there ever since. Teddy is short, husky, and soft-spoken. He has the weather-beaten hide of one who has spent his life on, in, and under the sea. He was raised so close to the ocean that had he fallen from his window when a baby, he says, he would have landed in the surf. And he has never left the sea.

His youth from twelve on was spent with fishermen. He quit school early to fish and dive for conch shells to

sell the tourists. He came to know intimately the ragged
reefs that surround Bermuda in a hundred-mile circle, and
has looked down on dozens of wrecks where the fish hide
in rusted hulls. (A report to the British Admiralty in 1800
listed over three hundred wrecks near the islands.)

Teddy has found cannon bare of coral on the reefs in
spots where the coral growth has hardly increased since
the last ice age. He has found cannon completely cemented over with coral where it grows rapidly and tall
and breaks off in storms.

From his boyhood days, Teddy has been interested in
wrecks and it seems fitting that he should be the one to
bring up a famous treasure. He used the first Japanese
face mask in Bermuda waters while diving for conch shells.
Joining the British Navy early in World War II, he spent
five years diving from light mine sweepers. He gained experience in Singapore, the Bay of Bengal, and the Gulf of
Aden. Sometimes wallowing up to his armpits in the mud
in strong tides and unable to see an inch in front of his
face mask, he was happy to get home to the clear waters
of Bermuda in 1947.

Tucker and his brother-in-law, Robert Canton, had
ideas. They formed a partnership, bought a boat, rebuilt
and rerigged her with air compressors and hoisting equipment, and went into business. They made surveys for insurance companies, and salvaged copper, lead, brass, and
other salable material. They spotted wrecks and worked
them but most of the sunken ships were steel-hulled or
copper-bottomed.

One of the largest vessels lost in the area, the French
60-gun ship *Hermione,* was wrecked off the west end of
the islands in December 1838. The muzzle-loading cannon in her main battery weigh about 7,000 pounds each,
and fired shot six inches in diameter and weighing 64
pounds. The name of a famous cannon maker "Ruelle"

and the date "AN 1828" can still be read on the breeches
of the eleven cannon that remain on the wreck. Tucker
and Canton have explored her thoroughly and have recovered some fifty swords and cutlasses, flintlock muskets,
brass and copper fittings, and nautical instruments. The
Hermione when she sailed to her end was the last word in
armed sailing ships. She now rests in a sea so clear that
Peter Stackpole, famous underwater photographer of
Life, has filmed a color movie of Tucker and Canton at
work on the wreck.

In the Spanish galleon era, the island was called "Isle
of Devils" by the superstitious mariners. A pinpoint on
their crude charts, uninhabited, unlit, low on the horizon,
the "Barmudas" were a death trap for many a treasure
ship in foggy or stormy weather and on dark nights. The
islands lay astride the homeward path of the plate fleets,
the last landfall between Havana and Old Spain.

In 1955 Tucker and Canton made one of the most important discoveries of water-soaked wealth ever raised
from the sea in modern times. The treasures in gold and
jewels had lain on the ocean bottom for over 350 years
lightly covered with sand.

On a calm, clear winter's day in 1950, Tucker was out
in a small boat looking around the reefs when he spied
three cannon sticking up out of the sand. The following
summer he went back to the location and recovered six
cannon, a bucketful of lead musket balls, and a very old
anchor. The anchor had a large eye and originally had a
wooden stock—the kind used with rope before the days
of chain cable. The cannon were purchased by the local
Historical Society and they now repose on the lawn of
the Bermuda aquarium.

It was not until 1955 that Tucker and Canton thought
of returning to the wreck site on a pleasant Sunday to dive
on the spot and prospect the area. On the bottom, in a

depth of thirty feet or less, they dug around in the sand with their hands. It was only by luck that the first object recovered was a bronze apothecary's mortar, plainly marked "Petrus Van Den Ghein" with the date 1561. Mendel L. Peterson of the Smithsonian in Washington identified the maker as a famous Flemish caster of bronze bells and objects who died in 1561. The mortar must have been one of his last works. Spurred on by this find, Tucker and Canton gathered a bucketful of blackened silver coins, some stuck together in clumps by coral. One lump still had the remains of the pigskin pouch clinging to them in which they were originally enclosed. Then a small square of bright gold shone in the sand—a cube cut from a larger bar.

"This was the first gold I had ever seen on the ocean bottom," said Tucker. "It was as clean and bright as jewelry in a Fifth Avenue store. One corner had been sliced off either to assay or for small change. We hated to stop work but it was nine miles back to port so we quit for the day.

"We were really excited," Tucker continued seriously, "and returned to thoroughly comb the small pocket among the rocks where the relics had been uncovered. We tried an air-lift operated by eighty pounds' air pressure in a pipe but it was unsatisfactory. We tried a water jet, using a small hose and less pressure. Finally, we just dug with our hands and used a small paddle like a ping-pong bat, to fan away the sand. This paid off well—I later hung the paddle on the wall at home—I guess we are the only treasure divers to fan ourselves into a small fortune from a sunken galleon wreck!

"Over a period of days when we could work we found three gold buttons studded with pearls; a gold bar ten and a half inches long weighing thirty-six ounces; two rounded lumps of gold weighing twenty-three and nineteen ounces; something over two thousand Spanish and French silver coins, and a second small square of gold.

"We uncovered some breech-loading culverins or swivel guns; hand grenades; a steel breastplate; sounding leads, in which the British Museum was most interested; a terra-cotta inkwell in the form of a lion's head; brass hour glasses and a pair of navigator's brass dividers; a set of nested brass weights; and the finest prize of all—a bishop's gold pectoral cross studded with seven emeralds, an almost priceless relic. It is of native Indian workmanship and from the ends of the cross bar hang two small golden nails. Whether a bishop was wearing it on his homeward trip to Spain or whether some wealthy patron of the church was carrying it as a gift may never be known.

"We also recovered some interesting pottery of native Carib make. One cruet for vinegar or oil is red clay with green glaze. A small six-inch pitcher with a spout is set on a ten-degree angle so that its center of gravity makes it less likely to tip over when used on shipboard. It was made by a left-handed potter who held it in his right hand while he molded the clay handle with his left; this can be detected by his fingerprints. Nothing like it in style has been seen before.

"A collection of Carib Indian weapons was being carried by some passenger to show the folks in Spain. One ceremonial spear five feet long is carved in an intricate design for about two feet along the handle. We also found bows and arrows. These weapons were fire-treated to harden them, and the water and worms that attack ordinary wood have had no effect on them.

"One of our strangest finds was human bones—scattered ribs, finger, forearm, and foot bones—now undergoing tests in England. Bones generally dissolve after five years under the sea and it is unheard-of to recover them after some 350 years. One British bone specialist has suggested that the bones are possibly those of some dignitary whose mummified body was being returned to Old Spain for burial. Could they have been the remains of the bishop who wore the emerald cross? The latest dated coin found on the site is a Spanish piece-of-eight of 1592, so the wreck must have happened at some later time, probably in the late 1590's. If church records list some bishop lost at sea on his return trip during the period, we may be able to date and name the wreck.

"We uncovered a pair of woman's leather shoes in the sand which fell apart when disturbed, but not before Pete Stackpole made photographs of them. I believe the ship hit the rocks, lay there for a short time, and then split apart, letting the material fall through her broken hull. There was no sign of timbers or the major parts of a ship. Apparently the wooden parts drifted away. We found only rock ballast, with the relics scattered around in the sand, the cannon and anchor on top. We moved everything and cleaned out the pothole, so I doubt whether anything more of value remains. It was an easy place to work, as there was no large coral; the water is not over thirty feet deep and in some places is so shallow that we could stand with our heads above water. The ship could not have been a large one, as her armament consisted of six large cannon, four breech-loading swivel guns, and some matchlock muskets."

The gold bars and cakes are as bright and clean as the day they were cast. They are marked with the circular stamp of the Royal Spanish Tax Collector, a circular design showing castles, lions, and a pomegranate denoting Castile, León, and Granada in a shield surrounded with the legend "PHILLIPVS.II.D.G.REX." This stamp denotes that the king's *quinto* or royal fifth had been deducted. The long bar is stamped "PINTO," the name of the mining locality in Colombia (then Nuevo Reino de Granada) from which the gold came. One of the rounded ingots is stamped "ESPANA" and the other is stamped with the name "D°HERNANDZ" (Diego, or Domingo, Hernandez) the assayer. One of the small squares of gold, cut from a larger bar, is stamped with the monogram PHVS for PHIL-LIPVS above a large pomegranate, denoting Nuevo Reino de Granada. The various bars are also individually stamped with the Roman numerals XX, XXI, XXII, and XXIIII, probably the lot numbers.

Tucker and Canton made treasure history when they fanned a fortune from the Bermuda reef. The island authorities have laid claim to their treasure but it seems sure that the finders will be well rewarded for their careful and intelligent work in the field of marine archeology.

The marine archeology project of the Smithsonian Institution, U.S. National Museum, is lending its help in many ways to the discoverers of historic wrecks. Mendel L. Peterson, acting head of history at the Institution, first began his explorations in 1951 when he met Edwin A. Link, who now finances the project. Peterson says:

The wreck sites are a vast storehouse of historical objects. It is believed that a systematic exploration, recovery, preservation, and study program will result in three significant gains: first, a large collection of precisely dated objects will be formed constituting a valuable reference for archeologists working ashore and in other wreck sites that are not so precisely dated; second, a collection of objects peculiar to maritime use will be assembled, many of which would be unobtainable from land sites; and third, studies in the archives of Europe on documents relating to shipwrecks in the Florida area will bring to light important facts concerning naval history of the Florida Straits area which is intimately connected with the early maritime history of the English-American colonies and the United States.

The identification of a shipwreck site may proceed from one or two directions: An unidentified shipwreck may be located, objects from it salvaged and listed, identity of nationality, period, and size of ship established from the objects found on it, and this evidence compared against shipping records of known losses for the area in which the wreck was located. In this way the wreck of *H.M.S. Winchester* was identified and more recently H.M.S. frigate *Looe*.

In the summer of 1951, I participated in an expedition with Mr. Link on his *Blue Heron* in the investigation of a shipwreck on a small reef some five miles off the Florida Keys about twenty-five miles southwest of Marathon, Florida. Only one fact was known about the wreck: the year before it had been discovered by Bill Thompson of Marathon and Dr. and Mrs. George Crile, Jr., of Cleveland, Ohio, and some uniform buttons and copper coins had been recovered. Among the coins was a half-ore piece of Sweden dated 1720. The reef on which the wreck lay was shown as "Looe Reef" on the charts. The expedition members dived on the wreck site for two weeks in thirty-five feet of water and recovered a large amount of material. These objects led to the conclusion that the vessel was a British ship that sank after 1720 and probably before 1750. The ship carried twelve- and six-pound cannon in her main battery and sank as a direct result of accident and not in naval action, since the plugs were found in the gun barrels. A crowned rose on one of the cannon substantiated the conclusion that the ship sank before 1750, as the emblem was not used commonly after the death of Queen Anne in 1714 and the normal life of an iron barrel at sea was not much over thirty-five or forty years. The mark of the broad arrow as well as the crowned rose on cannon and cannon balls also indicated that the ship was British. Permanent iron ballast cast to fit the hull also proved she was a warship.

Mr. Peterson later checked a register of British ships lost in America in the eighteenth century and found the entry: "February 5, 1744, *Looe*, 44 guns, Captain Ashby Utting, Commanding, lost in America."

The conclusion was obvious. The reef, like others in Florida, had been named on the charts from the wrecked ship. Shortly after this discovery, the Criles traced the history of the *Looe* through letters and reports by Captain Utting in the Public Record Office in London and thus learned the whole story of her wreck on her last cruise.

"Another method of identification of shipwrecks," continues Peterson, "may come from documents describing a particular wreck and sometimes charts giving the location of the wreck site may be studied first, and with this information an electronic and visual search is made of the area in which a ship is known to have sunk. In this manner the attempt to find the wreck of the *Santa Maria* was carried out, resulting in the discovery of the anchor which *could* have been hers."

About the time of the *Looe* discovery another wreck on Delta Shoals near Marathon was spotted by Charles Slater while skin diving. Slater saw cannon and what proved to be an ivory elephant tusk in the coral in twenty feet of water. He succeeded in breaking out the large ivory tusk and took it to Art McKee's Fortress of Sunken Treasure at Treasure Harbor, Plantation Key. By the time an expedition could be organized to work on the wreck, Hally Hamlin, Marathon designer and builder of a two-man submarine, visited the wreck site and recovered a cannon. By the time McKee and Slater with Wes Bradley and F. A. Ruff arrived at the wreck, Dr. George Crile, Jr., with Mrs. Crile and their six children, the guests of Captain Bill Thompson in the charter boat *Bon Ami*, had spied a tusk and two cannon on the ocean floor. Before the Crile party could blast the wreck with dynamite, McKee's party arrived and everybody pooled forces. Dynamiting was vetoed and the salvaging was done by McKee in his diving gear. After two days, twelve ivory tusks, the largest four feet eight inches in length; three cannon; silver plate; blackened pans and buckets from the ship's galley; and grapeshot and lead were recovered. Corroded manacles and slave bracelets, an ancient clay pipe, and a piece of human bone bore mute evidence to the human cargo that went down with the ship.

"The bone was the first I ever saw from a sunken ship," says McKee, "and its preservation was no doubt due to its being covered by sand. The cargo of ivory and the slave bracelets are good proof that the ship was a slave trader but her identity or date of loss have not been established. The ivory tusks were well preserved."

The following year an expedition to the wrecks of the *Looe* and the ivory slave trader was arranged by Dr. Crile with James Rand and Daniel T. Moore of Cleveland, John M. Shaheen of New York, Captain Bill Thompson of Marathon, Edwin Link, and Mendel L. Peterson. McKee and Wes Bradley of Homestead were invited to conduct the diving and get the relics out of the wrecks for a sixth share in the recoveries. McKee summed up the trip in these words:

"We worked on the bottom in six-hour shifts but the slave-trader wreck looked as if it had been dynamited since our previous trip, for the coral ledges had caved in on the area. We found some rifle butt straps, brass, and more cannon balls and bar-shot. Only two coins were recovered but Link with the *Blue Heron* raised some cannon, and we got a lead hull marker, in the shape of a Roman numeral IX, for our museum and also some cannon balls. It took a tough twenty-six hours breaking out rubble and jetting in the five days Wes and I spent on the bottom, and results were hardly worth the effort. But that's the way it is in this business. You never know what may turn up and whether you will hit pay dirt."

During the summer of 1957, a group of New Jersey skin divers made history on two cargo ships wrecked off Point Pleasant Beach, New Jersey. Their story of accidentally finding the wrecks and of their efforts was told to me by Jack Homer and Bob Franklin while I photographed some of the relics.

On the Fourth of July 1955, Jack Homer of Lavalette, New Jersey, and a few skin-diving friends took the holiday to spend a day on the water near Manasquan Inlet. They water-skied for a while and lazed around in the sunshine off Point Pleasant Beach. About three hundred yards off shore they drifted near two fishermen in a rowboat. The line of one was hooked onto something too solid to be a fish and Homer shouted, "Don't break your line—I'll dive down and release your hook!" Homer slipped a face mask on and dived down into the water, following the fishline to the bottom. It was hooked into a sunken wreck. Releasing the hook, Homer surfaced, and received the angler's thanks.

When the fishermen left, Homer's party donned their underwater gear and went down to look over the wreck. Her ribs were sticking out of the sand and silt but the hull, apparently about sixty feet long, was full of mud through which a pile of debris showed. On top were slabs of what looked like slate ballast, which turned out to be 70-pound bars of block tin. The hull was loaded with cargo in bales, barrels, kegs, and cases.

The group of young men, Jack Homer, Bob Franklin, Jack Baker, Ed Patrick, and other skin-diving friends devoted the rest of the summer to examining and working the wreck. A little farther off the beach they located another wreck, or a section of the first. This was also loaded with cargo.

Bob Franklin says of the wreck: "It was much larger than the first and rather broken up. She was about a hundred and fifty feet long and raised above bottom about twelve feet. In the hull was a long cylindrical object we thought was a boiler; when we examined it, it turned out to be about a hundred large spun brass pots nested together. The cargo is stacked in the hull without much growth over it. We have crawled into the hull and are gradually unloading the cargo. Even the wood in the barrels is in fairly good shape and I took one apart carefully. It was oak and packed with flatirons. They were still wrapped in the paper in which they were packed but when they were exposed to the air and washed off with water, the iron turned to paste and washed away. They smelled of sulfur and a chemist friend at the High School tells us that the cast iron had turned to iron sulfide.

"We recovered about a dozen pigs of tin which assayed 99 per cent pure. We brought up lead eight feet wide and twenty feet long, rolled so tightly that when it was unrolled we could read the chalk marks on the inside made by the shipper. As we looked, the marks faded and the lead turned black. We have found spun brass pots of all sizes, brass hooks, broken crockery, a case of jack-knives, and casters for furniture. Thousands of brass pins are scattered through the goods and we thought for a minute we had found gold coins shining in the sand. They are bright brass buttons marked 'EXTRA RICH LONDON' and inquiries in London lead us to believe that the maker is still in business. All the goods seem to be of British manufacture.

"It is like a detective story," Franklin continued, "trying to identify the wreck and her age. We sent some of the articles to the Smithsonian Institution and Mendel Peterson has dated the wrecks about 1800 to 1830. The British Museum is also helping us. The insurance records or companies no longer exist but we have found early reports of the wreck-master who had charge of salvage in the area, which may help us identify our find."

In late September 1956, another salvage crew, led by Captains John Berringer and Joseph Magill in the commercial dragger *Kingfisher*, anchored over the wrecks and started salvage. A three-sided battle for ownership is now on among the Homer skin divers, the *Kingfisher* group, and the New Jersey State Bureau of Navigation. Meanwhile the state has appointed the skin divers as custodians with the right to raise the balance of the cargo and report to a State Receiver until the case is decided.

"We do not want to destroy the wrecks," Homer states, "but hope to add to the historical records of Monmouth County. We still have a lot of cargo to salvage. It is very heavy and hard to break out and raise to the surface. We have a new boat with an air pump and can lift up to three thousand pounds. In the meantime, as more relics come up, we are searching through old newspapers, libraries, and family records for information that may help to identify the wrecks. They lay in only thirty-five feet of water about three hundred yards off Point Pleasant Beach where Bob Franklin operates a diving equipment and photo shop, so it is no trouble getting to the site when the weather is good."

When Jack Homer performed his good deed on the Fourth of July 1955, by diving to release a stranger's fish hook, he did not know that he would uncover New Jersey colonial history.

A couple of uniform buttons and a copper coin found by the Criles on a reef led to the discovery of the wreck of the *Looe*.

Such small things lead the true researcher under water into the greater discovery of relics which tell the tales of long-forgotten adventurers on the sea and the times in which they lived and died.

CHAPTER 10

Vigo's Mud-Covered Millions

The greatest loss of gold and silver in naval history: Vigo, Spain, October 24, 1702

"The sandy bottom was clean and bright. Some of the ship's crew in their diving-dresses were clearing away half-rotten barrels and empty cases from the midst of blackened wrecks. From these cases and from these barrels escaped ingots of gold and silver, cascades of piastres and jewels. The sand was heaped with them. . . . Laden with their precious booty the men returned to the Nautilus, *disposed of their burden and went back to this inexhaustible fishery of gold and silver.*

"I understood now. This was the scene of the battle. Here on this very spot the galleons laden for the Spanish government had sank."

—*Jules Verne,* Twenty Thousand Leagues Under the Sea

THE RICHEST of all sunken treasures lies in the mud of San Simon Bay, a stone's throw from shore in a spreading lagoon bordered by sandy beaches. Here lie the sunken hulls of a great Spanish fleet of galleons whose legendary cargo has drawn salvage adventurers from many corners of the world for two and a half centuries.

The tale of how these galleons were lost and their great treasure came to the mud of Galicia, instead of to the coffers of the king, is not a fairy story. It is recorded history. The sites of these treasure ships were never marked down in blood on a chart handed down by some dying pirate; but have been accurately plotted on hydrographic charts by generations of salvage crews. The fantastic value of the treasure's riches was not the hallucination of the sole survivor of the crew; it is recorded in documents in Spanish archives. The sunken hulks are not strewn over shark-infested coral reefs; they rest under the calm waters of a shallow inland bay. The treasure is not guarded by fierce moray eels and octopuses, but is watched over by oysters and sardines.

In the year 1702, on the coast of Spain, certain events took place which could be called "A Tragedy of Errors." Two kings, a queen, admirals, generals, statesmen, a naval hero, a chaplain, a loose-tongued consul, a world-renowned mathematician, with a great chorus of soldiers, sailors, marines, and diplomats, dressed in the colorful costumes of England, Holland, France, and Spain, were the characters. These actors performed against backgrounds of smoke, flame, explosions on land and at sea. At stake was 3,400 tons of gold and silver. And luck more than once changed the plot.

If you would like to own part of this treasure, there is no need for you to dig or dive for it. Here is the story:

In 1702 the War of the Spanish Succession had begun with England and her allies, the Dutch, arrayed against Philip V, first Bourbon King of Spain, and Louis XIV of France. Queen Anne of England commissioned Sir George Rooke as Vice-Admiral. Rooke in the *Royal Sovereign* of 110 guns, with thirty English and twenty Dutch fighting ships, and the Duke of Ormonde with thirteen thousand troops, sailed to the Mediterranean and besieged Cadiz.

The assault on Cadiz ended in disaster; battered and discouraged after their defeat, Rooke and his forces set sail for home and disgrace. But luck sailed with them aboard the *Pembroke*, in the form of a naval chaplain.

No treasure fleet from Mexico or Peru had sailed for Spain for three years, and gold, silver, and valuable cargo had been piling up at Cartagena, Porto Bello, and Vera Cruz. The Spanish flota was delayed until a fleet of French men-of-war arrived to convoy them on their plodding way. There were forty ships in all, including twenty-three treasure-laden Spanish galleons, stuffed with the accumulated three years' cargo from the mines of New Spain. Word leaked to England: "The Spanish galleons are coming overladen with riches," and, "This is the richest flota that ever came to Europe."

Sir Cloudesley Shovel with a British fleet of twenty-seven ships-of-war sailed to head them off. The flota was in a tight spot—it was headed for Cadiz, where Rooke and his forces lay off the harbor—and Shovel was waiting at sea. Before they could fall into either trap, a Genoese vessel that had been in Cadiz harbor and was now headed for Portugal met them, warning them of their danger. A hurried consultation was called among the naval officers and it was decided to make a run for Vigo, in Galicia. This was a safe refuge, as they could dodge the English and still keep far enough from France to spoil any designs that Louis XIV might have on Philip's treasure.

The fleet made Vigo safely and anchored in sheltered San Simon Bay, far inland past the narrow Straits of Rande. The forts at the Straits were manned, the militia called out, and a heavy chain boom stretched across the entrance to the inner harbor. Then the Spanish officials became so tied up in red tape that there seemed no way of unloading the treasure. The Cadiz authorities maintained that nothing could be disembarked at Vigo—that to unload the fleet was their privilege, and that the ships should be safe in the harbor at Vigo without discharging their cargoes. When the enemy had gone away, they could sail for Cadiz.

Never was so much treasure so foolishly endangered. The delays and arguments among the Spanish authorities gave the Anglo-Dutch fleet a chance to learn where the galleons lay.

Admiral Shovel had missed the flota at sea, Sir George Rooke had not captured Cadiz. The Spaniards had not put the riches ashore, and the English and Dutch fleets were on their way home, when a small but important event changed the whole play of history.

The ship *Pembroke* stopped on her way homeward at Lagos Bay for fresh water, and here we have an eye-witness account from Midshipman Nathaniel Uring:

. . . . On the 19th Sept. 1702 we left Cadiz, and set sail homewards. When we arrived off Cape St. Vincent, a detachment of six Third-rate Ships was made for the West Indies; we steering heavily home after a fruitless expedition, in which our chief Commanders got but little credit. Several of the transports having had no opportunity of watering in the Bay of Bulls, the Admiral had order'd Capt. Hardy in the *Pembroke,* to take such vessels under his care, and to convoy them to Lagos Bay, in order to water there: And on the 21st the Chaplain of the *Pembroke* being on shore, and by the advantage of speaking French, fell into conversation with the French Consul. . . . The Frenchman was full of his boasts of his master's power, and amongst the rest, gave broad hints of the arrival of the Spanish Galleons. Before they went, a gentleman from Lisbon . . . wanted to go on board the fleet; to him Mr. Beavour, the Chaplain, sent an offer of carrying him on board the *Pembroke;* and the stranger informed him that Admiral Château-Renault with 30 Men-of-War and 22 Galleons was arrived in Vigo.

Captain Hardy on hearing this news set out to find the fleet and on the 6th of October informed Sir George Rooke, who called a council of war and resolved to steer for Vigo. "Gladness appear'd in every face; the Chief Officers, no doubt, glad of an opportunity to retrieve their credit for their ill-conduct at Cadiz, and the rest of the Officers and sailors big with the expectation of the plunder of the Spanish galleons," writes Uring.

Early on the afternoon of October 24, 1702, the rumble of cannon echoed in the heights overlooking the Straits of Rande where the ships of the Anglo-Dutch fleet were bombarding Spanish shore defenses. The Spanish forts of Rande and Bestins defending the entrance to the straits crumpled under the bombardment. Their walls were jerry-built from earth and stone and they mounted between them only fifty-five guns. Even as they fought the stronger warships, a flank attack from shore by four thousand English marines under the Duke of Ormonde overwhelmed Rande's three hundred fifty French and Spanish defenders. Bestins fell soon afterward.

The passage into the straits was now open. A squadron under Admiral Hopson raced past the silent forts onto the last obstacle before the French warships: a floating chain of tree trunks and cables stretched across the narrows of Rande to stop the enemy. Driven by a strong wind, Hopson's eight ships smashed through the floating boom and sailed into the center of a line of twenty-one French warships arrayed in a long crescent across the mouth of San Simon Bay a few hundred yards beyond.

From his flagship, Le Fort, the French Admiral Château-Renault counterattacked with fireships, as the narrow arena made evasive maneuvering difficult. Burning fireships grappled with Hopson's attackers, and soon his flagship, the Torbay, was blazing. His other warships tore a gap through the French line and raced across San Simon Bay toward the trapped galleons.

Don Manuel de Velasco knew then that the naval battle was lost. To the last the Spanish Admiral had hoped that the boom and the French warships would keep the hungry English from his galleons and their treasure. Now, with the attackers only a mile away, he could see there was no escape. The order to jettison cargo went out from the *Capitana*, flagship to the numerous galleons. Treasure chests were hastily dumped into the bay, but the work had hardly begun when the Anglo-Dutch squadron closed in. Velasco gave a final order to scuttle the galleons. Their crews' discipline broke as seacocks were opened and ornate cedar decks set ablaze. Panicky Spanish sailors tore open chests of silver below deck, fought for places in the lifeboats, and leaped into the water. In a few minutes the galleons were settling slowly into the bay, flames and smoke belching forth over their towering decks and regal sails. The disheartened French soon followed the Spanish example.

In the melee the English and Dutch crews boarded the abandoned vessels. Some of the galleons and warships were saved from flames and captured as prizes. Most of the ships, however, were beyond rescue, and late into the night the bay was jarred by explosions as flames reached the powder and the ships burned to the waterline and disappeared in clouds of steam.

The next morning English marines captured the nearby village of Redondela, seizing a large part of what silver had been previously put ashore and stored awaiting shipment inland. French and Spanish troops watched from surrounding hills, too disorganized to counterattack.

Although the battle of Vigo Bay lasted only a few hours, casualties were heavy. The French fleet of twenty-one ships was reduced to fifteen sunken wrecks and six captured prizes. All the Spanish galleons were scuttled with the exception of five or six which were taken as booty. Over two thousand Spanish and French were killed and about two hundred taken prisoner. The English lost

115 in the *Torbay* and about forty of the shore party.

The booty divided between the English and the Dutch amounted to about $35,000,000. The English took two or three large galleons and five French warships. The Dutch received the warship *Bourbon* and five Spanish vessels, of which three were probably galleons. After the battle the victors consolidated their loot and repaired H.M.S. *Torbay* and the damaged prizes to make them seaworthy.

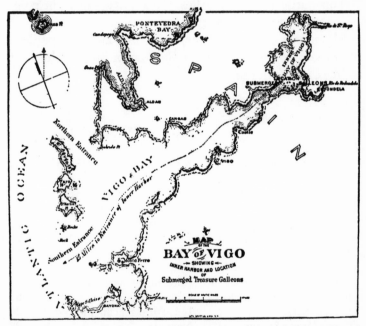

Bay of Vigo. Submerged galleons are near entrance to inner bay, at upper right.

On October 28, Admiral Cloudesley Shovel arrived with his squadron, and three days later Rooke and Hopson sailed for England. Shortly afterward prisoners of war were exchanged, and Shovel's fleet set sail escorting the captured vessels manned by skeleton crews. The galleons *Tauro* and *Santa Cruz* reached England with a mighty freight of bullion in their holds, but the largest of the captured galleons was lost at sea. This prize of H.M.S. *Monmouth,* loaded with about half of the English loot, struck a submerged rock pinnacle not shown on the charts and sank immediately with some three hundred tons of treasure off the mouth of Vigo Bay. (The Atlantic Salvage Company are now on her trail and believe that when they locate her they can salvage the treasure.)

This battle was the costliest naval engagement in point of material losses in history.

The names of the galleons, armament and commanders of the armada sunk in Vigo Bay, according to the best sources, is as follows:

Galleon	Commander	Guns
Jesus Maria Joseph (*Almirante*)	Manuel de Velasco, Admiral	44
Santissima Trinidad (*La Buffona*)	Jos. Chacon, Vice Admiral	54
Nuestra Sra. de las Animas (*La Capitana d'Assogos*)	Fern'do Chacon, Captain	54
San Juan de Baptista	Alonzo Lopez	50
Santo Cristo de Maracaja	Vincenti Alvarez	40
Santo Cristo de Buen Viaje	Francisco Blanco	36
La Santa Cruz	Alonzo Iparrere	36
Nra. Señora de del Rosario (*Nostredam de Mercy*)	Antonio Monteagudo	30
Nra. Señora de las Mercedes	Francisco Barragan	36
Santo Domingo	Ignacio Asconohuette	30
El Toro (*Santa Susana*)	Noguera	26
Nra. Señora de los Dolores	A. Gomez de Uliza	31
Nra. Señora de las Angustias	Miguel Cano	24
San Diego	Juan Diego	12
La Sacra Familia	Bernarde de Veira (de Vara?)	12
Felipe Quinto	Martin	8
Jesus Maria José y las Animas (probably *La Sacra Familia* ?)	Vera (Viera ?)	12

Two tenders, *La Trinidad* and *El Tambor*. To show difficulty in names and spellings in different records, one source names *L'Adjuan Bexta* or *Bextra*, which John Potter suggests is the *San Juan de Baptista*.*

Most of the bullion that reached England was silver and only £267 in gold was received at the mint. In the *Historical Letter*, 1702, is printed: "We do not, as yet, exactly know the amount of the booty taken at Vigo: we are sure that they have taken a value of 1,200,000 pounds Sterling in silver, with a great quantity of gold ingots." Of the English share only one-half went to the government. The other half, by decision of the Council of June 6, 1703, was divided among the forces that took part in the battle.

To stimulate patriotic sentiment, it was ordered that the gold and silver should be coined into money bearing the word VIGO below the bust of Queen Anne. The task of producing the coins fell on the famous Sir Isaac Newton, who, in 1699, had been made Master of the Mint. A few shillings with the new inscription appeared late in 1702, but the bulk were coined in 1703: crowns, half-crowns, shillings, and sixpences of that date were produced in such quantities that they are rather common. In gold, a few five-guinea, guinea, and half-guinea pieces were struck.

If you care to own a piece of this treasure, look for it at your coin dealer's—it will have a most interesting history.

At the time, recovery was believed to be so easy, the Crown wanted a 95 per cent share of any treasure raised. But the problem of finding scattered coins and bars in

---

* Wright, I. A., *Further English Voyages to Spanish America*, 1583-1594. London 1951. Note p. lxxxv: "The fact that ships were called by their own names (and usually had at least two, one sacred and one profane), by their owner's, by their captain's and sometimes by their pilot's, makes certain identification sometimes extremely difficult."

the sunken and burned hulks in fifty feet of water and mud was actually so great that little was done.

It is estimated that the treasure of Rande is worth at least $115,000,000 today!

Why hasn't more of it been salvaged? The reason is mud. San Simon Bay receives the flow of two muddy rivers which, year after year, deposit silt. Today it covers the wreckage of the galleons with thirty to fifty feet of mud and ooze. At the time of sinking, there were no diving suits available. Salvage was done with grapnels and drags.

Fifty or more salvage attempts have been made since 1702. Between 1723 and 1748 there were nineteen attempts, the most important being that of Alexander Goubert & Co. in 1728. Goubert succeeded in dragging ashore one ship, which turned out to be a French warship and not a treasure galleon. He quit in disgust.

In 1748, Juan Antonio Rivero made his second try (the first was in 1732) and recovered about 200,000 silver pieces-of-eight. About 1772, an Englishman, William Evans, worked with a diving bell of his invention and succeeded in recovering "many coffers of pieces-of-eight." Details are unknown.

The Dickson expedition arrived from England in 1825 aboard the brig Enterprize with a complement of thirty-three members. It is quite possible that this was the most successful of all, although the official records show nothing of intrinsic value in the quantities of cannon, wood, etc., raised from the five sunken wrecks over which Dickson worked. A letter written by one of the Spanish employees of this group complained that while Spanish divers were sent down in the diving bell during the daytime to clear off wreckage and mud, at night the English went down alone, and often when the local workers returned in the morning to work they found the deck of the ship strewn with "blackened ingots." After nearly a year of work, Dickson's sudden departure from Vigo caused a flurry of rumors that continue to the present time. The English crew caused their Spanish overseers to become intoxicated one night and put them ashore "for their own safety." The following morning the *Enterprize*—and those blackened ingots—were gone. Unsubstantiated rumors conclude that Dickson shortly afterward built a mansion in Scotland named, appropriately enough, "Dollar House."

Saint-Simon Sicard, a Frenchman, was reported to have recovered some gold and oxidized silver ingots in 1827.

The Magen-Berthe expedition arriving in 1869 aboard the *Julien Gabrielle* tried out some new inventions, including a large diving bell equipped with electric lights and a submarine electromagnet. During the next year the divers located and worked on eight wrecks, bringing up from the mud five heavy silver plates about an inch thick, called "tortas." Several of their salvaged cannon were displayed at the Musée de l'Armée in Paris. This expedition's work was interrupted by the outbreak of the Franco-Prussian War and its members were thrown into jail.

In 1869, Colonel John E. Gowen, an American, who had made a reputation by raising the Russian fleet sunk in the harbor of Sevastopol during the Crimean War, formed a company with English capital. When he arrived at Vigo to start work he found that the Magen-Berthe company was at work under a Spanish concession.

Colonel Gowen and American interests appeared with the Vigo Bay Salvage Company and the first models of the diving suit. Over the protests of local fishermen, submarine dynamite charges were exploded on the hulls of some wrecks, damaging them and nearby oyster beds and killing numerous fish. Results, as far as treasure went, were disappointing. This was the *Dido* operation.

The Vigo Bay Treasure Company, aboard the salvage

ship *Austin Knight,* took over in 1885 with some of the previous American personnel. Official reports of salvage describe only the usual cannon, wood, etc., yet there are strong indications that this group found treasure. For one thing, they successfully applied for renewal of their concession and continued their work for several years. At the same time the number of applications for the concession sharply increased. By coincidence, friction grew between local officials and the Navy, with the latter claiming that the local Customs were not keeping them sufficiently informed of the success of the salvage operators and hinting possible collusion. When, in 1886, the Americans finally withdrew (having *officially* recovered nothing of value), after expending large funds in maintenance, they gave the local fisherman guide a handsome bonus. They lifted only one mud-filled galleon off the bottom after cradling it with chains. They would have salvaged this ship, had its structure not been so damaged by the *Dido's* explosive charges that it broke and fell back into the mud. Some of its contents may have fallen out and been recovered.

The twentieth century saw the arrival of Mr. José Pino, the most indefatigable of the many seekers for treasure at Vigo. A respected inventor at only thirty-five years of age, he arrived in 1903 aboard the *San Clemente.* With him was Carlo Iberti, twenty-eight, who began a lifelong study of the treasure which resulted forty years later in the most authoritative book published on the subject. Pino brought several new inventions, including a "hydroscope"—a telescopic tube lowered from the surface with a compartment at the bottom from which an observer could look out through portholes. His ship was also fitted with strong pumps and electromagnets, and manned by experienced divers. While constantly under the surveillance of the Spanish destroyer *Audaz,* Pino's group raised much salvage, and charted the location of most of the wrecks. Twice, during his salvage work, he raised a galleon from the bottom, only to have it break up and slip back into the mud. Changing tactics, he tried tunneling down through the mud bottom into a covered galleon, but was forced to quit after penetrating fourteen feet, as the plastic mud threatened to clog the entrance.

In 1907 the Pino contract was extended to 1915 and Iberti said they had recovered "the anchors, including that of the *Misericordia of Santa Cruz,* cannon of various sizes, gun carriages, wheels, mortars, silver spoons, mariner's compasses, cannon balls, statuettes of inlaid gold, engraved pipe holders, Mexican crockery, plates and bars of silver, some weighing as much as eighty pounds; gold coins from the Mexico City Mint and ingots from Peru."

Pino's company continued its salvage efforts on and off until World War I broke out; they returned again in 1924 and a final time in 1928 with the ship *Sais.* Iberti indicates in his book that recoveries made by Pino amounted to 20 per cent of the total of all salvage made at Vigo.

Following Pino, the next concessionaire was W. van Wienen, a successful Dutch salvage operator. He owned a patent on an apparatus designed expressly to overcome the bay's mud—a big telescopic metal tube, sealed at the top and equipped with evacuators to remove mud at its open base. Lowered onto the bottom over the site of a galleon, it was intended to bore down through the muddy bay bottom until workers within the base of the machine could break into the interior of the galleon. The start of World War II terminated van Wienen's work before his ingenious device could be tried out.

The Spanish Ministry of Marine granted a three-year concession on August 16, 1955, to Ventures, Ltd., an American-owned corporation for salvage rights in San Simon Bay and the Straits of Rande. Mr. John S. Potter,

Jr., President of the associated Atlantic Salvage Co., Ltd., says: "We have raised so far several cannon, hundreds of cannon balls, pottery, beautiful porcelain pieces, a lead sounding weight of 25 pounds, much wood from various galleons, etc. It is certain that these galleons were crammed with cargoes so rich as to seem incredible to anyone who has not studied their manifests himself, and even to those of us who realize that the tremendous Spanish Empire was maintained largely by those riches freighted from the mines of the New World.

"I have made a full year's research through the archives in Madrid and Seville. The documents covering this armada were destroyed by fire in Seville years ago. When I arrived in Spain, I had visions of nearly entire galleons, far under the muddy bottom. This is not true. From our surveys on the bottom in the bay, I believe that all that remains of the galleons today is their shattered hulls, and in some cases only a few ribs and planks. Their treasure cargoes are scattered under the surrounding mud.

"I know that the *Monmouth's Prize** sank with her cargo intact. She was the richest single galleon in the flota and should hold at least $4,000,000 in bullion, mostly in silver.

"We have interviewed dozens of fishermen, studied currents and tides, made hundreds of long submarine dives covering large areas of the bottom and are now on her trail. We think her remains lie in the open sea, quite a way from shore, in water probably 150 feet deep. Our divers can work at this depth, wearing aqualungs. She has never been searched by previous salvage groups. We expect to find her soon and once we do, hope to raise the

* The English called each captured galleon by the name of the vessel taking it. The *Monmouth* captured a galleon heavily loaded with treasure, and on the return trip from Vigo to England the *Monmouth's Prize* struck on a sunken rock and immediately sank. As there were several frigates on each side of her, all the men were saved but two. This wreck has never been located.

treasure that has been in her strong rooms since 1702. In our search for both the *Monmouth's* galleon and the deposits of precious metal under the mud of Rande, we will employ electronic methods developed during the past decade and never before available for this work. With these instruments to guide us, we believe we can break through to the galleons' treasures."

While the fishermen in the nearby Baiona Islands tell tales of octopuses caught in the vicinity with coins stuck to their suction discs, the *Monmouth's* galleon is waiting for John Potter's divers with three hundred tons of treasure. And down under the Bay of San Simon, well scattered beneath their blankets of mud, the Vigo treasures are sleeping a sleep of centuries, awaiting the day when a flesh-and-blood Captain Nemo will reach down into their ancient bowels and wrest forth their immense treasures for a world that has long forgotten the magic of the old buccaneering words: doubloons . . . moidores . . . and pieces-of-eight!

CHAPTER 11

Loot from Lima

The world's most popular treasure island is Cocos. A pinpoint in the Pacific of international fame where gold, silver, and jewels of the buccaneer Captain Davis, the pirate Benito Bonito of the Bloody Sword, and the Loot of Lima are said to be hidden. Over four hundred expeditions in a century have sought the caches of $65,000,000 and one single gold doubloon has been found.

Was the treasure removed?
Was it ever hidden there?
Can modern science salvage it?

THERE IS an old saying in South America: "Treasure runs from the seeker."

For a century, seekers have been running after the treasures of Cocos Island. Hundreds of expeditions have visited the island, financed by wealthy explorers or the public. Millions have been spent and myriads of searchers have toiled, tunneled, blasted, dug, and starved in an effort to lay their hands on three fabulous caches of gold, silver, and jewels reputedly valued at $65,000,000.

It seems we ne'er shall hear the last of "Cocos Island Treasure";
The tales of charlatans have led to follies out of measure.
They all "have known just where it was"—but still the caves of
Cocos
Refuse to yield their opulence, but keep it to provoke us.

206

Crew after crew of sanguine ones upon the isle have landed,
  Dug in each indicated spot, and—come back empty-handed.
        —Excerpt from a lengthy poem printed in the
        San Francisco *Daily Morning Call*, March 19, 1872

Since this verse appeared eighty-five years ago, nothing has changed except the face of the island, and the treasures of Cocos are still running from the seekers.

Cocos Island, sometimes confused with the Cocos-Keeling Islands, lies in latitude 5° 32' 57" North, longitude 87° 2' 10" West, in the Pacific Ocean. It is about halfway between San Francisco and Valparaiso, Chile, and some three hundred miles from Punta Arenas, Costa Rica. Its area is about twenty square miles. Cliffs from two hundred to six hundred feet high rise abruptly from the ocean and there are mountain peaks at the interior, the highest of which has been surveyed at 2,768 feet. There are only two safe landing places and anchorages. One is named Wafer Bay after the buccaneer-historian Lionel Wafer, who landed on the island with Captain Edward Davis in 1685. Wafer described the place as small but pleasant, with water pouring down in a cataract, "as out of a bucket . . . making it a charming place, and delightful to several of the senses at once." Chatham Bay, to the east, is also a good anchorage and watering place.

Covered with a dense, tropical growth, the island is hot and humid. There is a long rainy season. The high land and interior of the island have never been thoroughly explored. In times past, it has been used as a penal colony by Costa Rica; a few people have tried, unsuccessfully, to live there; because of its value as a watering place it was well known to buccaneers, pirates, whalers, early navigators, and yachtsmen. Its chief claim to fame rests on the publicity it has received as a treasure site.

So many expeditions have been organized and so many

shares of stock have been sold; so many books have been written and so many diggers have returned empty-handed that laid end to end they would cover the entire island. Hardly a year passes but fresh groups of eager treasure seekers set sail for Cocos, in the belief that they will be the lucky ones to bring home the treasure. Cocos Island belongs to Costa Rica and digging must be done with government permission.

This is the saga of the treasure of Cocos, as printed in the prospectus of Cocos Island Treasure, Ltd., in 1931 when they were offering 40,000 shares of stock at two dollars per share:

"The story of the treasures which lie hidden on this romantic and beautiful island is one which is colorful in the extreme and covers a period of nearly three centuries. It brings together notorious pirate chieftains, roisterous buccaneers, stately galleons, Spanish grandees and cavaliers, heroes and patriots, common thieves, mutineers, murderers, priests, and soldiers of fortune. Its ramifications extend from the South Seas to the Spanish Main, from mid-Pacific to the South Atlantic, from Madagascar to New England. Through it all one hears, in imagination, the refrain:

> Fifteen men on the dead man's chest—
> Yo-ho-ho, and a bottle of rum!"

The reader should remember, of course, that this is the publicity writer of the stock sellers as he paints a rosy picture of the treasures waiting on Cocos Island. But let us see what they are:

"First comes the story of the most notable of all buccaneers associated with the island—that extraordinarily stout buccaneer, Captain Edward Davis, an English pirate, who, though he lorded it over all his fellow-pirates and their leaders, is credited with having never exhibited cruelty, inhumanity or brutality, and who was implicitly trusted by all those who were under him.

"Passing over all his previous exploits, we discover him sailing out of Chesapeake Bay with an 18-gun ship, the *Revenge*, after capturing a fine Danish ship, sinking the *Revenge* after removing everything aboard the prize, re-naming the latter the *Bachelor's Delight*, and then sailing leisurely up the coast of South America, taking Spanish ships and looting Spanish towns.

"Eventually Captain Davis sighted Cocos Island—of which Lionel Wafer, the buccaneer-surgeon and naturalist, gives a picturesque description—where he buried his treasure and careened and cleaned his ship.

"Later, when Davis became the leader of no less than a thousand buccaneers, he made many captures and looted the Nicaraguan city of León. But, before long, he found that to control a thousand wholly irresponsible buc-caneers was too great a task even for a man of his attain-ments. He broke away with a selected company and, head-ing direct for Cocos Island, added several hundred thou-sand pieces-of-eight to the cache already there. Still later he and his merry men captured the town of Guayaquil, from which they departed with gold and jewels valued at MANY MILLIONS OF DOLLARS—all of which was also immediately added to the hidden hoards of Cocos.

"In 1818, Captain Grahame, a British naval officer [who in some narratives has become Benito Bonito of the Bloody Sword, a colorful alias, but confusing to readers] who had served with distinction under Lord Nelson and had taken part in the battle of Trafalgar, was sent to the Pacific in command of H.M.S. *Devonshire,* to conduct a survey of the coast between Cape Horn and Panama. Instead of carrying on the survey, Captain Grahame and his crew

soon adopted a career of piracy, and carried on with great
success. In due course complaint was made to the British
government, and a warship was sent to deal with Captain
Grahame and his pirate crew. Instead of capturing the
pirates, the warship was defeated by them, and the surviving officers and crew were given the option of joining
the pirates or walking the plank. They became pirates!

"The *Devonshire* having suffered severely in the battle,
Grahame transferred his augmented crew and equipment
to a Spanish vessel which he had captured, and continued
his career until the British naval authorities, realizing with
whom they had to deal, dispatched three warships to
effect his capture. Eventually he was cornered in the Bay
of Buena Ventura, a battle was fought, and his ship sunk.
Attempt to escape by the boats was defeated, and all
hands were captured and taken to England. Captain Grahame and his officers were executed, and the rest of the
crew were transported for life to Tasmania.

"Among those of the crew transported for life was a
young woman who had accompanied Grahame on his
adventures. After serving twenty years in Tasmania she
was liberated, became married, and, when quite an old
woman, went to the United States of America to try to
interest someone in the recovery of the buried treasure.
According to the tale she told, a tunnel had been made
and, at the end of it, a huge chamber had been excavated,
in which all the booty had been stored to keep it secure
until it could be safely taken away for disposal.

"Captain Grahame had a chart with the compass bearings of the treasure cave, and this he always carried on
his own person. When he saw that his capture was imminent he gave the chart to the girl, saying that it had a
better chance to escape search in her care than in his.
This proved true, and she saved the chart, to use it many
years in an effort to recover the treasure. Her effort was

unsuccessful. In the time elapsed since her capture considerable change had occurred in the appearance of Wafer Bay. One of her identification marks was a huge mahogany tree, near which they had a camp and where she, with a doctor and wounded or convalescing men, frequently stayed when Grahame and his ship were at sea. This tree, and all other accessible timber, had been cut down by the whalers, who used Cocos Island as a source of wood and water.

"Although the treasure was not found, the woman's story was not discredited by those who financed the expedition. Her intimate knowledge of the island, its plant life, animal life, and particularly the bird life, could have been obtained in no other way than by considerable periods of residence there. Furthermore, in connection with the digging of their treasure cave, she described a soil condition which is most unusual, but which has been encountered by a subsequent expedition digging in the area described in the chart.

"Although the chart escaped the search of the British officers, some idea of the location of the treasure cave must have been obtained from other members of the crew, for the first expedition to seek treasure on Cocos Island was sent by the British Navy to recover the loot hidden by Captain Grahame.

"During the whole of his career of piracy, Captain Grahame used Cocos Island as a base of operations, and there the contents of his captured treasure galleons are still buried.

"The *Devonshire* treasure is said to comprise three hundred and fifty tons of material, consisting of bullion from Lower California, Mexico and Peru, and is conservatively valued at SIXTY MILLION DOLLARS.

"During a revolution in Peru in 1833, the authorities of the City of Lima and the wealthy residents of the city sent the state and private valuables to the seaport, Callao, to prevent their falling into the hands of the insurgents. At Callao they were placed with a guard of soldiers, on board the brig *Mary Dier*, Captain Thompson, for safe keeping, pending the outcome of the trouble ashore. Under cover of darkness, Thompson and his crew murdered the soldiers and sailed for Cocos Island, where the treasure was hidden. The treasure consisted of the state valuables, including all the gold and silver vessels and golden images from the great Cathedral of Lima, valued at THIRTY MIL-LION DOLLARS. Thompson led a pirate's life for some years, until his ship was captured. Thompson and one of the crew escaped; the rest were hanged."

That is the tale of the treasure of Cocos and how it got to the island. It has been told and retold with many variations and ramifications for a hundred years. Any resemblance to historical fact is strictly accidental. But the tales have been taken as true by hundreds of treasure hunters and thousands of investors who have lost millions. In justice to the backers of the expedition from whose prospectus the above treasure details were taken, this fine print was included:

... it is all a speculation, or venture, and ... shares are not offered or recommended by us as an investment.

One London syndicate that milked the ever-green public of many thousands of pounds described the Cocos Island treasures in fewer words but in larger print:

Buried by Bonito in 1818 & later, gold bars and specie worth ELEVEN MILLION DOLLARS. . . . buried by Thompson, TWELVE MILLION DOLLARS, buried by Davis, THREE HUNDRED THOUSAND POUNDS WEIGHT IN SILVER DOLLARS, SEVEN HUNDRED AND THIRTY-THREE BARS OF GOLD, ALSO SEVEN KEGS OF GOLD COIN.

They then generously add by repeating: ". . . buried by the notorious Bonito . . . THREE HUNDRED AND FIFTY TONS, consisting of bullion from Lower California, Mexico and Peru."

To keep the Cocos treasure hunting activity alive for over a hundred years, there very naturally had to be documents or eyewitness tales to back up these statements. The principal source of information was the Captain Thompson documents. These were handed down from Thompson to Keating to Mrs. Brennan (Keating's third wife) to Captain Thomas Hackett to Captain Gus Whidden to August Gissler.

A character named Nicholas Fitzgerald, who claimed to have known Keating, appeared on the scene with a letter in 1894; also a man named Captain Boag, Bogue, or Boig. Innumerable characters claiming to have the *only true* map, information, or knowledge of the treasure's location have sold either their services or their information to unwitting dupes in the last fifty years.

The Thompson-Keating Documents

An unsigned, undated letter owned by Keating and presumably written by Captain Thompson:

In the year 1835, when I was 18 years old, I shipped on the barquentine *Mary Dier*. After we had discharged our cargo in Valparaiso, we sailed up the coast and anchored one night in Callao.

There was war at the time; in the fort was gathered a lot of money and valuables belonging to the government and the people. An attack of the enemy was expected any time and as the fort was not very strong, the officials removed all the valuables on board the *Mary Dier*, thinking that the enemy would not dare to attack a British vessel.

We were tempted by all these millions, and that night we overpowered the Peruvian guard and got rid of them, slipped our cable, hoisted sails and stood out to sea.

The next morning at daylight we saw that we were chased by an armed vessel. Our ship was a fast sailer and everything alow and aloft was in first class order. Although it was blowing pretty hard we hoisted every stitch of canvas and gained on the pursuing vessel. The next morning at daybreak we were clear of her.

We shortened sail and now had another problem to solve. What should we do with the treasure? Many plans were proposed and as quickly rejected by some. At last we agreed to bury the stuff on Cocos Island.

Coming to the island, the treasure was conveyed in ten boat-loads to the beach. Then we looked for a place to bury it.

Reaching back from the shore, where we made our landing, was a piece of level ground about two acres. This ground laid on the foot of a mountain. Down its side ran a stream. We followed the stream very near to its head, on the level ground at the foot of the mountain. Here we selected the spot and buried the treasure. Some was in boxes and some in hides and it was supposed to be worth many millions.

We did not stay long on the island. Our intention was to go into Panama for more provisions and to find out if we could pick up any news from Callao.

The fourth day after we had left the island a squall struck us and we lost most of our sails. In this crippled condition we drifted for three days. Being close to the coast, we thought the best way would be to leave the *Mary Dier* and reach land in the long-boat. While we were getting the boat out, we saw a sail heading towards us and before long we were prisoners on board the Peruvian ship. Eight of our eldest men were shot at once, us three youngest they kept till we would show them where we had buried the treasure.

On board the Peruvian was fever, so the ship went into the Gulf of Panama. We laid there three weeks and a good many died, including one of us three. We two others knew that we would be shot anyhow by the Peruvians, even if we had shown them where we had buried the treasure.

About a mile from us laid a barque, a whaler, we had heard. Being not so well-guarded any more we thought we might try to swim to the whaler. One dark night we went down on the cable and swam for the whaler. There were many sharks around but we did not care, here at least we had a chance, but in the Peruvian no chance at all.

We reached the whaler right enough and climbing up the cable we found the man on watch on the forecastle head, who was not a little astonished to see two naked boys appear in front of him. We told him that we had run away from the Peruvian, and that if we were caught again we would be shot.

"Oh! said he, deserters! well, just stay here a while, I'll get you some clothes and show you a hiding place where Old Nick himself could not find you."

It was not long before he came back with some clothes, some ship's bread, and two bottles of water. We followed him into the hold, crawling over many barrels.

He stopped before a barrel and said, "Here it is. I am the cooper on the ship and this empty barrel will make you safe, if not comfortable. The head works on a hinge so you can crawl in and out. If the Peruvians come aboard and search the ship, close the lid, you'll have plenty of air," and he left us in the barrel.

We tried the barrel for size and with the lid closed we could not stand it for long. Even in the hold it was very hot and uncomfortable. We stayed there almost a week with the cooper bringing us rations and water daily, but no search was made. When the whaler, the barque *James Morris,* left port and we came on deck, we were signed on for the cruise back. When we anchored in Kona, Hawaii, my chum jumped ship. I stayed until the ship arrived in New Bedford, where I was paid off. (Unsigned.)

With the above anonymous and undated letter was the following statement from John Keating, written from St. John's, Newfoundland, on March 1, blank year:

As my health is failing and also my memory I now write the particulars, fearing I should forget.

My statement is this:

Thirty-eight years ago I made a voyage with Capt. Humphreys to Havana. There came a man to me asking if the captain would take on another hand? I asked the captain and he told me to bring the man on board. On the voyage to this port he told me about the treasure and that if we could find somebody in St. John's who would fit out a vessel to go around the Horn to the Island, we could get it. I went to two prominent merchants and they told me they would talk to the man.

Captain Boag found the man's statement quite correct but as they could not spare the money just then, they told us to wait a while. The man stayed with me three months.

He told Mr. Pretcherd to furnish him a vessel and if he could not ballast it with money and treasures, they could shoot him, as he would only be one man against the crew. Mr. Pretcherd asked him how far the money was from the water. The man told him if he would come to the island he would see how far it was from the water but not before.

While he was staying with me a rumor got around that he was a pirate, so he left for London. From there he wrote to me to come and see him, which I did. Afterwards he left for Calcutta. Boag and me went home.

In Newfoundland, the two merchants fitted out a vessel, and we took half a load of fish to Rio. Here we waited six weeks for another captain named Gault to arrive, who joined us and we sailed.

We were not out longer than two weeks before the two captains fell out. They did not abuse each other before the crew but wrote insulting letters to each other. The crew heard of all this and mutinied. Captain Boag arranged then with me to go to the island and have a look around and then go to Panama and get a vessel of our own and leave Gault with his ship.

When we came to the island we did not have much trouble in finding the treasure, but Boag said we should take out only enough to conceal in our clothes. Nobody in the ship knew that we had found the money.

A little afterwards we sailed for Panama. In Panama, Capt. Boag and I took a boat to pull onshore; the boat capsized and Boag got lost. I hired two mules and a guide to go across the isthmus. The ship in command of Captain Gault sailed for the Pearl Islands, for a load of pearl shells.

When I reached Newfoundland I got £1300 for the money I had taken from the island.

I drew a rough sketch of the island while there, as there was no chart in my time. I stated where we anchored and where the treasure was buried.

This statement is a fair one clearer than I had when I undertook the same.

                                        I remain, respectfully
                                        (signed) John Keating

Keating died in 1882, and on his deathbed drew up a plan of the island from memory and made the following statement:

August 6th, 1882

Matthew Henderson—John Phillips—witness to the signing of these papers on John Keating's dying bed. On the map you will find marked No. 1 means a cave, it is off the ground not down in the ground—it is on the surface. The grass grows high on this level, when you are at it you cannot see it. I was there a good while before I found it my back was resting against the stone that formed the door.

I took away the stone and took £1300 which I concealed in my clothes. I replaced the stone back in its own place as I found it and left it the same way as I did four years before.

There was no person with me at the time. I left the vessel this day alone and I returned to the vessel, no person knew that I had found the money, if they did my life would have been in great danger. They said that they would take my life if I did not share equal. When I heard this it put me on my guard so I kept all a secret.

On No. 2 marked on the map, a place called Morgan's Point, are $5,000,000 worth buried. By the side of the river in Anchorage Bay are 3 pots of gold coin. I could not bring it to bear to go the third time.

This is my last and full statement, so help me God.

(signed) John Keating

The above documents seem to be at the bottom of all the Cocos Island expeditions and have been circulated and quoted from hearsay until many variations of the Thompson-Keating story exist.

It would seem that Keating made trips to the island in 1844 and again in 1846. He then arranged a third trip with Captain Thomas Hackett in 1880 but Hackett died of yellow fever in Havana before sailing and Keating soon followed him. The North Sydney, Newfoundland, *Herald* of December 1, 1880, carried this item:

This is to certify that I have given to Thomas Hackett all the papers and all the information that I ever possessed necessary to find the treasure buried on Cocos Island, and that Richard Young nor anyone else has any information that will help them to find the said treasure.

Signed: John Keating

Witness: Geo. B. Ingraham.

These papers came into the hands of Captain Fred M. Hackett, a brother of Thomas, in the year 1890.

The complete treasure-hunting history of Cocos Island would cover thousands of pages. Many famous names have been connected with it: wealthy tycoons and corporation presidents have backed expeditions; many famous naval officers, officials, and explorers have dug on the island; thousands of armchair hunters have invested their savings in Cocos Treasure stocks; adventurers without capital have worked their way across oceans in small boats just for a chance to reach the place; many have suffered hardship, heat, humidity, and starvation—some have died there. The strange fascination of the place has led all who have visited the spot to return, sometimes again and again. Cocos diggers never seem to give up. It is not unusual for some ex-Cocos veteran to break into print years after his visit with a story similar to this news item of November 1945 from Melbourne:

Captain Max Stanton, master of the freight steamer *Islander* now at Melbourne, owns a battered parchment map, outlined in human blood, on which is traced the path to a $65,000,000 hoard.

Stanton, Chief Officer of the *Discovery* in Morton's Antarctic Expedition of 1930-31, led a treasure hunt once before on Cocos Island in 1934. He said that search failed because "spooks interfered."

But they found old hinges and other relics which convinced Stanton that the treasure, supposed to consist of Inca gold and Spanish cathedral plate from South America is there.

August Gissler's Story

The most loyal Cocos Island booster of all time was August Gissler, a German who first learned of the island

in 1888 when a sailor. The story he heard of the original
treasure cache was one of the many that had circulated around the world for many years.

Gissler did not know it but treasure hunters were op-
erating early and unsuccessfully on Cocos on funds raised
in San Francisco as can be seen from a long satirical poem
"The Legend of Cocos Island, Being the Revelations of an
Ancient Mariner Concerning Sixty-five Millions of Buried
Treasure" which appeared March 19, 1872, in the San
Francisco *Daily Morning Call*. The complete poem is too
long to quote here but the ending will show what the
West Coast newsmen thought of Cocos Island treasure
expeditions.

Again our ancient mariner, his curious yarn still spinning,
Swears if he gets another show he's confident of winning;
    Explains the reason why the former expedition busted
Was that he feared the crew could not with so much wealth be
        trusted.
    He formed another company, and got some interested,
While others heard the wondrous tale, and doubted, but invested.
    "I'll titilate their hopes," thought he, "till they go up like rock-
        ets:—
If there's no treasure on the isle, there is in people's pockets!"
    But those who'd been already sold, concluded it was played
        out—
"No more of Cocos pie for us!" they said and wisely stayed out.
    The company sold all their stock, then bought a gallant schooner,
And started out once more to woo the fickle jade Fortuna.
    They say this wealth's been there too long,
    But now they're bound to free it
And when they bring the treasure home, may we be here to see it.

In spite of the pessimism in some circles, there are always true believers, and August Gissler was one. While
in Hawaii in 1888 he met a man named Bartels, who
owned a map of Cocos Island and together the two adventurers decided to try their luck. They reached Val-

paraiso, when Bartels weakened and left Gissler to carry
on.

Gissler interested a Captain Howland, superintendent
of the whaling company, and a few people who had heard
the treasure story. A company was formed and a small
party sailed with a Captain Olsen in February 1889. They
sighted Cocos in eighteen days but drifted becalmed for
two weeks more before they reached the island in the
longboat. Bartel's chart in Spanish read, when translated:
"This island lies in lat. N. 5 deg. 27 min. long. W. 87 deg.
It is a healthy place. In the year 1821 we buried here
a treasure of immense value. After we had buried the
treasure we planted a coconut tree on top and took bearings by compass which showed location to be N.E. ½ E.
to the east mountain and N. 10 deg. east to the west
mountain." All agreed the treasure spot would be easy to
locate.

While Captain Olsen and the barque lay anchored
in Chatham Bay, Gissler and the crew worked ashore.
They patched up a tent from old canvas and palm
leaves, but it gave them little protection from the torrential rains which soaked them day and night. With the map
as a guide they endeavored to run lines. Trees and underbrush were so thick that it was impossible to sight across
country. For the first few days they chopped down palms
and underbrush to clear a trail. The process was too slow
and back-breaking, so they cleared only underbrush.
Climbing a tall tree, they found the correct line with the
mountain and after a week managed to lay out their lines
until the spot X was found. None of the palms were coconut palms. They dug under each palm tree in the vicinity with no results.

While hunting wild pigs for food, they discovered a
vine-covered and deserted cottage. On the door, in English and Spanish, a note read:

On the 31st of January 1884 Captain Schwers of the steamer NEKO found this island uninhabited and took possession of it in the name of the German Emperor.

At Wafer Bay, a tunnel was found driven about thirty feet into a hill by a previous expedition. They decided to try their chart here.

The level land in Wafer Bay covered about ten acres. A river entered on the south side and there was a beach of fine sand some three hundred yards long. On two sides, the land was steep up and down, and behind the level land were two small mountains. Continuing their survey by the chart, they arrived at a spot about two hundred yards behind the level area, in a small gulch. There were many palm trees but not one coconut palm From this spot no mountains could be seen.

If the treasure was here, the pirates must have landed in Wafer Bay. Why then, did they draw their lines to X on the chart from Chatham Bay? The crew who had been left digging at Chatham were sure they were in the right location; they had discovered a mark "D.C." on a rock. They undercut the rock, tumbled it away, and dug beneath the spot, but found nothing.

Captain Olsen had agreed to wait with the vessel for a month and the time was up. But the men and Gissler were sure of success, so Olsen sailed, leaving on the island, to dig, Gissler; Mike, a sailor; Anderson, a marine engineer; and Holm, a Swedish Naval Academy graduate.

More than a hundred names of ships were found chiseled or painted on rocks around the stream, some dating back to 1740. Many were from New Bedford, Martha's Vineyard, Providence, and Bristol . . . whalers who had stopped to fill their water casks. Several British men-of-war had also paid visits to the island and left names and dates. Gissler noted a rock marked G S B 1400 with "1844" below the S B, and another at the foot of the mountain,

moss-covered, which when cleaned showed SxS. CIEN D
I with "x" below the D I. The meanings of these marks
were not known but as they were near shore and the diggings, it was thought they referred to the treasure.

For the next month the party alternately dug and
for food chased pigs. The rain fell continually. For coconuts, it was necessary to row around to Dampier head,
land in a cove, and climb a three-hundred-foot cliff. At
the end of another month, they were living on coconuts,
stewed vines, and wild pork, varied with crabs and
boiled booby birds.

They then decided to build a 32-foot schooner to
reach the mainland. For a month they cut timber and
hewed logs for the frame. They assembled these near
their shack on a hill, fitted and marked each part and
carried the pieces down to the beach to reassemble. A
smaller, 11-foot, flat-bottomed boat was also constructed,
to sail near shore. Mike looked at the small boat and said,
"Anyone who goes outside the headlands in that gets a
free passage to Davy Jones."

Their clothes were in rags. Their shoes had long since
fallen apart and all had sore feet. Mike made a new suit
out of an empty bread bag by cutting out each corner to
put his legs through. With two holes for his arms and a
drawstring around his neck, his "ball costume" outlasted
any clothes he ever owned.

At the end of September, with their schooner nearly
completed, a ship appeared. It proved to be the barque
Clorinda with friends from the mainland. Gissler and
company moved to the ship and were comfortable and
well fed for the first time in months. Digging was continued. A whaler arrived and stayed a week. Provisioned
by the whaler, Gissler and his crew dug with no results
for another three weeks, and finally left the island. This
ended August Gissler's first try for the treasure on Cocos

Island, but it was only the beginning of his life there.

For the next twenty years Gissler spent his time living on the island or promoting the place both as a treasure spot and as an island Paradise.

Gissler made his second trip to the island in 1890 and bored, dug, and searched for three months. He then came to the United States and traveled across the country in an attempt to interest investors in the treasure. In June 1892, he cleared San Francisco in the yacht *Hayseed* and reached Cocos 101 days later after a rough cruise. He found that an expedition from Vancouver, British Columbia, had been digging on the island in his absence but had left before his arrival.

The Vancouver hunt was one of many which were to follow from British Columbia. The party sailed in the schooner *Eliza Edwards,* captained and owned by S. F. Mackenzie and his brothers, Duncan and William. It was backed by Mr. Van Bremner, a retired banker. They spent 61 days in their search, most of the time being spent in tunneling 120 feet into a cliff and then sinking a 20-foot shaft at the northeast corner of Wafer Bay.

A crew from Panama in the schooner *Lucia* landed and dug upstream and inland about this time and Gissler spent a month following leads on a map obtained from a Costa Rican official.

Gissler's family in Germany were in the paper business and he was called home on family affairs and spent some time there, during which he was married. In December 1894, he was back on Cocos with his new bride and a party of colonists. Houses were constructed and agriculture begun. The next three years were spent building, digging, and trying to make a permanent settlement.

Before Gissler left for Germany in 1894 he had been made Governor of the island and granted half of its area by Costa Rica. The colonizing and agricultural plans were developed for a good reason. Back of the plan, which was worked out by Gissler and a Mr. Ehlers, the president of the current treasure company, was the idea that if a permanent colony could be established and the soil regularly worked and dug, sooner or later the treasure would be turned up.

After Gissler brought his colonists from Europe, Ehlers took four families and some single men from the United States. To Cocos they carried building materials, tools, farm implements, poultry, cattle, and seeds. Truck gardens and coffee were planted, homes were erected, and a real effort was made to make the colony self-sustaining and successful.

In spite of these efforts, made at great expense, the Costa Rican officials would not arrange regular boat service between the island and the mainland. Largely as a result, the colony gradually broke up and by 1897, much to Gissler's disappointment, the agricultural experiment was ended.

But the Gisslers stayed on as permanent residents although part of their time was spent in trips to Costa Rica, the United States, and Europe in further efforts to arouse interest and capital toward the island's future welfare.

"Monte Cristo" Harford

The years 1896-97 made history for the island. The colony had broken up and Gissler had exhausted all his information on where the treasure might be hidden.

Then the Costa Rican steamer arrived on one of its rare visits and put ashore a character named Harford accompanied by his "man Friday." Gissler learned from the steamer captain that Harford was a down-and-out beachcomber in Punta Arenas. He had impressed the officials with a cock-and-bull story about knowing where the treasure lay and the captain had been ordered to land Harford and his Negro, Jim, on the island.

Harford refused to give Gissler any information—he only stated that he had obtained his knowledge from his grandfather, who had been a pirate. Jim was set to work digging near an old excavation made in 1877 by the San Francisco party in the schooner *Roescoe*. After a few days, Gissler decided that Harford knew nothing and ignored him.

The *Aurora* Expedition

In May, the *Aurora*, a schooner out of Victoria, British Columbia, appeared and anchored in Chatham Bay. The expedition was captained by Fred Hackett and was made up of a group of ex-sealing captains, including Captain Gus Whidden. They had brought a Mrs. Brennan, Keating's third wife and widow, who had verbal information from her husband on the treasure. Captain Hackett had Keating's charts.

Gissler as Governor of the island and representative of Costa Rica's interests in treasure produced his agreements and the party signed. The *Aurora* party went to work with a great flourish but after two weeks' toil were ready to give up and ask Gissler's advice. They produced the Keating charts, one made by him while on the island and the other drawn from memory. Mrs. Brennan's verbal instructions from her husband were: "Go around Morgan's Point. Stay on that side and follow up the first brook you come to until you get to the point. The treasure lies on the point."

Even with Keating's records the *Aurora* party, worn out and discouraged, sailed home to Victoria on July 25. They carried Harford with them, to the relief of Gissler, and left Captain Gus Whidden and W. Livingstone on the island to continue the search.

The Victoria *Colonist* of August 17, 1897, devoted a long article to the *Aurora* expedition.

Captain Hackett thinks . . . that he was somewhat astray in his bearings of the place where the treasure was stored. He had no prescribed bearings to follow, only the directions of a hand-made chart. The bay was a large one, and in it are several smaller bays. To the wrong one he believes now that he went, but . . . he is firmly of the opinion that the men left on the island will perchance stumble on the buried treasure. There were only a few inhabitants, one of them, an American named Charles Harford, being a passenger to Victoria on the *Aurora*, and another, a German named August Gissler, who manages a large coffee plantation of 50,000 plants. He has been on the island since 1889 and spent $15,000 of his own money in hunting for the treasure. He is described by Captain Hackett as a gentleman in every sense of the word, including a splendid education.

Harford's Claims

In the same interview, Harford is described as very reticent about what he had done and his tale varied with each narration. He claimed to have located the bullion for the Costa Rican government who landed him on Cocos ten months before and then ignored him. He was in rags when taken off by Captain Hackett. He also claimed that the *Aurora* hunters were right over the treasure spot and he was afraid they would find it.

Harford made front-page news again on September 7, 1897: "Monte Cristo Harford Will Again Undertake a Trip to Cocos Island: Careless of Silver He Asks Only for the Gold and Jewels." The *Colonist* reporter was puzzled as to why the Costa Rican officials should ignore Harford, if he knew where the treasure lay.

Harford may not have answered questions quite truthfully, for, as he himself says, "with so much at stake, a little lying is justified." He frankly admits having lied to Gissler and to the members of the Hackett party, and the reporter had no right to think himself better than they.

When asked, "How do you know the treasure is there?" Harford answered, "Know it is there? Seeing is believing, I guess. If you saw twenty million dollars in gold bricks, would you go to the Klondyke? There are jewels on the island, also, and I have found the stone which is the key to their hiding-place.

"I have a chart here, but I don't need it now. After spending nine months on that island do you suppose I want to go back for fun? No, sir. I was almost starved and have rheumatism, but I don't ask anyone for a dollar. In a few days I will have five thousand dollars and I will fit up an expedition of my own. I just want ten or fifteen good men to protect the treasure, which weighs forty tons. Some people think I am crazy. Let them think what they like.

"Two or three expeditions left this part of the world, and you should see the tunnels they made. In walking around the island a man must clear away the underbrush or he will fall in a hole. Several parties wanted to fit up expeditions for me, but I will charter a steamer and will bring the jewels and gold here. The silver is too heavy to handle and we will have enough without it. My ambition is to have a photograph taken with the treasure in front of the picture. I know where it is and will go for it when I am ready. Hundreds have interviewed me since my arrival. One person advised me to consult a medium and tell her everything. Others call me a humbug, but I ask for nothing. Hackett can have the silver, it is in bars three feet long and is buried only two feet beneath the earth.

"My friends will wear diamonds from Guideleppe's crown. I am an old pensioner; belong to the G.A.R. My age is fifty-five. Seems like a fairy story? Yes, but seeing is believing."

"Why didn't you bring back some of the gold?" queried the reporter.

"I was single-handed," answered Harford, "without means of self-defence, and had I shown any, Gissler could have had me at his mercy."

And buttoning up his overcoat, which for a live Monte Cristo was very shabby, the hero of Cocos Island left the reporter to meditate on the story he had just heard. But this was not the last of Harford.

The British Navy Tries for the Treasure

Back on Cocos Island, things had quieted down for a while but peace did not last long. August Gissler had gone to Costa Rica in an endeavor to arrange regular boat service with the government, and had left Mrs. Gissler on the island.

Into the bay steamed the British man-of-war H.M.S. *Imperieuse*, in command of Admiral Palliser and anchored offshore. Over Mrs. Gissler's protests, the British tars swarmed ashore armed with picks, shovels, and rifles and set to work digging at the northeast corner of Wafer Bay. Directing the search with the naval force was none other than "Monte Cristo" Harford. He had met the Admiral, sold him his story of the treasure, and sparked the idea of a naval dig. Admiral Palliser and H.M.S. *Imperieuse*, called "Captain Shrapnel and H.M.S. *Haughty*" in many narratives, steamed off in three days none the richer, but the navy and Harford were not finished.

It was not long before another British warship, H.M.S. *Amphion*, Captain Finnis, appeared in Wafer Bay and anchored. Admiral Palliser had met the *Amphion* at Acapulco, transferred Harford for another free ride and ordered Captain Finnis to Cocos for a ten-day treasure hunt. Finnis apologized to Mrs. Gissler for intruding on the island but orders were orders and he could hardly refuse the Admiral's instructions. The *Amphion's* tars dug and delved for the allotted time and then departed, taking Harford with them—the Gisslers hoped for good.

Admiral Palliser was apparently reprimanded by the Admiralty and Cocos Island was placed out-of-bounds for the British Navy. The Admiral, however, had been bitten by the Cocos treasure bug and made another expedition to the island with some companions, on his retirement, in the *Lytton* in 1904.

It was not for another thirty years that a naval vessel officially stopped at Cocos. Then the U.S. cruiser *Houston*, carrying President Franklin D. Roosevelt on a fishing trip, stopped for lunch ashore. It was said that F.D.R.

granted the sailors shore leave with a wave and a "Go ahead boys and find the treasure!" But it was only in fun.

Another British Columbian Expedition

The Pacific Exploration and Development Co., Ltd., was organized in Victoria, British Columbia, in 1901, with Captains Fred M. Hackett and A. B. Whidden. With them was Justin Gilbert carrying a "gold finder" that would locate only gold and a "silver finder" that would locate only silver, or so the inventors claimed. It was claimed also that the instruments had pinpointed small quantities of metal at a distance of two hundred yards or more and "that they will undoubtedly indicate a deposit of the size to be searched for, at a distance of some miles."

Another instrument, the invention of Mr. Daniel D. Enyeart of Washington, was carried which had located an 8-inch ledge of ore 136 feet below the ground. These instruments were supposed to "do the work in twenty minutes which would require months and possibly years to accomplish without them."

The "gold and silver finders" found nothing and the party returned, leaving investors short $7,500. The investors had believed the sales talk, which asked, "Is it not worth investing $10 with the chance of its returning $10,000?" The answer, as usual, was "No!"

Meanwhile, August Gissler was living on Cocos trying various locations and clues and welcoming new arrivals. The Gisslers were never lonesome as there was generally one party and sometimes two or three appearing with "the only correct map" to dig at the point marked "X."

One morning, marks were noticed on an old palm tree. They were overgrown with moss and age but when cleared, the letters, carved years before, plainly read: "THE BIRD IS GONE."

What did this mean? Had someone found the treasure
and removed it? Or had some treasure hunter, finding
nothing, *thought* it was gone? This was more likely, for if
anyone had found and taken the treasure, he would
hardly have taken the trouble to notify later hunters.

The Tale of Captain James Brown

In 1902, a Captain James Brown appeared in San
Francisco with a story that he was the only man alive who
knew where the Cocos Island treasure was located. And
it was not on Cocos at all!

Brown was a striking and dominating personality. He
was over six feet in height, and must have originally had
great strength. His face was that of an old Viking, with
thick, bushy beard, prominent cheekbones, and flashing,
deep-set blue eyes. He had an expression of determina-
tion and daring, craft, and immense self-confidence and
had a quick and uncontrollable temper. He also spun a
very impressive tale.

Captain Brown's story interested a number of business-
men. In his younger days he had been one of the crew of
the piratical schooner *Black Witch,* and in 1850 had
fallen in with the son of the original captain of the *Mary
Dier.* They had gone to Cocos and dug up the treasure
deposited there in 1821.

"That is the reason," Brown told his backers, "that all
these searchers since 1851 have failed. We dug it up and
carried it off, and no one will ever find any of it now on
Cocos Island, unless they turn up a few old coins which
we may have scattered in our haste."

Brown's tale was that after getting the precious cargo
aboard, the vessel sailed for the "Pacific Islands," some of
which were entirely uninhabited. On one of these the
pirates landed and reburied the Cocos treasure. Their immense wealth only seemed to whet Brown's shipmates'

appetites for more. And so, with the overpowering lust for gold in their hearts, they made for Australia, lured there by reports of the fabulous amount of gold that was being taken from the placer mines. Reaching Australia in 1853, they found a large part of the community mad with excitement and utterly reckless in their methods. Immense cargoes of gold dust, bullion, and, later, coins were on their way to England, sometimes in unprotected ships.

Brown's pirate pals managed to put aboard two of these ships some unprincipled crew members, who overpowered the officers at sea and captured the vessels. The gold was transferred to the *Black Witch*, the victims killed, and the ships scuttled. All sail was then set for their treasure island, where a second landing was made and the stolen gold added to the ex-Cocos hoard.

Then followed a period of drinking, fighting, slaughter, artful poisoning, and gradual extermination—a fit end to such men. Brown claimed that he took no part in the violence but that the pirate captain deliberately fomented trouble in order to get rid, as far as possible, of witnesses and sharers in the plunder.

Finally but three remained of the original crew of fifty. The survivors were the pirate captain, the steward, and Brown, whose strength, courage, and knowledge of navigation had raised him to the position of mate. The *Black Witch* had been badly damaged by fire during a drunken brawl, and she was scuttled. All traces of human life on the island were destroyed. The three survivors fitted the longboat with food and water, ballasted her with several hundred thousand dollars in gold, and after a speedy but rough voyage, Brown, the sole survivor, landed on the Australian coast. He reluctantly told how the captain had killed the steward and how in self-defense he, Brown, had shot and killed the pirate captain.

Brown spent the next few years in Australia, mining and

sheep raising, then went to London, where he opened a
large bank account with his pirate loot. He later moved to
Providence, Rhode Island, but lost most of his wealth in
an effort to smuggle arms to the Cuban insurgents. Now
at age seventy-two he was willing in exchange for their
financial support to offer a large share of a colossal fortune
to his San Francisco friends.

A company was privately financed, the schooner *Herman* was purchased and provisioned, and the expedition
slipped out of San Francisco on July 20, 1902, for an unknown destination.

Trouble began almost at once, and practically all the
trouble was old Captain Brown. He was suspicious and
autocratic—bullied the crew and insulted his backers, who
tried, without success, to humor him. He became more and
more unbearable.

The first stop was Honolulu, where the party expected
to pick up a letter of credit. They had little cash and when
Brown ran up bills for five or six hundred dollars and the
treasurer lost his cash from his pocket, a libel was placed
on the ship. Brown was in a continual huff against everybody but delighted reporters with his tales of past exploits
and career, proclaiming that he was the only man on
earth to know the secret of the famous Cocos treasure.

He then had a pessimistic period and announced that
the expedition was "hoodooed," that the "fifty dead men"
on the island were "working against them," and that if
they should ever reach their goal, which he doubted, they
would never live to get away. He kept a loaded revolver
under his pillow and complained that he expected to be
murdered in his sleep. By days he flew into rages at the
slightest look and threatened to fight duels with his backers. The captain could not put up with the crew, and vice
versa, and as a result the crew left the ship and libeled it
for their wages. Finances were finally arranged, the

treasure party sailed by steamer for San Francisco, and Captain Brown and the *Herman* sailed for Samoa.

By January 1903, the *Herman* reached Port Jackson and the company had raised another $8,400 to continue the cruise. They planned to sail for the treasure island in March but Captain Brown became more and more secretive and demanding. He was now threatening to sell the ship, which was registered in his name. He then informed his backers that he would leave the party and go alone. He was forestalled in his plans after court litigation and the whole company cruised to Tahiti, arriving in July 1903.

The American Consul, the Honorable W. F. Doty, helped iron out differences and gave Brown a final chance to take the expedition to his mysterious treasure island. Brown would not, and probably could not, tell them or take them to it and it was decided that he had never known where the island was.

The *Herman* was sold at Tahiti for $8,250 and the party returned to San Francisco by steamer. Captain James Brown traveled in the steerage with the crew and the humiliation was almost more than he could stand. One of the party decided that "being an extremely vain and sanguine man, Brown thought he *might* find the treasure, and when we reached Honolulu he was prepared to try. His knowledge was merely hearsay based on information and perhaps some chart furnished by a member of the pirate crew. Had he *tried* to find the island and failed, we should have had little complaint and he nothing to apprehend. His knowledge being hearsay, the chances were about a thousand to one he would fail. He knew he did *not* know, and after his outrageous conduct, he feared to send us further on a wild goose chase lest we should return and take vengeance on him."

Captain Brown, on his return to San Francisco, spent two weeks in jail, for striking the steward on several occasions while at Samoa. When he was released he brought suit for $75 per month salary, as supercargo from Sydney to Tahiti. He had waived this claim when he broke his contract to pilot the expedition to Treasure Island. A countersuit was filed against the captain for $20,000 which was the price of the company's acquaintance with him.

When last seen in San Francisco, Brown was starting East by rail on a "tourist ticket" and as a parting shot informed his ex-partners that Mr. Gould was waiting for him back east to take him in his yacht to Treasure Island.

Whether Brown ever inveigled an Eastern tycoon into another trip to his imaginary island I do not know. But seated before a wood fire one night with my friend Brian Boru Dunne in the lobby of the La Fonda in Santa Fe, New Mexico, we found our talk turning to pirates and treasure.

Dunne spun a yarn about a great hulk of an ex-pirate named Brown and a New York backer he had met in the "Pacific Islands" years before. The backer had taken Captain Brown to the area on a promise that the Cocos Island treasure could be recovered but was having trouble with the captain. Brown seemed vague about just which island it was on, although he presumably knew, or claimed to know.

Finally Brown was pinned down and told to put up or shut up. He picked an island and was taken ashore to point out the spot. "It's right around here," said Brown, who was on his last legs, and then he collapsed, clutching at his heart, and passed out. The effort of pointing out the spot was too much for his overtaxed constitution. Anyway, that was Brian Boru Dunne's story and I have no reason to doubt it.

The *Rosemarine* Expedition

Few of the true Cocos Island believers, including August Gissler, placed confidence in stories that the treasure had been hijacked and moved to another resting place. Expeditions continued to appear in ever growing numbers as the twentieth century began.

The *Rosemarine* expedition of de Montmorency, Gray, and Dormer was using information from Nicholas Fitzgerald, a harbormaster of St. John's, Newfoundland, which had been previously obtained by Admiral Palliser: "On the north end of the island you will find a creek. Go to the bottom of this creek and from high-water mark with your pocket compass in hand, walk fifty paces west; then face north, a bare rock or bluff will be in view; walk right up to it and hunt for a small hole just large enough for your thumb to go into. Shove a crowbar into this hole and the stone will turn, leaving room enough for one man to enter the cave."

Keating's statements differed entirely from this but they tried the directions. Digging was carried on around both Chatham and Wafer Bays until the yacht crew refused to work further. When peons were hired from Costa Rica the digging was continued. Gissler knew of a rock with a hole and showed it to Gray, but landslides made it impossible to investigate the area without moving tons of rock and earth.

The Earl Fitzwilliam Calamity

Perhaps the largest and best-equipped expedition to leave England in search of treasure since the days of Sir Francis Drake sailed quietly from Southampton in October 1904. Calls were made at the Cape Verde Islands to coal; at Rio de Janeiro; at Montevideo; Fortescue Bay; Valparaiso; and Punta Arenas. To all who inquired, the

trip was explained as a scientific expedition for rare or-
chids and minerals. Many weeks later, the ship turned up
in Panama. Several of the party were in bandages and
obviously seriously injured. When they arrived in England, they eluded newsmen, and the true story of
their adventures was not published until thirty years
later.

This was the expedition of some fifty members that
sailed in Earl Fitzwilliam's large yacht. They arrived in
Chatham Bay in December 1904, and August Gissler
thought when he saw the yacht that the British Navy had
returned.

Gissler met the party, introduced himself, and said that
as he was Governor of the island, they could not dig without his permission. The Earl had stopped at Punta Arenas
on the way to Cocos and when Costa Rican officials refused to give him a concession to dig, he told them his party
was strong enough to capture and hold the island if necessary. The Earl told Gissler the same thing but after a
few Scotch-and-sodas peace was arranged.

On New Year's Eve, 1905, Gissler sent a few bunches
of bananas to the Earl's party with an invitation to spend
New Year's at Wafer Bay with the Gisslers. Just before
dark the peons returned and reported that there had been
a terrible accident. Five men had been seriously injured
or killed by a blast. Many more were badly hurt and the
Earl had received a severe scalp wound.

By daylight the next morning Gissler went to Chatham
and found the bay deserted. On a high bluff close to a
waterfall on the east side of the bay there had been a
gigantic landslide. Tons of rock and dirt had buried a
large area. If any treasure was on the site, it was now
safely buried.

Thirty years later, Mr. David T. Smith, a member of

the group, described in *Blackwood's Magazine* the expedition to what he called "El Dorado."

When the expedition landed on Cocos they found that some of the most important marks on their chart had been obliterated by earthquakes and tropical rains. A council of war was held. It was decided to land a strong party, fully equipped to camp ashore and work while the ship went away on other business.

As day succeeded day, and the doubloons refused to reveal the secret of their grave, it became evident that Nature had so changed the island that in all probability the treasure was buried deep below the ground. "The stables of thorough-bred hunters which had loomed so large in our imaginations grew dimmer in outline. . . ."

They decided to blast, and a heavy charge of powder was placed at the foot of a large rock. "The explosion was not loud, and the effect was not so great as expected. We rushed to the cliff. I was easily the winner, and had just reached the goal when—crash! The earth beneath me shook, the whole face of the rock seemed to rise up, twist, and lean over. . . . Stones weighing tons and pounds hurtled past and over me. . . .

"Someone had miscalculated in setting the fuses. I was up to my waist in rubble. I had not a bruise or scratch on my body; but of a dozen men on the hillside I alone was standing.

"The first man to rise was our leader, staggering about blinded by blood from a ghastly wound running right across his scalp. He tried to take command of the situation, refusing all offers of attention. We had to fill him with brandy to keep him quiet and enable us to dress his wound. . . ."

Hours of work under a scorching sun were spent rescuing and dressing the injured. The tide came in to the base of the cliff, and some of the badly injured had to be floated a hundred and fifty yards round the beach to camp.

The ship returned just as the medical stores ran out, and the doctor on board was able to perform many operations. The party was hurriedly taken off the island and the most seriously injured were left in the American Hospital in Panama. The remainder returned to England by Royal Mail steamer.

For days attempts were made to run the various members of the party to earth and discover what had happened, but the secret was well preserved.

"There had been a certain amount of diplomatic trouble," Smith concludes. "We were not popular in Government circles. Tradition tells of a summons to Buckingham Palace, of a heavy wigging from the king. Edward VII was a great Englishman and very human; when it was over he rose from his chair. 'You know perfectly well you ought not to have done it, but—by God, I wish I had been with you.' "

Back on Cocos Island

The Arnold Gray–de Montmorency party were back for their third time, and sorry to have missed meeting the Earl. Eighteen more peons were imported by Gray to speed up the digging, and they began to get in each other's way. To remedy this, they were divided into short shifts of six men each. This pleased the peons who now spent most of the time loafing and sleeping. One laborer died suddenly and caused a yellow fever scare and an epidemic of sham illness. The *Rosemarine* soon left; Mr. and Mrs. Gissler were called to Germany by the illness of his brother. After nine months Gissler visited England, raised more capital and returned to America. He traveled from the Atlantic to the Pacific and then back to Florida, where he purchased a suitable ship at Key West to run regular Cocos-to-mainland service.

They sailed for Port Limón, ran into gales; the yacht sprang a leak and the water tank burst. One night the ship ran on to a reef and the Gisslers were rescued by daylight by North Cay fishermen. Luckily, the ship had been insured by Lloyd's who paid Gissler's London associates. A vessel was purchased in England and shipped in parts to Panama where it was reassembled.

The Gisslers returned to New York and found a cable telling them to return to Cocos immediately as another expedition was heading for the island with a concession arranged between the British consul and the Costa Rican government. Gissler refused to recognize the concession and his relations with Costa Rica nearly reached a breaking point. Peace was finally made in London through the Foreign Office, and six months later the Robinson party arrived.

The Robinson Party

The members of this group had told friends in London that they could walk right up to the treasure and get it in less than a day. After digging for three days with Gissler's permission, they produced their map. It had been copied from a magazine article which Gissler had seen months before. The Robinson visit was a short one.

There had been political changes in the Costa Rican government and their attitude had changed toward Gissler. He returned to London to reach an understanding with his backers, and his island days came to an end.

The Gisslers moved to New York City, and there he continued his endeavors. In 1925 an agent, J. J. Campbell of Belvidere, New Jersey, was working to interest the U. S. government in taking over Cocos as a submarine and air base and coaling station. The island's proximity

to the Panama Canal made it valuable in the defense of
the area.

Before August Gissler died on August 8, 1935, he said:
"The treasure is on the island, but it will take money and
a great deal of effort to unearth it. The work, once started,
must be pushed strictly to an issue, otherwise some diplomatic land-sharks will reap the benefit of my work and investigations during the past twenty-two years. All this
time, I have gone through many hardships and dangers
but I am willing to do so again and this will not keep me
away. As soon as I obtain a guarantee that I can finish
work, I intend to start anew."

August Gissler considered Cocos *his* treasure island
and his belief in the treasure never wavered. He was the
only man to find treasure on Cocos and he carried it with
him always in his pocket—it was one lone Spanish gold
doubloon.

CHAPTER 12

Hocos-Pocos-Cocos

*The facts of one of the four hundred and forty-four
expeditions to Cocos Island to recover the vast
treasure reputedly buried there by pirates*

*"At every strike of his spade he laid bare a golden
ingot; diamond crosses sparkled out of the dust; bags
of money turned up their bellies, corpulent with
pieces-of-eight, or venerable doubloons; and chests,
wedged close with moidores, ducats and pistareens,
yawned before his ravished eyes and vomited forth
their glittering contents."*

—Billy Bones and His Chest,
by Washington Irving

THE ALL-TIME high in the Cocos Island
treasure boom hit London in the 1920's and '30's. Articles
appeared regularly in the daily papers about treasure islands, the buccaneers, pirates, Captain Shrapnel, Benito
Bonito of the Bloody Sword, and Captain Thompson of
the *Mary Dier.*

There were expeditions to the Jesuit gold mines, the
Sacambaya treasure of Bolivia, the Montezuma treasures
in Guatemala, and the gold of Peru. But for most of the
hunters, Cocos Island was the goal.

Syndicates promoting Cocos Island, called "The Treas-

ure Island Expedition," "Cocos Island Treasure, Ltd.,"
and "The Romance Expedition," were all busy. Sir Malcolm Campbell, the Speed King, had a go at Cocos and
was so enthusiastic that he later became a Director of a
British Columbia venture. Treasure hunters were dashing
off for Cocos and each had *the only correct* chart or clue.

The most modern and scientific of the expeditions
claimed to have given up old pirate charts and were ad-
vertising that they would spot the gold in an hour or a
day, once they landed on the island with their geophysi-
cal and electromagnetic apparatus. A few depended on
clairvoyance and luck—one used a gramophone spring.

The London *Daily Mail* printed a cheerful bon voyage
to one expedition, as follows:

Armed with hope, the public school spirit, hope, metal diviners,
and a little more hope, fourteen man and a cabin boy (*Yo, ho,
ho, and a bottle of rum*) will set sail next week on a voyage calcu-
lated—if it succeeds—to make the treasure trips of Drake look like
a church collection on a rainy Sunday in Aberdeen!

Undeterred by the fact that a score of expeditions have returned empty-handed from digging and blasting in the sun baked
soil, Captain A. Max Stanton and Mr. G. Cocknell, of Coventry, will
lead their merry men and Master Leslie Green, of Appledore, the
cabin boy (*Yo, ho, ho, and a bottle of pop*) aboard the fifty-ton
motor schooner *Romance* and hoist anchor on October 12. While
previous expeditions have taken electrical devices to trace the resting place of the treasure, or charts marking with a cross the place
where the cache was *not* found, the present company is taking Mr.
G. C. Barwood and two other metal diviners to tell their comrades
where to dig.

Yo, Ho, Ho and willow twig!

The stock-selling syndicate called "The Treasure Island
Expedition," promoted by Lieutenant F. W. Keeley and
Lieutenant George Williams, later of Panama fame,
headed their prospectus:

HOW TO TURN £1 INTO £50
AND
HOW IT CAN BE SUCCESSFULLY ACCOMPLISHED

The London *Daily Mail* ran frequent headlines reading:

TREASURE HUNT BUNKUM
WARNING TO THE PUBLIC
DO NOT SUBSCRIBE

At the same time, a Vancouver, British Columbia, syndicate at work on Cocos Island under a concession from Costa Rica was asking for further funds from the public at two dollars per share, to continue their search.

While enthusiastic adventurers were sailing under the auspices of old salts and ex-naval officers, whose integrity was unquestioned, the greenhorns, excited by pirate lore and tales of gold, were clamoring to take off. Trawlers, ketches, yachts and schooners—anything able to carry a party and equipment—found a ready market. Cocos was overrun with diggers. The ever-green public bought thousands of shares and waited for news that their syndicate had brought up the swag.

Discouraged, tired, and penniless treasure searchers began to drift home with stories of cutting through mats of vines in bogs where insects swarmed, while torrential tropical rains soaked them continually and their food moldered. A few were optimistic and promptly began to plan for another trip—with new backers.

Into this hectic hunt came "Treasure Recovery Limited" with an issue of 180,000 shares at five shillings each, and in small type the warning, "These shares must be regarded as definitely speculative . . . a very attractive gamble."

Their prospectus was well printed and illustrated with engravings of priceless Inca gold relics (in some museum). The history of the treasure, which we have referred to earlier, was (as usual) told vividly, and with little of truth.

"Gold bars and specie worth ELEVEN MILLION DOLLARS from rifling churches in Peru: TWELVE MILLION DOLLARS buried by Thompson; buried by the notorious Bonito of the Bloody Sword THREE HUNDRED AND FIFTY TONS; by Davis the buccaneer THREE HUNDRED THOUSAND POUNDS WEIGHT IN SILVER DOLLARS, SEVEN HUNDRED AND THIRTY-THREE BARS OF GOLD, also SEVEN KEGS OF GOLD COIN."

All on Cocos Island!

The prospectus continues:

"The Search for the Treasure

"Faded parchments, crudely constructed charts, cryptic clues, etc. which have harried generations of treasure-seekers, are eliminated from the program. The modern scientific methods to be employed render clues superfluous. . . .

"Under expert supervision, by proved electrical and electromagnetic methods, all areas likely to conceal treasure will be thoroughly and systematically explored . . . with apparatus of not less than nine alternative methods, seven of which are selected whereby no conductive metals may escape detection."

Treasure Recovery Ltd. had been fortunate in securing a well-balanced and seasoned field force, including:

Col. J. E. Leckie, C.M.G., C.B.E., D.S.O., F.R.G.S., Mining Engineer, Member Canadian Mining Institute, Pacific Treasure Expedition, M.Y. *Silver Wave* 1932.

Commander F. A. Worsley, D.S.O., O.B.E., R.N.R., who

had been on two British Antarctic Expeditions in 1921 and 1925.

Commander Joseph Russell Stenhouse, D.S.O., O.B.E., D.S.C., R.N.R. (Ret'd), who had been Captain on Shackleton's Antarctic Expedition in 1914-16 and Royal Research Ship *Discovery*, 1923-28.

Commander F. C. Finnis, Stratford Dowker Aird Jolly.

Captain C. O. Polkinghorne.

S. MacFarlane Arthur and others.

These men were surely experienced. It would be difficult to find anywhere a more likely lot of "sea dogs" for this sort of research. If anyone could bring home the elusive treasure of Cocos, they could.

Shares were offered at five shillings and at the first stockholders' meeting on May 18, 1934, it was reported that over a thousand applications were received and 33,433 shares had been sold.

Progress reports were issued regularly and report No. 2 stated that "shareholders are no longer engaged in a speculative investment but in a sound businesslike enterprise capable of returning enormous profits all out of proportion to the amount of their investment."

Report No. 3 announced that a magnificent twin screw steam yacht, the *Queen of Scots,* of about 700 tons, had been loaned to the expedition at no charge whatsoever because the owner preferred 3 per cent share of any treasure recovered. With this news it was announced that "other very promising prospects for treasure were known to the Directors, such as the city of Old Panama, the pre-Inca city of Chan-Chan, two cities near Machu Picchu in Peru, the Islands of Teshgo and Trinidad off the coast of Brazil, etc." These treasures were estimated at a value of £13,000,000. Shareholders could now increase their holdings at 9 shillings a share (up 4 shillings in 30 days).

By July 1934, the *Queen of Scots* was about to be docked for inspection (by invitation only). And "The Managing Committee and the Field Executive do not regard their quest as romantic, dramatic or spectacular— *they have no doubt whatever that the treasure exists and that they will positively recover it.* It may be only a matter of weeks after the arrival of the Expedition at Cocos Island before the first big strike is made."

Soon the first report to omit the scientific apparatus appeared and a new angle was mentioned. "For those of our clients who are interested in clairvoyance and psychic phenomena, Miss Gene Dennis, who has astonished critics with the uncanny accuracy of her forecasts into the future, has volunteered the information that the expedition will be successful, and, further, has marked a chart of the island with crosses where the treasure will be located."

In August, the *Queen of Scots* sailed for the island, "carrying with her the most serious and business-like expedition that has yet been organized, fully equipped with the latest devices that science can produce. Shares will be in great demand. Partial success will spell fortune. Do not part with your shares."

The next news came in the form of a cable from Punta Arenas announcing that the party had landed on Cocos on September 26. "Continuous rains—surf—shark infested water—party safely ashore—impenetrable bush everywhere—prospecting commenced—all optimistic."

The optimism was a little premature. The next reports came via the news columns: October 13, San José, "Treasure Hunt Forbidden—Force Sent to Remove British Party." The treasure party had landed under the impression that the island was a sort of No-man's Land, but the Costa Rican government sent fifty police to defend national rights. The two boatloads of police were reported lost on the way but finally reached the island a week late, all suffering from mal-de-mer. They landed, pulled down the British flag and placed the eighteen members of the party under arrest. All the equipment, including radio, electric plant, and stores, was seized.

After many cables between Foreign Offices and profuse apologies by the treasure hunters to Costa Rican government officials the party was allowed to leave for England on the *Queen of Scots*.

It was then discovered that the treasure-hunting concession from Costa Rica was held by a Vancouver, British Columbia, syndicate until October 1935.

Upon the arrival of the *Queen of Scots* at Southampton, the captain would allow no one on board but told reporters that he, for one, was glad to leave Cocos Island: "If we had stayed longer the Costa Ricans would have taken the ship, too."

Treasure Recovery Ltd. officials still claimed that the island was free soil and if they had run up a British flag, it was only as a Boy Scout would have done it at camp. The British Foreign Office refused to enter into an international argument. A bulletin was issued to stockholders calming them with the statement that the famous seeress, Miss Dennis, had predicted that the expedition would meet with armed intervention in a foreign country. As this had now come true, her predictions that treasure would be found should also come true.

Another ship was chartered, *Veracity*, not as palatial as the *Queen of Scots*, but cheaper to operate. A working agreement was made with the Vancouver concessionaires. Harmonious relations were established with Costa Rica, and the directors were congratulated for their grit and tenacity. "With the enormous amount of treasure that exists, there is ample to satisfy the Costa Rican government, the Canadian Company, and still leave an enor-

mous profit for distribution among the share-holders of
Treasure Recovery Ltd."

The way was now clear. The *Veracity* set out on her
journey and, after encountering unusual weather conditions en route, arrived at Punta Arenas, Costa Rica, on
June 6. She took on board all the confiscated stores, etc.,
of the previous trip and also the Costa Rican armed force
as provided for in the transfer of the concession. Cocos
Island was reached on June 9. The camp was set up
again and scientific exploration work resumed where the
previous research stopped.

The Field Executive was instructed to adhere rigidly
to the original program, ignoring so-called "clues" which
had been the only guide of former treasure hunters on the
island. As stated in the Prospectus, "all such clues, no
matter how accurate their recording, become misleading
in after years, owing to various changes that occur. Modern science having provided such highly efficient apparatus for the locating of buried metals and minerals, 'clues'
form no part of the Company's program."

In the same report, this interesting story appeared:

Discovery of the Benito Bonito Treasure— Bergmans' Story

One very interesting and important diversion in the Company's
set programme has been made, the circumstances being as follows:—

In the month of February last, the company was approached by
one, P. A. Bergmans, whose story was that in the summer of 1929
he sailed out of San Pedro (the port for Los Angeles) in the yacht
Westward. This vessel had belonged to a Mr. C. W. Young of
Seattle, and it may be that she was renamed. She was chartered by
a party of the movie colony, and on their business visited a number
of places in Lower California, and then continued south towards
Panama. The date of the charter was 28th July, 1929. The captain of the *Westward* was H. Peterson of Portland, Oregon.

Coming down the Nicaraguan coast *Westward* was caught in a

hurricane and foundered with all hands, Bergmans and Captain Peterson alone surviving. This disaster took place on the 25th September, 1929, a season of the year when strong squalls (known as *papagaya*) come down from the Andes. The *papagaya* comes after sundown and without warning, at least to those without local knowledge, and even a well-built sailing vessel, caught unprepared, is liable to founder. *Westward* was on charter and probably in a none too seaworthy condition.

Bergmans and Peterson got away in a small boat and drifted for three days, when they sighted an island, but they only made land two days later with great difficulty. They had landed on Cocos Island.

Peterson became ill and they occupied the ruins of the settlement abandoned by a German named Guiesler [*sic*], who had lived as a hermit 18 years on the island.

Two weeks after Bergmans and Peterson's landing on the island, Bergmans, in his wanderings, put his foot on a spot that gave way under his weight, leaving a small hole not larger than a footprint. This rather strange occurrence aroused his curiosity, and he examined the spot, shouted through the opening, and to his surprise, got back an echo. Naturally, he became more curious and eventually he discovered it was the entrance to a tunnel or natural cave which on investigation proved to be the hiding place of long buried treasure. He saw stacks of gold and silver, bar and coin piled loose on the floor, quantities of golden ornaments for altar use, numbers of gold statues resembling those found in Roman Catholic Churches, large lots of jewelry and precious stones, two large chests which were left unopened—and the skull and bones of a man.

The floor of the tunnel or cave measured approximately 40 paces by 15 (i.e., 40 yards by 15 yards). More important still, he found parchments bearing the name of Bonito, some of which he states he took away and left in a safe deposit in San Francisco.

(*Note:* It should be remembered that Benito Bonito throughout his remarkably successful career of brigandage, used the Island of Cocos as a safe deposit for his plunder, estimated at £11,000,000 in value.)

Bergmans and Peterson removed about half a sackful of the treasure and secreted it in two selected spots on the Island and then resealed or covered up the entrance to the cave.

On the 16th October, 1929, a derelict ship's boat drifted ashore on the island, and on the 30th November, 1929, Bergmans and Peterson set out on it to make the mainland. They were picked up on the 4th December, 1929, by a German steamer *Nachwezeld* (Bergmans is not sure of the spelling). The captain of the steamer was a Carl Heindritch. The *Nachwezeld* was bound through the Panama Canal to Boston.

Bergmans and Peterson showed to Captain Heindritch the valuables they had with them [from the cave], and subsequently Heindritch left his ship at Boston and went to New York to introduce them to an underworld firm of dealers, named, so Bergmans states, Strauss Bros.

Strauss Bros. paid them $56,000 for their treasure (probably less than a quarter of its value), which amount was divided between the three of them, on 27th December, 1929.

Peterson went to his home in Portland, Oregon, where he died in a hospital in 1932. The captain of the tramp steamer threw up his job and proceeded to enjoy his share of the proceeds, and in April, 1930, Bergmans sailed for Europe on the S.S. *Cleveland.*

In March, 1934, Bergmans returned to the U.S.A., and at the Chicago World's Fair (where he was connected with the Belgian section) he made the acquaintance of a Colonel Hunter, a prominent Chicago lawyer. Colonel Hunter, after a five months investigation of Bergmans' story, despatched him in the yacht *Nautilus* to Panama, and Colonel Hunter himself, with five others, joined the yacht, by air, in the Panama Canal—the yacht then leaving for Cocos, ostensibly on a pearl-fishing expedition.

On the voyage Bergmans was warned by the yacht's cook, with whom he had become friendly, that his life was in danger, and this warning, together with Bergmans' own suspicions, decided him to pretend that he was unable to re-locate the site of the treasure.

Eventually, the *Nautilus* returned to Panama, and in Colon Bergmans was badly beaten up and taken to a hospital in a serious condition. Under the Panama Canal regulations the yacht was not permitted to sail without him, and it was detained until he was discharged from the hospital. Bergmans was then taken to the Island of Trinidad and put ashore.

While in the hospital Bergmans met an English seaman named George Lane, and was befriended by him. Lane was a British Naval Rating lent for service to the Colombian government for the training of engineers for their new gunboats. On his discharge he joined Bergmans, as previously arranged, and paid his passage to Europe, traveling with him.

Since the disposal of the valuables to the Strauss Bros., Bergmans has been shadowed by that firm's agents, in the belief that more valuables were to be obtained from the same source. Bergmans has also been kept under observation by the Colonel Hunter party, and he now greatly fears the vengeance of the Hunter group should he disclose the whereabouts of the treasure to others.

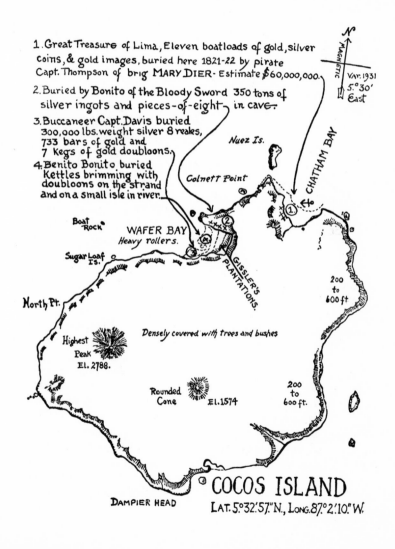

1. Great Treasure of Lima, Eleven boatloads of gold, silver coins, & gold images, buried here 1821-22 by pirate Capt. Thompson of brig MARY DIER · Estimate $60,000,000.

2. Buried by Bonito of the Bloody Sword 350 tons of silver ingots and pieces-of-eight in cave.

3. Buccaneer Capt. Davis buried 300,000 lbs. weight silver 8 reales, 733 bars of gold and 7 kegs of gold doubloons.

4. Benito Bonito buried Kettles brimming with doubloons on the strand and on a small isle in river.

VAR. 1931 5.°30' East

Nuez Is.

CHATHAM BAY

Colnett Point

Boat Rock

WAFER BAY
Heavy rollers.

Sugar Loaf Is.

GISSLER'S PLANTATIONS.

North Pt.

200 to 600 ft

Densely covered with trees and bushes

Highest Peak El. 2788.

Rounded Cone   El. 1574

200 to 600 ft.

COCOS ISLAND
DAMPIER HEAD   LAT. 5.°32'.57."N., LONG. 87.°2'.10." W.

Bergmans has entrusted to Lane certain information regarding the site of the treasure to be used in the event of his (Bergmans') death.

We have seen copies of the local newspapers describing the attack on Bergmans by the Hunter people after his failure to locate the hiding place. He bears evidence of the rough treatment by a long and very ugly scar on his forehead.

A representative of the company has been through all the letters and documents entrusted to Lane, who shares Bergmans' knowledge. Our agent concluded that Bergmans' story was true. Not actually being on the island with Bergmans, but with his own knowledge of the place, he is quite convinced that we have a man who has actually seen the treasure and removed a small portion of it. It must be remembered, however, that Bergmans is still going in fear of his life from gangsters hired by the Hunter crowd, who have dogged his every movement since they knew of his association with our company, and it has been difficult to convince him of his personal safety. There was the possibility that he might return to the Hunter crowd and save his skin that way.

Our member is satisfied that the information imparted to Lane is correct and he has the two treasure locations as he knows them. One, where the two small lots were hidden by Bergmans, although close to the camp, is not known to anyone on the island. The site of the cave is in the vicinity of Wafer Bay.

Bergmans is now in San José, Costa Rica, and should soon be working in co-operation with the Managing Director on Cocos, but there is no disputing the fact that he is in a very nervous condition—in constant fear of his life—Lane, his bodyguard, separated from him—the Hunter crowd, the Strausses, the German captain of the tramp steamer, and the Vancouver Company, are all on the watch.

All possible precautions have been taken by the Company to circumvent any possible interference. Lane is now on the island, and as soon as he and Bergmans are brought together, both working under the observation and supervision of the Company's Managing Director and the members of the Field Executive, all guarded by the Costa Rican armed Force, very startling developments may be expected.

Inside the organization something must have been stewing. No progress was reported on the island—possibly due to complications in the efforts to get Bergmans calmed down and allay his fears of being shadowed by spies. Whatever cloak-and-dagger work was in progress was not reported, but after a three-month blank period an Extraordinary General Meeting of shareholders was called. The subjects considered were: repatriation of members of the expedition; agreement with Bergmans; accusations by the Chairman against the Controller of Operations; personal financial transactions between the Chairman and the Company; retention of company-owned equipment by Mr. Jolly and Captain Polkinhorne; and "that the present Directors with the exception of Mr. R. H. Studdert be removed from office and replaced with others . . ."

The report of this meeting was not printed. A new Board of Directors was elected consisting of Messrs. Baron, Bevan, Arthur, Mendelssohn, Thorp, and Bergmans. The explorers, scientists, Lieutenants, Captains, Colonels, and Commodores were apparently thrown overboard to the sharks. The new Directors believed that Mr. Bergmans' information held the only sure road to early and complete success.

The company now had a map showing the site and approach to the cave and a plan of the island giving the general location of the treasure cave—and obviously neither could be shown to stockholders. But a description of the contents of the cave, exactly as written by Bergmans and signed by him, read:

When arriving in cave you will first notice on your left the form of a person (sceleton) [sic].

Further on the left are sacks with gold nugets [sic] and more sacks further inside on the same left.

You will have to walk on silver coins and other metals which is filled up in abundance.

On the right from the entrance are seven little barrels containing gold coins and in the farther and middle are eight boxes or trunks and many different pieces of ornament from churches, together with statuettes.

Two of the boxes have been opened by me and jewels have been removed.

Notice an old shirt was used to make a sack from, but was later left in the cave and gold nugets [sic] of all sizes are spread on the ground in order to use two of the bags to fill them with jewels.

Along with this exciting information came a plea to the shareholders for further loans to finance a return to Cocos Island on the *Veracity*, which was then anchored at Punta Arenas.

Meanwhile, news from Paris was announced by Reuters:

PIRATE'S GHOST TO LEAD TREASURE HUNTERS
Woman Medium Said to Be the Contact
Hidden £300,000,000 to Undo the Evil of His Life

A German yachtsman, Hubert Mazenick, announced that he was starting for Cocos Island, taking with him Margo Schneider, a girl spiritualist. Margo had brought Mazenick into touch with Benito Bonito the pirate, who had given them precise information about where his treasures were hidden.

Margo saw his spirit one evening [explained Mazenick].

He came alone in his finest pirate costume, spoke to us for a long time, and begged us to go and dig up the treasure hidden by him during his adventurous existence.

"There are four dumps," said Bonito, "representing about £300,000,000. Dig them up and with all this money you shall repair the harm I did during my life."

In three months' time I shall be back with the treasure [declared Mazenick confidently].

A hundred others have tried Cocos Island and failed. Some of them came within a few yards of the treasure. Sir Malcolm Campbell had to give up the search.

But we shall go straight to the place. I shall say, "There it is," and the £300,000,000 will be ours.

Whether the promoters of Treasure Recovery Ltd. tried to hire Mazenick, the lovely Margo and Bonito's ghost, is unknown, but it is doubtful as they already had Bergmans among their Directors.

It was April 1936 before the *Veracity* left Punta Arenas, and then she sneaked away without clearance papers, not for Cocos but for Balboa, because of reported "subversive activities."

During the loading an attempt was made to sink her by leaving a seacock open and she was flooded to a depth of eight feet. On arrival at Balboa damage to the ship's copper sheathing was found and certain members of the crew were showing disaffection. Costa Rica wanted $1,800 at once for past use of government launches, and Mr. Arthur received a warning that if the *Veracity* showed up at Punta Arenas or Cocos again, she would be seized by the Costa Ricans and held against the government's claim.

This was on April 20, 1936, and ended the reports.

Mr. Studdert reported later that when Bergmans arrived at Punta Arenas by steamer, he declined to go to Cocos Island as he believed his life was in danger. Eventually, after much persuasion he went, but beyond pointing to a spot on the beach where he claimed to have buried the loot he removed in 1929 he did not disclose any place where treasure could be found. Bergmans, who was in poor health, was on the island for about seven weeks and then returned to Punta Arenas for medical attention. Some time later he left and vanished into oblivion.

In the High Court of Justice, Chancery Division, Mr. Justice Crossman presiding, No. 00260 of 1936, a statement of the affairs of Treasury Recovery Limited was filed. On the 19th day of November, 1936, an eight-page report signed by the Official Receiver appeared. The syn-

dicate ended owing its shareholders £63,832/18/4. Not
so much as a buccaneer's button had been found. Which
proves (or does it?) that the Loot of Lima still lies buried
right where Captains Davis, Bonito, Thompson, and company planted it.

Your compiler dislikes unhappy endings. He would
much rather give here a blow-by-blow description of
Arthur, Studdert, and Bergmans in the pirate cave wad-
ing up to their knees in gold doubloons and jewels. It
is particularly sad that no one recovered the old shirt—
some of the shareholders could have used it.

CHAPTER 13

Treasure Trove

THE TREASURE associated with galleons, pirates, and buccaneers came from the mineral wealth of mines in Mexico and Central and South America. From the sixteenth to the nineteenth century Spain held in the New World the greatest treasure house that had ever been known. Gold and silver flowed by tons to the foundries and mints and to Old Spain in ingots and coins. Pearls, emeralds, and precious stones were also found in quantity.

The values of the galleon cargoes can only be estimated but when records in the archives have been discovered, an idea of the sea-borne wealth is proven.

When Sir Francis Drake missed at sea both of the galleon flotas that reached Spain in September and October of 1585, he failed to capture bullion and coin officially manifested at a value of $5,683,523. This was about evenly divided between the King's revenues and sums for private individuals. And this figure does not take into account "unmanifested" bullion and jewels which sometimes amounted to more than was manifested. The figures show only "cash" revenues to the Crown and "cash" receipts on account of private persons.

Besides this vast sum, there were on board for the king, 506 pounds' weight of pearls and 107 pounds of emeralds. A 6-pound sample lump of silver from a new mine in Caxatambo was also on board.

This great heap of treasure reached San Lucar, Spain, inside of a thirty-day period and was no doubt as quickly siphoned from King Philip II's coffers into the pockets of the officials and moneylenders.

When the Spaniards arrived in the New World, the Indians knew how to separate silver and gold from the rich ore by fire, but they knew nothing of how to refine it. Much of the gold was washed from the sands of streams in dust and nuggets and this was easily worked into various forms by Indian artisans. As the gold was not used as barter but merely for ornamentation, rich hauls have been made over the years from grave digging and Inca and Aztec gold ornaments have been gathered by many museum expeditions for historic value while priceless ornaments have gone to the melting pot for their gold value by weight.

The Spaniards went "gold crazy" on their arrival and sent the Indians into the bowels of the ground to follow the veins of ore. The returns were fabulous but the native population, slaving underground in the heat, wet, and mud for their exacting taskmasters, died by thousands.

The Spanish method of refining silver was by amalgamating it with quicksilver. The ore was crushed and ground to dust. It was then passed through a fine sieve. The powder was put into pottery vessels and placed over furnaces where salt was added to separate the earth and dross from the silver. Quicksilver was then strained through linen into the ore and stirred so that it would thoroughly amalgamate with the silver. Before furnaces were used, the ore and quicksilver were mixed in large troughs and stirred for about twenty days until well mixed. When it was found that heat speeded up the process, the process of amalgamation could be completed in five or six days. The ore was then washed in water-filled vessels and stirred so that the dross and earth ran off with the water and the heavier amalgam remained at the bottom. This was strained and molded into cone-shaped lumps or loaves of about one hundred pounds' weight. Earthen pots were placed like caps over the loaves which were set over a hot fire. The quicksilver passed off in vapor which condensed against the sides of the earthen cap and was drawn off by a pipe, while the pure silver remained in a lump. From two of these loaves a bar of silver weighing about thirty-three pounds was recovered.

The purity of the refined silver thus obtained was very high. Borings from a 60-pound ingot recovered by Charles Brookfield and Arthur McKee, Jr., from a sunken galleon off Key Largo, Florida, assayed 999 thousandths pure. Another bar weighing 75 pounds assayed 999.1 thousandths pure silver with an additional trace of gold. Sterling silver by comparison is only 925 thousandths fine.

The purest of the pre-Columbian gold has been reported to have been so soft that artisans could work it into shapes like lead, almost by hand, although this seems like an exaggeration.

When Careri, an early writer, visited the silver mines at Pachuca, Mexico, in 1698 he reported that the Santa Cruz mine was 672 feet deep. The ore was brought to the surface by wheels and rope moved by four mules, and as one bucket came up loaded an empty one went down. The Navarro mine was 585 feet deep and the Indians brought up the ore on their backs, at imminent danger, climbing up many ladders, or rather notched posts. They were paid half of a piece-of-eight (four reales) a day and at night were allowed to carry up one load and share it with the mine owner.

The same writer visited a nearby mountain where he found a small city of thatched huts and no less than twelve thousand Indians working the mines. There were some thousand mines in the vicinity and one of them, the Trinity, employed 900 to 1,000 miners daily. In ten years forty million pesos in silver was produced at that mine. When the Trinity became too dangerous to work, a shaft was sunk nearby which became just as rich.

In 1698 the King's tax of one-fifth of the metal mined amounted to about six million pieces-of-eight and in 1691, the chief assayer stated that the king's share was some eight million. At least four times as much silver was mined in Peru at that time. The purchasing power of such vast sums in those days was tremendous.

The Real del Monte mine was doubtless worked by natives long before the time of Cortez and Montezuma. From time immemorial it was the law of Mexico that a mine belonged to the one who worked it. Whenever he abandoned it anyone might take it. Thus the Real del Monte mine was worked by many owners, the most noted of whom was named Terreros. He took advantage of the law that a mine owner could own but the first five hundred feet in depth till he had exhausted that, when he might begin on the second five hundred. Not far from Real del Monte was the Santa Brigida mine and he decided to cut into the second five hundred feet of that mine by tunneling from the bottom of the shaft of the Real del Monte. On the way he struck one rich vein after another until in the eleven years which it took him to complete the tunnel, he became the richest man in all Spain.

To show his gratitude he gave the King a million dollars in silver and in 1762 presented the Spanish Navy with two ships of war fully manned and equipped. His other benefactions amounted to many millions of dollars, and not long before his death he was remembered by the King with the title of Count.

The descendants of Terreros worked this mine till the revolt of Hidalgo swept the country bare, and it was abandoned. An English company, knowing how rich it had been, put $20,000,000 in machinery and labor into it and lost $3,000,000 in the following twenty-five years before they abandoned it.

In 1775, Father Flores, a Dominican priest, who in his zeal had pushed far into the frontiers of San Luis, was at last compelled to abandon his work because of utter unproductiveness, hopelessness, and nonsupport. Gathering his most precious personal possessions in a bundle, he set forth to return to civilization. The first night, he built a fire out of the green or water-soaked wood with great difficulty, but at last it was glowing hot and he slept by it all night, wrapped in his blanket. A fierce storm near morning blew away every particle of the fire, and when he arose there was gloomy prospect that he could make another. But on the bare earth where the fire had been, there were some shining white particles of metal. He examined them and found the outcroppings of a vein of silver. Then he remembered the dream of his boyhood, which had led him to the spot, in which an angel appeared and told him that he would be buried in a silver vault under a great church which he would erect in the far wilderness of Mexico.

Without disclosing his secret, he worked the mine alone for five years and the ore brought him $3,000,000. With this he opened it up on an extensive plan and before his death he had paid the royal fifth to the King of Spain amounting to more than $20,000,000. The rest of his fortune he spent in settling emigrants upon well-equipped tracts of land, and in due time he rested according to his dreams in the silver vault underneath the great stone church he had built. Today his mine is only a cave for the small animals that remain in the nearby fields and woods.

There were hundreds of mines in the mountain regions worked by natives or priests who were contented with a bare sufficiency for support. Many of these are believed to contain fabulous riches equal to those whose one-fifth once made Spain the richest government and nation in the world.

The Santa Eulalia mines in Chihuahua are still rich producers and the church still receives one sixty-fourth from the oldest of them as a result of a curious compact. In 1706 several desperadoes, confined in the prison, killed the guards and escaped to the mountains, where they defied every effort at capture. As their crimes were particularly atrocious, the vigilance of the authorities never relaxed and a large reward was offered to the Indians for the robbers' scalps.

The desperadoes fortified themselves in a cavern having secret outlets deep in the almost inaccessible mountains, and made the region uninhabitable.

One day a few years later, an Indian came to the padre of the village bearing a letter which stated that the outlaws desired forgiveness of church and state, not only because they now desired to live right for the rest of their lives, but because the saints had prospered them so that they could make the padre and the governor rich beyond their wildest dreams.

The absolution and the pardon were soon secured, for which a vast amount of silver ore was turned over and a pact made that one sixty-fourth of the entire output of the mine should be set aside for the building of a great Cathedral. In a few years the Cathedral of the City of

Chihuahua was begun and completed and equipped at a cost of $2,000,000. The yield was above $2,000,000 a year for nearly a century.

Then the Apaches overran the country and the mines were abandoned for many years.

CHAPTER 14

Tips For Treasure Seekers

I f you are bitten with the treasure-hunting bug or get gold fever, stop a minute before you grab a shovel or diving helmet and take off. There is no rush. If the treasure is really where you think it is, it will wait till you get there.

The history of treasure hunting is crammed with cases of misguided seekers chasing off to far corners of the earth to uncover trove that never existed.

There is no sure formula but at least any treasure worth seeking is worth documenting as to its existence, past history, and the likelihood of recovery. The factual history of treasure hunting on Cocos Island alone puts all fictional accounts of the game to shame. It is hard to believe that sensible people in these modern times could spend so much and fumble so badly.

Millions of dollars have been squandered in following the "exact directions" to the spot marked "X" on some tattered chart. The chances of finding wealth near your own home are better than a thousand-mile trip with a map drawn on porpoise hide by a defunct pirate's mate.

Accurate maps and information regarding buried treasure and lost mines are nonexistent. If they did exist the treasure would not be lost.

This writer once discovered between the pages of an old atlas, previously in the library of an eighteenth-century British Duke, a typical treasure map. It was on old paper in faded ink and had all the earmarks of a legitimate document. After keeping it in the archives for a few years as a curiosity, I presented it to my friend and treasure hunter, Edward Rowe Snow. When *Life* wrote up Snow's expedition to a Canadian island where he uncovered the hand of a skeleton holding a few gold "Half-Joes," the map was used in the article. Hundreds of letters were sent to Snow by readers who decided that they recognized the island. The strange part was that all but two students of pirate lore placed the island in different parts of the world. Two readers (in Florida and Michigan) both hit on what they thought was the right spot by their deductions from the date 1699 and the initials "J.W." of the supposed maker. An expedition was planned to go to the island and dig up the loot of Captain Kidd, at the spot marked "X."

Before the hunters took off Snow advised them to write me for the facts about the chart, and as an old skeptic I told them to check the chart first as to paper, ink, and handwriting. The map was sent to the Smithsonian Institution and I quote from their report:

Your letter . . . has been referred to the Map Division, Library of Congress. Mr. Frederick R. Goff, chief of the Library's Rare Books Division, is of the opinion that the map is drawn on wove paper, which was not made before 1782 and little used before 1800; that the writing on the face of the map does not appear to be of the type employed at such an early date; and that even the ink indicates a much later date than 1699.

The conclusion is that the map is a fairly recent production, for which the maker used a flyleaf from an old book, but chose a book by no means old enough for the purpose.

The above is typical of hand-drawn treasure maps reputedly drawn by Captain Kidd or some other pirate. The fake was caught by checking the map, and the hunters saved time, money, and disappointment.

There are many modern treasure maps which show the approximate location or area in which *reputed* lost treasure and mines lie. Some are based on historical records or marine charts, in the case of sunken ships. They are all interesting and some are decorative and well worth the cost to frame or study. In years to come many of these maps will be collector's items, when they go out of print.

The U.S. Coast and Geodetic coast and harbor charts as well as the navigational charts of the U.S. Navy Hydrographic Office show the positions of wrecks which present hazards to navigation. They are obtainable from the Department of Commerce or the Navy Department in Washington, D.C.

The commonly accepted definition of treasure trove is, "Coin, bullion, gold or silver articles, found hidden in the earth *whose original owners are unknown.*"

The rights to treasure trove vary in different countries. In England and Scotland the rights to treasure trove have been held by the Crown for centuries and finders are ordered by law to report any discoveries to the local coroner. "The Law and Practice of Treasure Trove," by G. F. Hill, in *The Antiquaries Journal,* London, July, 1930 (Vol. X, No. 3), goes into the British law very thoroughly.

State laws in the United States vary, but in general the finder is allowed to keep treasure. In Louisiana treasure is divided between the landowner and the finder. Some states like Florida will grant hunting licenses to search on state property in general or exclusively for definite areas for a fixed fee and a percentage of the treasure if recovered. The U.S. Treasury Department will grant salvage rights to sunken ships in government waters or buried treasure on public lands.

The income taxes will have to be paid if you dig up a potful of treasure or raise a ton of gold from a sunken ship and it is best not to try to outwit the law. There are many cases on record where the courts have declared finders of U.S. legal tender in paper money, silver and gold coins, and jewelry entitled to the full value of the treasure. When the treasure belongs to some individual or estate, finders have generally been rewarded with a percentage.

In case of any doubt, it is best to look into the law before going too far and to consult an attorney. Proper legal advice and signed agreements with all parties concerned may save long litigation and heavy expenses.

A pamphlet, *Treasure Trove Law,* is obtainable from J. Jensen, 34 Pilgrim Road, Natick, Massachusetts, that may be helpful if you are serious about digging.

Many treasure expeditions working in populated areas have been interrupted in their digging or salvage operations by rival expeditions, interlopers, curiosity seekers, and crowds of onlookers. A serious treasure hunter digging on a government reservation writes:

"The area is a prohibited one, and we operated on temporary permits, issued first two days at a time and later for fifteen days, renewable and approved by the head of the area.

"We had been operating for some time and were about to bring in additional heavy equipment when a newspaper got wise and broke a story on the matter. The public swarmed in from the neighborhood and even from nearby states. Roads were blocked in violation of regulations and in spite of prohibitory government signs posted along the highway. This brought the authorities marching down on us. After an extended conference, it was decided by 'the brass' that we should discontinue operations, unless and until we could get a clearance permit from Washington. We applied as directed but got a reject. The project has been abandoned, at least for the present."

Moral: Keep away from newspaper or other publicity. It can spoil your sport.

The finders' rights in treasure are sometimes disputed. The most recent argument over a hoard has yet to come to trial in Municipal Court in New York City. When Pearley Dickens, a construction worker, pried out the bricks in a chimney while razing an old house, $2,300 tumbled out. Dickens turned the money over to the N.Y. Police property clerk. After ninety days he claimed the money but found that the realty company which owned the property had entered a counterclaim contending that the money was not lost but "abandoned" and therefore belonged to them. Until the suit is settled the police are holding the cash.

Edward Smith, an odd-job trucker, was luckier. On June 18, 1956, Smith found $5,162 in an old kettle that lay in an empty lot in Brooklyn where he was dumping debris. He also promptly turned the money over to the police and in December, after six months had expired with no claimants appearing, Smith was happy to have the money turned over to him—a nice Christmas present for the Smiths and their two children.

Moral: More treasure is stumbled upon near home than

is dug up with pirate maps. It may not be romantic but gold is gold wherever you find it.

In case you are one of the lucky finders of silver and gold of the Spanish Colonial era, or early American coins, *do not* hurry to sell your treasure for its metal value. To collectors and museums old coins are generally worth many times their bullion value. The numismatic value, of course, depends on rarity, source, date, and condition, but even the commonest coins of early dates are worth more as coins than by weight as metal.

A doubloon weighing about an ounce in gold worth $35 can bring from $60 to $500 to a coin collector. A silver piece-of-eight containing 90 cents' worth of silver may sell for $3 or $100 or more, according to rarity and condition.

The American Numismatic Society in New York and the Smithsonian Institution in Washington both maintain museums of numismatic material. They have staffs of curators and are always willing to help identify and help with information on old and rare coins, medals, and paper money. They do not appraise or place values on coins but there are many coin dealers and collectors who can value single pieces or entire collections.

The American Numismatic Association, composed of thousands of coin collectors, maintains a library and publishes a monthly magazine, *The Numismatist*. The chances are that there is a Coin Club in your vicinity that meets regularly, and guests at meetings who wish to show their coins are always welcome.

To keep in touch with recent developments in treasure hunting you can join the Treasure Trove Club. Members receive the *National Prospector's Gazette*, which contains reports on finds and expeditions, a question-and-answer column, and lists of books and articles in current magazines. A. J. Stewart, Treasure Trove Club, 2922 164th St., Flushing 58, N.Y., can furnish information on the club. Another group of active treasure hunters is Associated Geographers of America, whose secretary is John W. Pounds, 2649 34th St., Santa Monica, California.

Adventure Magazine, 205 East 42nd Street, New York, N. Y., has a question-and-answer department called "Ask Adventure." The magazine's experts can answer queries on climate, geography, mining, metal detectors, diving, and other such matters. A. J. Stewart is the Treasure and Lost Mines Editor, and all requests for such information should be addressed to him.

CHAPTER 15

Pirate Treasure of Gold and Silver

TREASURE IS FOUND in many forms; in fact, any valuable manuscript, painting, jewel, antique that has a great cash value to a museum or a collector can be called treasure.

This section is devoted to bars and coins of the pirate period, the seventeenth and eighteenth centuries, and hence is limited and in no way complete. The literature of numismatics is vast and any seeker for knowledge in some particular coinage can refer to the books on the subject in any library.

Invariably, when an old coin is discovered, the finder asks, "How much is it worth?" The worth or selling price depends on the factors which are discussed on page 269. A common piece-of-eight from the Mexican mint of the period 1772-1821, bearing the portrait of the king, could be purchased at retail from a dealer until a few years ago for a dollar or less. Today it will bring from $3.50 to $10.00. This is largely because of an inflationary market and the increase in collectors, many of whom are endeavoring to form a complete collection of dates. Collectors

271

have begun to realize that this coin, so common in years past, was taken by the United States Treasury Department as the basis in size, weight, and value for the first dollars of this country.

Gold coins of the pirate period have also risen in value, because of the increase in collectors and the scarcity of gold coins in any form and largely because gold coins (even U.S. gold) can be owned if they are part of a coin collection. In years past (not too long ago), treasure found in the form of foreign gold coins was generally melted and sold secretly as bullion in an effort to cover up the treasure find. If you find a chest of gold doubloons, do not hurry to melt them, as they may be worth as coins many times their weight as bullion. A gold coin weighing an ounce ($35.00 in gold value) may bring from $50 to $500 as a rare collector's item. The T-men will not seize your coins, if they are foreign, but you will be expected to pay your income taxes on the profit from their sale.

Exact values of coins are hard to fix; they vary with the years and their popularity among collectors. Auction records are not too sure a gauge. The best way to find the value of a coin is to try to sell it. Naturally a coin dealer has to buy at wholesale and sell at retail and make a profit to stay in business. Prices listed in this section are based on approximate sales of similar coins from catalogues and auction records.

It is almost impossible to make clear the values today of such coins as doubloons, escudos, duros, pesos, moidores, "Joes," reals, chequins, and endless others. A few are illustrated in order to show their design, size, shape, and worth. When one reads that "a treasure hunter uncovered 500 French, Spanish, and Brazilian gold coins," one understands easily enough. But should the report read, "He found 500 Louis d'ors, pistoles, ducats, excellentes, doubloons, moedas, and cruzados," it sounds like double-talk.

The crudely shaped, poorly struck, and lumpy coins called "cobs," frequently mentioned, were made in that form at the mint and were seldom clipped after they reached circulation. The mints of the period were in private hands, and the officials and workers earned their pay from the amount of metal they made into coins. It was difficult and costly to make the blanks of metal in a round form of even thickness before they were struck with the design, and to speed up production, these irregular blanks were cut from flat bars and hammer struck. They were legal coinage as long as the design showed, even in part, and as long as they approximated the standard weight. The laws did not specify the exact weight of each coin but ordered that a definite amount of coinage be struck from a specified weight of metal. The silver coins of Spanish Colonial mints of the period 1536 to 1734 made in either rounded or "cob" shape vary considerably in weight, but when a large lot is weighed together they are generally of the correct average. More care was exercised with gold coins, but even then, some were made in "cob" shape. Merchants and money-changers of the period used scales to weigh coins, as the western storekeepers of '49 weighed gold dust and nuggets when these crossed their counters in trade.

The word "plate" is found in many narratives of the period. "We found on board the ship 112 bags and 6 chests of Dollars and one bag of plate." Or "Receiv'd from the prize one box of Plate and Virgin silver." Or "This prize had on board 606 lb. weight of Gold, and two chests of wrought plate, being a set of curious Plate lately purchased for a church, with several costly images of Saints . . . which we beat up close to make them lye snug in the chests" (Commodore Anson's capture of the Manila galleons in 1741). The dollars mentioned were pieces-of-eight and the plate was silver in bars or, when made into objects, "wrought plate." The annual treasure ships from America to Spain were generally called "the plate fleet" or "plata flota," as they carried bullion. In Spanish the word *plata* means silver.

Pieces-of-eight were dollar-size Spanish coins of silver, of eight reales' value. Coins were also struck in denominations of 4, 2, 1, ½, and ¼ reales. The 4 and 2 reales were sometimes called "4 bits" and "2 bits," and the ½-real pieces were called "picayunes" in Louisiana.

Gold doubloons were 8 escudos or 4 pistoles, the pistole being 2 escudos of Spain or a quarter doubloon, equal to 4 pieces-of-eight in silver.

Bibliography*

The material on numismatics is large, but a few of the best books covering the Spanish Colonial mints and coinages of the period 1500 to 1800 are listed here:

The Numismatic History of Mexico, by Alberto F. Pradeau (Los Angeles, 1938). Covers thoroughly the Mexico City mint and its coinages from the Pre-Columbian epoch to 1823. There are 23 plates illustrating the various coins. A Spanish edition was published by the Banco de Mexico, S.A., in 1950.

The Peruvian coinages and mint history are fully covered in *La Ceca de la Villa Imperial de Potosí y la Moneda Colonial,* by Humberto F. Burzio (Buenos Aires, 1945). Two hundred and twenty-six coins of the Potosí mint are illustrated and described.

"The Spanish Gold Treasure of El Mesuno," by C. S. Wilcox (*Numismatic Review,* December 1943) gives the history and illustrates the treasure from which coin No. 9 was taken.

The most complete series of illustrations of pieces-of-eight is in *Catalogo de Los Reales de a Ocho Españoles,* by José de Yriarte (Madrid, 1955). The book also contains a good bibliography on the subject.

Many references to coins of the period will be found in the publications of the American Numismatic Society, the *Coin Collector's Journal,* the *Numismatic Scrap Book,* and the *Numismatist.*

* See also full Bibliography, p. 275.

Plate A. Gold.

No. 1. Excelente of Spain, same size as a ducat. Shield and busts of Ferdinand and Isabella. Value $25–$35.

No. 2. Guinea of England. Bust of Charles II and shield. Value $30–$45.

No. 3. Doubloon or 4 pistoles of Spain, Philip IV. Shield and cross. Was equal to 16 pieces-of-eight in silver value. Value $150–$200.

No. 4. Pistole of Spain, or quarter doubloon. Value $50–$75.

No. 5. Dinar, or chequin or sequin, commonly called "Arabian gold" in colonial days. Value $10–$15.

No. 6. Moidore, or moeda, of Portugal and Brazil, Peter II, 1704. Shield and cross. The "4000" designates reis. Value $20–$30.

No. 7. Pistole or quarter doubloon of Lima, Peru. Pillars with PLVS (VLTRA) and cross with castles and lions. Philip V, (1727?). Recovered by Arthur Mc-Kee, Jr., from sunken galleon wreck. Value $75.

No. 8. Joannes, or "Joe," of Portugal and Brazil, John V, 1731. Bust and shield. In colonial days (1784) this gold coin was heavier than a doubloon and worth 8 shillings more. Value $100–$125.

Plate B. Gold.

No. 9. *(lower center.)* Pistole or quarter doubloon of Nuevo Reino de Granada, now Republic of Colombia, Philip IV, 1635. Part of El Mesuno treasure found in the Magdalena River (see p. 17). Value $75–$100.

No. 10. Half Louis d'or of France, Louis XIII, 1641. Bust and cross. Value $25–$35.

No. 11. Louis d'or of France, Louis XIII, 1642. Value $50–$75.

No. 12. Double Louis d'or of France, Louis XV, 1717. Value $35–$50.

No. 13. Doubloon of Philip V, Lima, Peru, mint, 1730. Cross with castles and lions and P.V.A. (PLVS VLTRA) across pillars. The 8 stands for 8 escudos. Value $150–$200.

No. 14. Doubloon or 8 escudos of Mexico, Philip V, 1736. Bust and crowned shield surrounded with chain and golden fleece. Part of Arthur McKee, Jr., galleon recovery (p. 43). Value $100.

No. 15. Doubloon or 8 escudos of Nuevo Reino de Granada (Colombia), Ferdinand VI, 1759. Value $75.

Plate C. Gold.

No. 16. Brazilian gold bar dated 1802. The marks are stamped and not cast into these bars. They show source, quality, weight, and assayer's and official seals. Value $750–$1,000.

No. 17. Brazilian gold bar dated 1813. Value $750–$1,000.

No. 18. Gold bar dated 1746. The marks are *cast* into this bar. It shows no official stamps. Recently discovered in small numbers. Value ?.

No. 19. 100 escudos of Spain. The largest coins made in Spain. Segovia mint, Philip III, 1609. Possibly unique. Value $6,000–$7,500.

PLATE C

Plate D. Silver. Pieces-of-eight reales.

No. 20. Spain, Seville mint, Ferdinand and Isabella, undated, circa 1560. Shield and arrows and yoke. Value $50–$100.

No. 21. Mexico mint. First dollar-size coin struck in America. Circa 1572–1598. Shield and cross with castles and lions. Value $35–$75.

No. 22. Mexico mint, Philip IV, struck 1623–1666. Value $25–$50.

No. 23. Lima, Peru, mint. First coinage of Peru. Philip II, undated. Shield and Pillars with PLVS VLTRA. Exceedingly rare. Value $300 (?).

No. 24. Lima, Peru, mint, Charles II, dated 1688. Rare. Value $75.

No. 25. Potosí (then Peru) mint, Charles II. Rare in this condition. Value $100.

Plate E. Silver. Pieces-of-eight reales.

No. 26. Mexico mint. Obverse of one piece with shield, and reverse of another piece with cross. Charles II. These come in very crude shapes and are called "cobs." Value $35–$50.

No. 27. Mexico mint. Obverse with shield showing fleur-de-lis imposed denoting Philip V, first Bourbon king of Spain. Reverse of another piece showing cross with castles and lions. Value $35–$50.

No. 28. Lima, Peru, mint, Charles II, 1700. Very rare date. Value $50.

No. 29. Madrid, Spain, mint, Philip V, 1714. Value $60.

No. 30. Madrid, Spain, mint, Charles III, 1773. Value $20.

No. 31. Mexico mint, Ferdinand VII, 1822. Value $5–$10.

26

27

28

29

30

31

Plate F. Silver. Pieces-of-eight reales.

No. 32. Potosí (then Peru) mint. From McKee sunken treasure galleon. This piece was completely covered with coral, and photo shows it as split in half and opened. Upper part is shell and lower part is remains of coin (1724 ?) which has changed to silver sulphide. Of no numismatic value.

No. 33. Potosí (then Peru) mint, Louis I, 1725. Compared with No. 32, the design of No. 33 can be seen. However, this coin is exceedingly rare and valuable, as Louis I reigned for only eight months in 1724 and few coins were struck under his rule. (Because of slow travel of news, most of those struck in the New World were minted after his death.) Value $350 (?).

No. 34. Mexico mint. From McKee sunken treasure galleon. Coral covered, Philip V, 1733 cob. Of no numismatic value.

No. 35. Mexico mint. Philip V, 1733 cob. Compare with No. 34 to see design. This design was only struck during 1733 and 1734. Value $25–$40.

No. 36. Mexico mint. From McKee sunken treasure galleon. Philip V, 1732 pillar dollar, coral covered. Compare with No. 37.

No. 37. A fine example of the coin struck the first year, 1732, that a screw press was used in the mint. This is the famous "Dos Mundos" (Two Hemisphere) or pillar dollar. Value $250–$350.

32

34

36

33

35

37

Plate G. Silver eight reales.

These coins are all part of recovered treasure hoards and were left dirty as found. They are chiefly valuable to their owner for their historic interest but would probably bring from $10 to $75 each if sold today. In Foul Anchor Archives.

No. 38. Lima, Peru, mint, Charles II, 1699. From the Vigo Bay, Spain, sunken galleons. From Charles B. Driscoll Collection.

No. 39. Potosí (then Peru) mint, Philip V, 1719. Washed ashore on a Cape Cod, Massachusetts, beach. From Edward Rowe Snow Collection.

No. 40. Potosí (then Peru) mint, Charles II, 1675. From a hoard excavated in Peru. The writer obtained 158 pieces from the hoard. (For details see *American Numismatic Society Museum Notes*, No. I, 1945, pp. 81–99, Plates XVIII to XXI.)

No. 41. Mexico mint, Philip III, undated, circa 1600–1606. This coinage was first dated in 1607. From a large hoard dug up while excavating for a new Opera House in Mexico City. Included were smaller coins.

No. 42. Mexico City mint, Philip V, 1742. From a hoard found in Manila by Dr. P. I. de Jesus.

No. 43. Charles IV, with bust of Charles III, struck in 1789, 1790 in various mints in Mexico and South America. This one is rust covered from seepage from iron chest hidden in wall of adobe house in Santo Domingo.

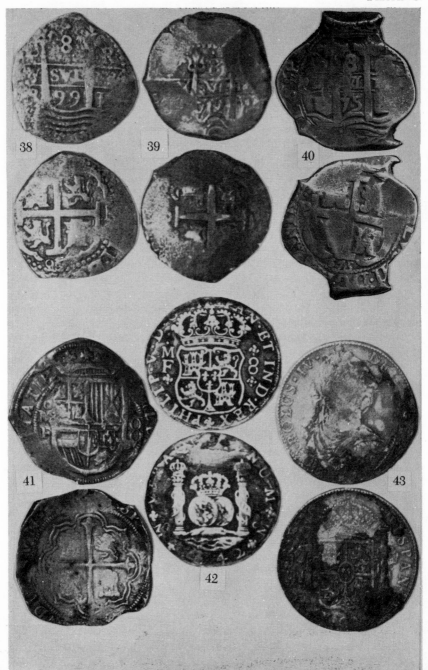

38 39 40

41 42 43

Bibliography

MY MAIN SOURCES have been the personal narratives of living treasure hunters gathered in many years of friendship, and correspondence with those I have not met face to face; plus one of the best libraries on the subject of piracy, buccaneering, and treasure hunting: the Foul Anchor Archives, at Rye, New York. The many libraries and institutions and individuals who have been very helpful have been credited in the preface or through the text. As this is not a scholarly book I have not included annotations, but the most important references to unpublished documents or unusual sources are given under chapter references.

The literature on the subject is so vast that a complete bibliography has never been published. Two great libraries: those of Philip Gosse, now owned by the British Maritime Museum in Greenwich, England: and of Charles B. Driscoll, now owned by the Wichita City Library in Wichita, Kansas, have never issued catalogues. I have never finished cataloguing the Foul Anchor Archives and although a bibliography of Exquemelin and Captain Charles Johnson have been in the works for many years, I doubt whether I will ever live to finish them.

The real cornerstone of all buccaneer history is *The Buccaneers of America* by Alexander-Olivier Exquemelin, a French surgeon from Honfleur, who served in the West Indies with Sir Henry Morgan and was an eyewitness to most of the events of which he writes. His book has been in print in many languages since it was first written in 1678 and was largely responsible for the world's learning of Morgan's raids on the Spanish. Exquemelin has been confused by various authors as being two people: Exquemelin (his real name), and Oexmelin (the French name used). He has also been named as one Hendrik B. Smeeks, an entirely different author of Amsterdam who wrote a fictitious shipwreck narrative in 1708. Students of Exquemelin can find the details of who he was and how his identity was discovered in "Who Was Exquemelin?", *Publisher's Weekly*, Vol. 152, No. 21, November 22, 1947, by R. I. Nesmith. This is based on Vrigman, L. C., *L'Identité d'Exquemelin*, taken from *De Kwestie "Wie was Exquemelin?"* volledig opgelost, Tijdschr. v. gesch. 47 (1932), p. 125-128.

Exquemelin's *Buccaneers of America* originally appeared in Dutch in 1678, was then translated into German in 1679, into Spanish in 1681. From the Spanish it was translated into English in 1684 and appeared in London in two separate and different books, one by William Crook and the other by Thomas Malthus. Sir Henry Morgan sued both publishers for statements which he considered defamatory. Malthus stopped publication and paid £200 damages but Crook apologized profusely and published a second edition (with some additional material) also in 1684.

A second volume was published in 1685 written by Basil Ringrose titled *The Dangerous Voyage, and Bold Attempts of Captain Bartholomew Sharp, and Others, in the South Seas, etc.* An octavo edition appeared in 1698 with additional narratives of the French buccaneers Raveneau de Lussan and Sieur de Montauban. French editions began in 1686, and differ considerably from the other editions. It has been said that the French edition was done from Exquemelin's original manuscript, whereas the Dutch publisher made many alterations in his translation.

The most famous source book on pirates appeared in 1724 in London under the name of Captain Charles Johnson, called *A General History of the Robberies and Murders of the Most Notorious Pirates*. It was very popular and went into a second edition the same year, a third in 1725, and a fourth in 1726. A second (no date) volume was issued in 1726 containing additional pirate lives and information. The writer believes that Captain Charles Johnson was a nom-de-plume of Daniel Defoe, and John Robert Moore in *Defoe in the Pillory* (Indiana University Publications, Humanity Series No. 1, Bloomington, Indiana, 1939) furnishes good evidence that Johnson and Defoe were one and the same person.

No one interested in buccaneering, piracy, and treasure should be without a copy in his library of both *The Buccaneers of America* and *A General History of the . . . Pirates*.

See *Eye to Eye*, No. 6, September 1951, published by The Graphic History Society of America, Washington, D.C., for a short bibliography of the above books: "Black Hearts and Bibliography" by R. I. Nesmith.

Nearly all present-day books on buccaneering and piracy are rewrites of Exquemelin and Johnson but here are a few that are well worth owning or reading:

Pirate's Own Book, Boston 1837 and reprinted until 1859. A modern reissue was made by the Marine Research Society, Salem, Massachusetts, in 1924.

Privateering and Piracy in the Colonial Period: Illustrative Documents, edited by J. F. Jameson (New York, 1923).

Notes on Piracy in Eastern Waters, compiled by S. C. Hill (Bombay, 1923).

The Pirates of the New England Coast, 1630-1730, by G. F. Dow and J. H. Edmonds (Marine Research Society, Salem, Massachusetts, 1923).

The History of Piracy (London, 1930) and *The Pirates' Who's Who* (London, 1924), both by Philip Gosse.

History of the Buccaneers of America, by James Burney (London, 1816).

On the Spanish Main, by John Masefield (London, 1906).

The Buccaneers in the West Indies in the Eighteenth Century, by C. H. Haring (London, 1910).

Pirates of the Eastern Seas (1618-1723), by Charles Grey (London, 1934).

Piracy in the West Indies and Its Suppression, by Francis B. C. Bradlee (Essex Institute, Salem, Massachusetts, 1923).

Dampier's Voyages, by Captain William Dampier, edited by John Masefield (London, 1906). Two vols. Has valuable appendix on Dampier's associates.

Sir Henry Morgan, Buccaneer and Governor, by W. Adolphe Roberts (New York, 1933).

Jolly Roger, by Patrick Pringle (London and New York, 1953). The best book in recent years on the subject in many ways.

The Great Days of Piracy in the West Indies, by George Woodbury (New York, 1951).

Piracy Was a Business, by Cyrus H. Karraker (Rindge, New Hampshire, 1953).

The Carolina Pirates and Colonial Commerce, 1670-1740, by S. C. Hughson (Johns Hopkins University Studies, Twelfth Series V-VI-VII, Baltimore, May-July, 1894).

Pirates Ahoy! by Charles B. Driscoll (New York, 1941).

For other books on piracy consult your own Public Library. There are hundreds, both fact and fiction.

Chapter 1. Dig for Pirate Treasure

Much of the material came from *The American Journal of Numismatics,* of the 1880's, in the Library of the American Numismatic Society, New York. Some material is from Exquemelin and Captain Johnson and the *Pirate's Own Book.* The Clement Downing treasure lead is taken from his *A Compendious History of the Indian Wars; with An Account of the Rise, Progress, Strength, and Forces of Angria the Pyrate, etc.* (London, 1737). Downing died leaving about $35 in his estate—apparently no one, including himself, took advantage of his tip on treasure.

Lionel Wafer's *A New Voyage and Description of the Isthmus of America* (London, 1699) and *Pirates of Colonial Virginia,* by L. H. Williams (Richmond, 1937) are quoted or used.

Edward Rowe Snow's *True Tales of Pirates and Their Gold* (New York, 1951) tells the full story of his treasure discovery on Cape Cod, and also that of Captain Bellamy and the wreck of his pirate ship *Whidah.*

News accounts of Gow and his crew are from *Parker's Penny Post,* July 5, 1725; and also from *The Real Captain Cleveland,* by Allan Fea (London, 1912): on Gibbs and Wansley in New York *Evening Post,* April 23, 1831, quoted from the *Morning Courier and New York Inquirer,* and in the New York *American,* same date, quoting the *Mercantile Advertiser.* The *Confessions and Execution of the Pirates Gibbs and Wansley,* etc., a pamphlet sold on the streets at the time of their trial and execution (1831), and *The Christian and Deist,* by the Reverend Herman Norton, who interviewed Gibbs in prison, were used as was the unpublished manuscript on *The Newport Pirates* by Elton Manuel of Newport, Rhode Island, who kindly donated his notes to the Foul Anchor Archives. Gibbs's skull discovery was reported by *The New Yorker* magazine, December 31, 1955.

The Lieutenant Williams material is from London news items in the scrapbooks of Hubert Palmer, of Kidd Museum fame, now in the Foul Anchor Archives, and the Williams-Driscoll correspondence (1920's and 30's) in the same Archives.

The Sneed treasure discovery of $625,000 worth of coins was reported in the *St. Petersburg Times* (Fla.) and was sent out over the AP wires and a day later in the same mediums was denied in an interview with Sneed who said his "statements had been misinterpreted" and the reports were "all a mistake."

The full story of the Castine treasure is in *The Castine Deposit* (American Numismatic Society, No. 100 of Numismatic Notes and Monographs, New York, 1942). "A Survey of American Coin Hoards," by W. A. Breen, in *The Numismatist*, January, 1942, lists besides the Castine Hoard, seventeen others, with descriptions and valuable references.

I have examined some hundreds of silver and gold coins recovered by Arthur McKee, Jr., from his sunken galleon wreck off Plantation Key, Florida; over one thousand reals of Charles and Johanna (1536-1572) in various collections; the Snow find (largely early U.S. silver half-dollars); over a hundred silver coins of Mexico uncovered while excavating for a new opera house in Mexico City; some two hundred pieces-of-eight of the period 1654-1689 of Lima and Potosí mints, from a Peru hoard, and nearly a hundred of the gold coins of Philip IV found in the Mesuno hoard, plus many small collections. This proves to the writer that treasure is found, although the details of where, when and by whom are in most cases difficult to trace down.

The Manila treasures mentioned are described in *The Numismatist*, November, 1952, "Buried Hoard in Manila's Walled City," by P. I. de Jesus; and in *Philippine Numismatic Monographs*, No. 9, 1953, "Further Report on the Manila Hoard," by the same author. Another find by the same author, "A Hoard of Mexican Silver Cobs Discovered in the Philippines," is discussed in *Philippine Numismatic Monographs*, No. 11, October, 1955.

Chapter 2. Spain's Golden Galleons

Materials for the chapter came largely from some three years' research and examination of relics and coins brought up from the wreck of the McKee galleon. These are preserved in McKee's Treasure Fortress, at Treasure Harbor, Plantation Key, Florida, which is open to the public. Readers interested in the Spanish treasure galleons and their history should consult C. H. Haring, *The Buccaneers in the West Indies in the XVII Century* (New York, 1910) and the writings of Irene A. Wright published by the Hakluyt Society of London, Series II, Vol. LXII, *Spanish Documents Concerning English Voyages to the Caribbean, 1527-1568* (1928): Vol. LXXI, *Documents Concerning English Voyages to the Spanish Main,*

1569-1580 (1932); and Vol. XCIX, *Further English Voyages to Spanish America, 1583-1594* (1951).

"Manila Galleons and Mexican Pieces of Eight" by Gilbert S. Perez, in *Philippine Social Sciences and Humanities Review*, Vol. XIX, No. 2, pp. 193-215, June, 1954, and "The 'Dos Mundos' Pillar Dollars," by the same author, in *Philippine Numismatic Monographs* (Manila, 1948), are both worthy of study. *The Coin Collector's Journal*, New Vol. II, No. 6, November 1944, "The Lima Pieces of George II of England," and Vol. 12, No. 3, May-June, 1945, "Cross Roads of South American Trade with the Orient," both by R. I. Nesmith, give information on the Manila-Acapulco galleons and treasure. These are not Florida, of course.

Also suggested are *They All Called It Tropical*, by C. M. Brookfield and Oliver Griswold (Miami, 1949), and *History Under the Sea*, by Mendel L. Peterson (National Museum, Smithsonian Society, Washington, D.C., 1954). If you are interested or find cannon you will want to consult *Artillery Through The Ages*, by Albert Manucy (Gov't Printing Office, Washington, D.C., 1949).

Armada Española, by C. Fernandez Duro (Madrid, 1895-1903, 9 vols.), is a source book for galleon wrecks, captures, and treasure losses. The official report of the 1733 loss of the annual fleet quoted is from the original by courtesy of the director of the Royal Academy of History in Madrid.

Chapter 3. Captain William Kidd—Pirate?

The story of Captain William (he has been called Robert and John) Kidd has been overwritten by authors in song, fiction, and story. As to whether he was or was *not* a pirate I leave to any reader to decide for himself. The literature on Kidd would fill a good-sized bookcase and has appeared regularly in the market for over two hundred and fifty years.

For popular reading I would recommend Ralph D. Paine's chapter on Kidd in *The Book of Buried Treasure* (New York, 1911); W. H. Bonner, *Pirate Laureate: The Life & Legends of Captain Kidd* (Rutgers University Press, New Brunswick, N.J., 1947); and H. T. Wilkins, *Captain Kidd and His Skeleton Island* (New York, 1937). Wilkins' documentary references and research are fine, and his story of Hubert Palmer and his Kidd Museum, with a treasure map in each chest bought by Palmer, is just about as entertaining as my story of Blackbeard's skull.

Jameson's *Privateering and Piracy* gives many Kidd documents, and Kidd's trial is covered fully in the *Trial of Captain Kidd*, in Wm. Hodge's "Notable British Trials" (Edinburgh, 1930), and Sir C. N. Dalton's *The Real Captain Kidd* (London, 1911). There are dime novels galore on Kidd and the best collection I know belongs to George French of Bloomfield, New Jersey.

The *Herald of Freedom and The Federal Advertiser* (Boston, November 17, 1788), containing a front page essay on "The Art of Digging Money," was sent to the Foul Anchor Archives by my friend, Norman Dodge of Goodspeed's, Boston, and the American Antiquarian Society of Worcester kindly photostated the issue of December 1, 1788, which contained Chapter II for my records.

G. P. Lathrop wrote in *Century Magazine* (December 1885) the story of Gardiner's Island titled "An American Lordship"; and R. D. Gardiner's article on "Gardiner's Island" appeared in *Colonial History of Long Island* (Papers read at the 33rd Annual Conference of the N.Y. State Historical Society, at Southampton, October 6, 7, and 8, 1932). Frank Monaghan contributed a paper at the same meeting called "Captain Kidd," most valuable for his viewpoint and others on Kidd's fame and character.

The documents from the Public Record Office files in London are reproduced with their permission.

Quotations from a poem by Richard Walsh are from a delightful and beautifully printed book, *Kidd: A Moral Opuscule*, The Verse (sic) by Richard J. Walsh and Illustrations (sick) by George Illian, published by William Edwin Rudge, New York, 1922. Fred Goudy, Bertha Goudy, Bruce Rogers, and others famous in good bookmaking had a hand and much fun in doing it, and my copy is not for sale.

The *Notable Lawsuit* by Franklin H. Head is taken from a copy in the New York Public Library and was checked for accuracy by Edwin H. Carpenter Jr. Although it is a hoax from beginning to end, it is outstanding as a typical Kidd yarn, and the best ever written—and I quote from Ralph D. Paine: "To be over-critical of buried treasure stories is to clip the wings of romance and to condemn the spirit of adventure to a pedestrian gait. All these tales are true, or men of sane and sober repute would not go a-treasure hunting by land and sea. . . . The base iconoclast may perhaps demolish Santa Claus (which God forbid), but industrious dreamers will be digging for the gold of Captain Kidd, long after the last Christmas stocking shall have been pinned above the fireplace.

. . . There are no conscious liars among the tellers of treasure tales. The spell is upon them. They believe their own yarns and they prove their faith by their back-breaking works with pick and shovel."

Chapter 4. The Treasures of Silver Shoals and the Isle of Mystery

Well-informed treasure hunters have by now discovered that the Mysterious Island in Waldo Logan's tale is Mona. At the time the chapter was written in late 1956 and checked by Waldo Logan for accuracy, we decided not to name the place as he hoped to interest a backer to go for the treasure. My last letter from him was received on January 9, 1957.

Waldo Hancock Logan died on January 11, 1957, in Miami, Florida, at age fifty-eight. He was a true treasure hunter and had spent a large part of his life in research and actual hunting and surveying locations, and he was well known in his field.

He was one of those adventurous men who work and dream and now that he has gone on the Great Adventure, may his spirit be with those of the pirates and buccaneers he knew so well.

The author has in his possession unpublished information written by Waldo Logan on details of procedure for further work on Mona Island which may be valuable to future expeditions. This information will be held private and not released except by the approval and permission of his heirs.

The attempt made by the *Faulcon,* Captain George Churchill, to find the Silver Shoals treasure galleons, was taken from a three-page manuscript letter "From on board his Maj^{tes} Ship the Faulcon, Jamaica S^{ber} ye 14th, 1683," signed Geo: Churchill. See "The Man Who Missed the Boat" in *Manuscripts,* Vol. VIII, No. 3, Spring, 1956, pp. 153-157. The original letter is now in the Pierpont Morgan Library, New York.

The details of the Phips treasure are told in *The Hispaniola Treasure,* by Cyrus H. Karraker (Univ. of Pennsylvania Press, Philadelphia, 1934). Contains a fine bibliography of sources.

The story of Sir William Phips, the poor boy of New England who became Governor and was knighted because of his salvage from the lost Spanish galleons on Silver Shoals, has been the basis of many tales. If you enjoy fiction based on fact, read *Silver Shoals,* by Hamilton Cochran (Bobbs-Merrill, New York, 1945); *The His-*

paniola Plate, by John Bloundelle-Burton (New York, 1895). Mona Island lies west of Mayaguez, Puerto Rico, in Mona Passage. It was a famous hangout for pirates and has been the scene of many searches for buried treasure.

Chapter 5. The Pirate's Skull

The facts on Snow's discovery of Blackbeard's skull, as he told them to my friend Captain Jafar Clarke, together with the historical events in Blackbeard's life, are based on history.

Blackbearded Edward Teach, or Thatch (sometimes called Drummond), has been the subject of so many histories, pamphlets, motion pictures, and television plays that it is unnecessary to list them here. No book on piracy or treasure would be complete without including him.

Chapter 6. Oak Island's Secret

The mystery of Oak Island has made it second only to Cocos Island in popularity as a treasure spot. It is visited annually by hundreds of tourists and the Nova Scotia Chamber of Commerce and Travel Bureau has kept it in the news regularly. The facts of its history are taken from the prospectus of the Oak Island Treasure Company (Boston, 1894) and from news items since that date. Its history can be found in Driscoll, Snow, and magazine files. A rare little book, written, typeset, printed, and bound by the author, Thomas P. Leary, in an edition of one hundred copies, *The Oak Island Enigma* (Omaha, Neb., 1953), is unusual as the author suggests that the pit contains the lost manuscripts of Sir Francis Bacon.

Another explanation came to the author from an ancient mariner in Toronto, whose knowledge of pirate and treasure lore is not to be taken lightly. "The original Oak Island yarn may have acquired its initial momentum from those three original jokers under a venerable oak. A few veiled remarks, flavored with sly winks over Scotch heather dew, would have started the searchers. As an *employment venture* there were enough Scotsmen in those parts to lend-a-hand for a cash consideration . . . there are those scheming twisters who lure and inflict themselves on all and sundry and appear with surprising alacrity when a shillin' is due for a split into half-farthings. So good luck to brother Greene . . . he and all of us need same."

Chapters 7 and 8. *Lutine* Gold; Hell Gate Holds the *Hussar*

Based on an unpublished typescript by Simon Lake, *Treasure Trove & Pieces of Eight,* in the Foul Anchor Archives, Rye, New York, and material in the U. S. Treasury Department.

Also printed records in the form of prospectuses and reports to stockholders: The Submarine Exploration and Recovery Co. (Bridgeport, Conn., 1920), *"Recovering the Natural Products of the Sea."*

Galley proof of "The Development of the Submarine," an interview with Simon Lake, August, 1933.

The Lake Submarine Salvage Corporation (Milford, Conn.), n.d., *Fortunes Under the Sea.*

The Submarine News (Milford, Conn.), June 6, 1916; September, 1933; October 10, 1936.

Prospectus: Deep Sea Salvage Corporation and The Argonaut Salvage Corporation; together with reports from The Lake Submarine Salvage Corporation, 1934-1935, and the prospectus of Underwater Recovery Corporation (New York, 1938).

The records of H.M.S. *Lutine* are from a manuscript report on the *Lutine;* Lake manuscripts; and courtesy of Lloyd's of London, who kindly furnished material by N. S. Binnendijk (of Lloyd's Agency, Amsterdam) which covered the salvage attempts Nos. 7 to 10, not included in the Lake records.

Chapter 9. History Under the Sea

Based on interviews and information furnished by Edwin A. Link, Mendel L. Peterson, and Arthur McKee, Jr., who have worked on many expeditions together.

Teddy Tucker's Bermuda salvage story was tape-recorded in an interview as was that of the Point Pleasant, New Jersey, salvage by Jack Homer and Bob Franklin.

F. L. Coffman, President of Quest Associates, furnished the information on his plans and equipment. His treasure charts are well known and his two books *Atlas of Treasure Maps* and *1001 Lost, Buried or Sunken Treasures* (Thomas Nelson & Sons, New York, 1957) have recently appeared.

Thanks for information and help go also to Charles M. Brookfield, Peter Stackpole, Fred Hamilton, Coles Phinizy, and W. C. Blaisdell.

The most complete and finest work on diving is *Deep Diving and Submarine Operations*, by Robert H. Davis, Kt., D.Sc., Birmingham University, F.R.S.A. (London, 1955), sixth edition. It is a complete manual of 693 pages with index, profusely illustrated with photographs, drawings, and charts. Part I covers the present state of the art of deep diving, dress, apparatus, hints, first aids, diving suits, tools, underwater warfare, etc., and is technical. Part II covers secrets of the deep, diving for treasure, salvage of sunken ships, diver's yarns and adventures, and the history of diving and early submarine vessels. Mr. Davis is credited with many of the inventions in diving and safety apparatus in use today and is the Chairman of Siebe, Gorman & Co., Ltd., of London, founded by Augustus Siebe, who invented the "closed" flexible diving dress in 1837.

On the subject of diving I can recommend:

Treasure Under the Sea, by N. B. Stirling (New York, 1957).

The Silent World, by Capt. J. Y. Cousteau (New York, 1953).

Treasure Diving Holidays, by J. and B. Crile (New York, 1954).

Up for Air and *Fathoms Below,* by Frank Meier (New York, 1940 and 1943).

Danger Is My Business, by J. D. Craig (New York, 1938).

A Narrative of the Operation for the Recovery of the . . . Treasure Sunk in H.M.S. Thetis at Cape Frio, on the Coast of Brazil on the 5th December, 1830, by Capt. Thomas Dickinson (London, 1836).

"The Yankee's Wander-World," *National Geographic Magazine,* January 1949.

"I Found the Bones of the *Bounty,*" by Luis Marden, *National Geographic Magazine,* December 1957.

Wonders of Salvage, by David Masters (London, 1944).

Diving with and without Armor, by J. B. Green (Buffalo, 1859).

I Dive for Treasure, by H. E. Rieseberg (New York, 1942).

Seventy Fathoms Deep and *Egypt's Gold,* by David Scott (London, 1931 and 1932).

Gold From the Sea, by James Taylor (London, 1943).

Ship Ashore, by Desmond Young (London, 1932).

Skin Diving and Exploring Underwater, by John Sweeney.

Free Diving, by Dimitri Rebikoff (New York, 1956).

Vastness of the Sea, by Bernard Gorsky (New York, 1957).

Ship Ashore, by J. E. Rattray (New York, 1955). Long Island wrecks.

Graveyard of the Atlantic, by David Stick (Chapel Hill, N.C., 1952). North Carolina wrecks—authentic.

To Hidden Depths, by Capt. Philippe Tailliez.

Dive: The Complete Book on Skin Diving, by Rick and Barbara Carrier (New York, 1957).

Men Under the Sea, by Commander Edward Ellsberg (New York, 1939).

Chapter 10. Vigo's Mud-Covered Millions

John Potter, Jr., President of the Atlantic Salvage Company, currently working at Vigo Bay, furnished much information and kindly edited the chapter. He also allowed use of material from his pamphlet, *The Treasure of Rande.* Potter is after the *Monmouth's* galleon, sunk at sea south of the Baiona Islands. If he and his associates can locate her and raise her treasure they will be well paid for their efforts.

Most of the Vigo history was taken from two prospectuses: *Narrative of the Circumstances of . . . and the Sinking of, the Spanish Galleons, with the Treasure on Board, in the Harbor of Vigo, Spain, in the Year 1702, etc.,* published by The Galleon Treasure Company (New York, 1874), and *Vigo Bay Treasure Company, Prospectus and Narrative . . . of the Sinking of the Spanish Galleons . . . and Project for . . . Recovery* (San Francisco, 1883). Both in the Foul Anchor Archives, Rye, N.Y.

Ralph D. Paine in *The Book of Buried Treasure* (New York, 1911), and Charles B. Driscoll in *Doubloons* (New York, 1930), each devote a chapter to the Vigo Bay galleons.

A History of the Voyages and Travels of Nathaniel Uring (London, 1726) gives an eye-witness account of the battle of Vigo.

The English coins of gold and silver struck from bullion taken to London are described in "The Vigo Pieces of Queen Anne, 1702-03," by R. I. Nesmith, in *Coin Collector's Journal* (New York, September 1945, Vol. 12, pp. 100-109), and in *Boletín Ibero-Americano de Numismatica* (New York, March-April 1951).

Chapters 11 and 12. Loot from Lima;
Hocos-Pocos-Cocos

Most of the material on Cocos Island was taken from the following sources in the Foul Anchor Archives, Rye, New York:

The unpublished typescript of *My Twenty Years on Cocos Island*, by August Gissler.

Prospectus of The Pacific Exploration and Development Co. Ltd. (Victoria, B.C., 1901) and *Cocos Island Hydraulic and Treasure Company* (Vancouver, B.C., 1910), both in the Provincial Library, Victoria, B.C. These and photostats of many newspaper items from the Victoria *Daily Colonist* were furnished through the courtesy of Mr. W. E. Ireland, Provincial Librarian and Archivist.

The scrapbooks of Hubert Palmer's Kidd Museum furnished a great many news items from the London newspapers on various expeditions, as did the files of Raymond Dow, Secretary of the Treasure Trove Club.

"Hocos-Pocos-Cocos," the tale of Treasure Recovery Limited, was taken from a complete series of reports made to stockholders over the period 1933-1936 while the company was operating out of London. In files of the Foul Anchor, Rye, New York.

The tale of Captain Brown is from *Our Search for the Missing Millions*, by "One of the Searchers" (San Francisco, 1904).

Cocos Island tales are told by so many different writers in books, magazines, and newspapers (and will continue until the end of time) that it would be impossible to list them here.

One of the latest and best, from a woman's viewpoint, is *Cocos Island Venture*, by Marie Briggs (Los Angeles, 1950).

General Treasure Literature

If you really are a treasure fan, either armchair or active, you will enjoy any books by Charles B. Driscoll, Edward Rowe Snow, A. Hyatt Verrill, and Harold T. Wilkins. They were all prolific writers on the subjects of pirates, treasure, and shipwrecks.

A few more books recommended are:

Bridges, T. C., *The Romance of Buried Treasure* (London, 1932).
Beard, C. R., *The Romance of Treasure Trove* (London, 1933).
Cooper, Gordon, *Treasure Trove, Pirates' Gold* (New York, 1951).
Goldsmith, F. H., *Treasure Lies Buried Here* (Perth, Australia, 1946).

Knight, E. F., *The Cruise of the Alert* (London, many editions, 1904, etc.).

Plumpton, J., *Treasure Cruise* (London, 1935). Cocos Island.

Penfield, Thos., *Lost Treasure Trails* (New York, 1954).

Quarrell, C., *Buried Treasure* (London, 1955). English treasure only.

Rosenthal, Eric, *The Hinges Creaked* (London, 1951). South African treasure.

Although no lost mines or Western stories have been included in this book, no library should be without J. Frank Dobie's *Coronado's Children* and *Apache Gold and Yaqui Silver:* may the publishers keep them in print forever.

If you enjoy fiction that will keep you awake nights read:

Adventures of Louis Blake, by Louis Becke (London, n.d.).

The Silver Oar, by H. Breslin (New York, 1954).

Captain Adam, by D. B. Chidsey (New York, 1953).

Rogues' Holiday, by Hamilton Cochran (New York, 1947).

Black Bartlemy's Treasure and *Martin Conisby's Vengeance,* by Jeffrey Farnol (Boston, 1920-21).

Thomas the Lambkin, by Claude Farrère (New York, 1924).

Double Treasure, by C. B. Kelland (New York, 1946).

On Board the Morning Star, by P. MacOrlan (New York, 1924).

American Captain, by E. Marshall (New York, 1954).

The Isle of Palms, by C. M. Newell (Boston, 1888).

The Frozen Pirate, by W. Clarke Russell (London, 1887).

Leonard Lindsay, by A. B. Reach (London, 1850).

Pirate Wench, by Frank Shay (New York, 1934).

Buccaneer Surgeon, by C. V. Terry (New York, 1954).

Carolina Corsair, by Don Tracy (New York, 1955).

The Ledger of Lying Dog, by W. G. Weekley (New York, 1947).

Captain Brand of the Centipede, by H. A. Wise (Harry Gringo), New York, 1864,

and last, but not least—

Howard Pyle's Book of Pirates (New York, 1921).

Index

Index of Coins (*see also General Index*)

Index of Ships (*see also General Index*)

General Index (see also Index of Coins and Index of Ships)